Lakota
Woman

Lakota Woman

by
Mary Crow Dog
and
Richard Erdoes

GROVE WEIDENFELD   NEW YORK

Published by Grove Weidenfeld
A division of Wheatland Corporation
841 Broadway
New York, NY 10003-4793

Published in Canada by General Publishing Company, Ltd.

Unless otherwise stated, all photographs are by Richard Erdoes.

Library of Congress Cataloging-in-Publication Data

Mary Crow Dog.
Lakota woman / Mary Crow Dog and Richard Erdoes. — 1st ed.
p.   cm.
ISBN 0-8021-1101-7
1. Mary Crow Dog.   2. Dakota Indians—Women—Biography.
3. Dakota Indians—Social conditions.
4. Rosebud Indian Reservation (S.D.)   I. Erdoes, Richard.   II. Title.
E99.D1M425   1990
978.3'62—dc20
[B]   89-24862
CIP

Manufactured in the United States of America

Printed on acid-free paper

Designed by Irving Perkins Associates

First Edition 1990

3   5   7   9   10   8   6   4

Contents

1   A Woman from He-Dog   3

2   Invisible Fathers   12

3   Civilize Them with a Stick   28

4   Drinking and Fighting   42

5   Aimlessness   55

6   We AIM Not to Please   73

7   Crying for a Dream   92

8   Cankpe Opi Wakpala   111

9   The Siege   128

10   The Ghosts Return   144

11   Birth Giving   156

12   Sioux and Elephants Never Forget   170

13   Two Cut-off Hands   186

14   Cante Ishta—The Eye of the Heart   199

15   The Eagle Caged   215

16   Ho Uway Tinkte—My Voice You Shall Hear   242

Epilogue   261

Lakota
Woman

CHAPTER 1

A Woman from He-Dog

A nation is not conquered until
the hearts of its women
are on the ground.
    Then it is done, no matter
how brave its warriors
nor how strong their weapons.

—*Cheyenne proverb*

I am Mary Brave Bird. After I had my baby during the
siege of Wounded Knee they gave me a special name—
Ohitika Win, Brave Woman, and fastened an eagle plume in
my hair, singing brave-heart songs for me. I am a woman of
the Red Nation, a Sioux woman. That is not easy.

I had my first baby during a firefight, with the bullets
crashing through one wall and coming out through the other.
When my newborn son was only a day old and the marshals
really opened up upon us, I wrapped him up in a blanket and

3

ran for it. We had to hit the dirt a couple of times, I shielding the baby with my body, praying, "It's all right if I die, but please let him live."

When I came out of Wounded Knee I was not even healed up, but they put me in jail at Pine Ridge and took my baby away. I could not nurse. My breasts swelled up and grew hard as rocks, hurting badly. In 1975 the feds put the muzzles of their M-16s against my head, threatening to blow me away. It's hard being an Indian woman.

My best friend was Annie Mae Aquash, a young, strong-hearted woman from the Micmac Tribe with beautiful children. It is not always wise for an Indian woman to come on too strong. Annie Mae was found dead in the snow at the bottom of a ravine on the Pine Ridge Reservation. The police said that she had died of exposure, but there was a .38-caliber slug in her head. The FBI cut off her hands and sent them to Washington for fingerprint identification, hands that had helped my baby come into the world.

My sister-in-law, Delphine, a good woman who had lived a hard life, was also found dead in the snow, the tears frozen on her face. A drunken man had beaten her, breaking one of her arms and legs, leaving her helpless in a blizzard to die.

My sister Barbara went to the government hospital in Rosebud to have her baby and when she came out of anesthesia found that she had been sterilized against her will. The baby lived only for two hours, and she had wanted so much to have children. No, it isn't easy.

When I was a small girl at the St. Francis Boarding School, the Catholic sisters would take a buggy whip to us for what they called "disobedience." At age ten I could drink and hold a pint of whiskey. At age twelve the nuns beat me for "being too free with my body." All I had been doing was holding hands with a boy. At age fifteen I was raped. If you plan to be born, make sure you are born white and male.

It is not the big, dramatic things so much that get us

down, but just being Indian, trying to hang on to our way of life, language, and values while being surrounded by an alien, more powerful culture. It is being an iyeska, a half-blood, being looked down upon by whites and full-bloods alike. It is being a backwoods girl living in a city, having to rip off stores in order to survive. Most of all it is being a woman. Among Plains tribes, some men think that all a woman is good for is to crawl into the sack with them and mind the children. It compensates for what white society has done to them. They were famous warriors and hunters once, but the buffalo is gone and there is not much rep in putting a can of spam or an occasional rabbit on the table.

As for being warriors, the only way some men can count coup nowadays is knocking out another skin's teeth during a barroom fight. In the old days a man made a name for himself by being generous and wise, but now he has nothing to be generous with, no jobs, no money; and as far as our traditional wisdom is concerned, our men are being told by the white missionaries, teachers, and employers that it is merely savage superstition they should get rid of if they want to make it in this world. Men are forced to live away from their children, so that the family can get ADC—Aid to Dependent Children. So some warriors come home drunk and beat up their old ladies in order to work off their frustration. I know where they are coming from. I feel sorry for them, but I feel even sorrier for their women.

To start from the beginning, I am a Sioux from the Rosebud Reservation in South Dakota. I belong to the "Burned Thigh," the Brule Tribe, the Sicangu in our language. Long ago, so the legend goes, a small band of Sioux was surrounded by enemies who set fire to their tipis and the grass around them. They fought their way out of the trap but got their legs burned and in this way acquired their name. The Brules are part of the Seven Sacred Campfires, the seven tribes of the Western Sioux known collectively as Lakota.

The Eastern Sioux are called Dakota. The difference between them is their language. It is the same except that where we Lakota pronounce an *L*, the Dakota pronounce a *D*. They cannot pronounce an *L* at all. In our tribe we have this joke: "What is a flat tire in Dakota?" Answer: "A b*d*owout."

The Brule, like all Sioux, were a horse people, fierce riders and raiders, great warriors. Between 1870 and 1880 all Sioux were driven into reservations, fenced in and forced to give up everything that had given meaning to their life—their horses, their hunting, their arms, everything. But under the long snows of despair the little spark of our ancient beliefs and pride kept glowing, just barely sometimes, waiting for a warm wind to blow that spark into a flame again.

My family was settled on the reservation in a small place called He-Dog, after a famous chief. There are still some He-Dogs living. One, an old lady I knew, lived to be over a hundred years old. Nobody knew when she had been born. She herself had no idea, except that when she came into the world there was no census yet, and Indians had not yet been given Christian first names. Her name was just He-Dog, nothing else. She always told me, "You should have seen me eighty years ago when I was pretty." I have never forgotten her face—nothing but deep cracks and gullies, but beautiful in its own way. At any rate very impressive.

On the Indian side my family was related to the Brave Birds and Fool Bulls. Old Grandpa Fool Bull was the last man to make flutes and play them, the old-style flutes in the shape of a bird's head which had the elk power, the power to lure a young girl into a man's blanket. Fool Bull lived a whole long century, dying in 1976, whittling his flutes almost until his last day. He took me to my first peyote meeting while I was still a kid.

He still remembered the first Wounded Knee, the massacre. He was a young boy at that time, traveling with his father, a well-known medicine man. They had gone to a place near Wounded Knee to take part in a Ghost Dance. They had on their painted ghost shirts which were supposed to make them bulletproof. When they got near Pine Ridge they were stopped by white soldiers, some of them from the Seventh Cavalry, George Custer's old regiment, who were hoping to kill themselves some Indians. The Fool Bull band had to give up their few old muzzle-loaders, bows, arrows, and even knives. They had to put up their tipis in a tight circle, all bunched up, with the wagons on the outside and the soldiers surrounding their camp, watching them closely. It was cold, so cold that the trees were crackling with a loud noise as the frost was splitting their trunks. The people made a fire the following morning to warm themselves and make some coffee and then they noticed a sound beyond the crackling of the trees: rifle fire, salvos making a noise like the ripping apart of a giant blanket; the boom of cannon and the rattling of quick-firing Hotchkiss guns. Fool Bull remembered the grown-ups bursting into tears, the women keening: "They are killing our people, they are butchering them!" It was only two miles or so from where Grandfather Fool Bull stood that almost three hundred Sioux men, women, and children were slaughtered. Later grandpa saw the bodies of the slain, all frozen in ghostly attitudes, thrown into a ditch like dogs. And he saw a tiny baby sucking at his dead mother's breast.

I wish I could tell about the big deeds of some ancestors of mine who fought at the Little Big Horn, or the Rosebud, counting coup during the Grattan or Fetterman battle, but little is known of my family's history before 1880. I hope some of my great-grandfathers counted coup on Custer's men, I like to imagine it, but I just do not know. Our Rosebud people did not play a big part in the battles against generals Crook or Custer. This was due to the policy of Spotted Tail, the all-powerful chief at the time. Spotted Tail had earned his eagle feathers as a warrior, but had been taken East as a prisoner and put in jail. Coming back years later, he said that he had seen the cities of the whites and that a single one of them contained more people than could be found in all the Plains tribes put together, and that every one of the wasičuns' factories could turn out more rifles and bullets in one day than were owned by all the Indians in the country. It was useless, he said, to try to resist the wasičuns. During the critical year of 1876 he had his Indian police keep most of the young men on the reservation, preventing them from joining Sitting Bull, Gall, and Crazy Horse. Some of the young bucks, a few Brave Birds among them, managed to sneak out trying to get to Montana, but nothing much is known. After having been forced into reservations, it was not thought wise to recall such things. It might mean no rations, or worse. For the same reason many in my family turned Christian, letting themselves be "whitemanized." It took many years to reverse this process.

My sister Barbara, who is four years older than me, says she remembers the day when I was born. It was late at night and raining hard amid thunder and lightning. We had no electricity then, just the old-style kerosene lamps with the big reflectors. No bathroom, no tap water, no car. Only a few white teachers had cars. There was one phone in He-Dog, at the trading post. This was not so very long ago, come to think of it. Like most Sioux at that time my mother was supposed to give birth at home, I think, but something went wrong, I was pointing the wrong way, feet first or stuck sideways. My mother was in great pain, laboring for hours, until finally somebody ran to the trading post and called the ambulance. They took her—us—to Rosebud, but the hospital there was not yet equipped to handle a complicated birth, I don't think they had surgery then, so they had to drive mother all the way to Pine Ridge, some ninety miles distant, because there the tribal hospital was bigger. So it happened that I was born among Crazy Horse's people. After my sister Sandra was born the doctors there performed a hysterectomy on my mother, in fact sterilizing her without her permission, which was common at the time, and up to just a few years ago, so that it is hardly worth mentioning. In the opinion of some people, the fewer Indians there are, the better. As Colonel Chivington said to his soldiers: "Kill 'em all, big and small, nits make lice!"

I don't know whether I am a louse under the white man's skin. I hope I am. At any rate I survived the long hours of my mother's labor, the stormy drive to Pine Ridge, and the neglect of the doctors. I am an iyeska, a breed, that's what the white kids used to call me. When I grew bigger they stopped calling me that, because it would get them a bloody nose. I am a small woman, not much over five feet tall, but I can hold my own in a fight, and in a free-for-all with honkies I can become rather ornery and do real damage. I have white blood in me. Often I have wished to be able to purge it out of me. As a young girl I used to look at myself in the mirror, trying to find a clue as to who and what I was. My face is very Indian, and so are my eyes and my hair, but my skin is very light. Always I waited for the summer, for the prairie sun, the Badlands sun, to tan me and make me into a real skin.

The Crow Dogs, the members of my husband's family, have no such problems of identity. They don't need the sun to tan them, they are full-bloods—the Sioux of the Sioux. Some Crow Dog men have faces which make the portrait on the buffalo Indian nickel look like a washed-out white man. They have no shortage of legends. Every Crow Dog seems to be a legend in himself, including the women. They became outcasts in their stronghold at Grass Mountain rather than being whitemanized. They could not be tamed, made to wear a necktie or go to a Christian church. All during the long years when practicing Indian beliefs was forbidden and could be punished with jail, they went right on having their ceremonies, their sweat baths and sacred dances. Whenever a Crow Dog got together with some relatives, such as those equally untamed, unregenerated Iron Shells, Good Lances, Two Strikes, Picket Pins, or Hollow Horn Bears, then you could hear the sound of the can gleska, the drum, telling all the world that a Sioux ceremony was in the making. It took courage and suffering to keep the flame alive, the little spark under the snow.

The first Crow Dog was a well-known chief. On his shield was the design of two circles and two arrowheads for wounds received in battle—two white man's bullets and two Pawnee arrow points. When this first Crow Dog was lying wounded in the snow, a coyote came to warm him and a crow flew ahead of him to show him the way home. His name should be Crow Coyote, but the white interpreter misunderstood it and so they became Crow Dogs. This Crow Dog of old became famous for killing a rival chief, the result of a feud over tribal politics, then driving voluntarily over a hundred miles to get himself hanged at Deadwood, his wife sitting beside him in his buggy; famous also for finding on his arrival that the Supreme Court had ordered him to be freed because the federal government had no jurisdiction over Indian reservations and also because it was no crime for one Indian to kill another. Later, Crow Dog became a leader of the Ghost Dancers, holding out for months in the frozen caves and ravines of the Badlands. So, if my own family lacks history, that of my husband more than makes up for it.

Our land itself is a legend, especially the area around Grass Mountain where I am living now. The fight for our land is at the core of our existence, as it has been for the last two hundred years. Once the land is gone, then we are gone too. The Sioux used to keep winter counts, picture writings on buffalo skin, which told our people's story from year to year. Well, the whole country is one vast winter count. You can't walk a mile without coming to some family's sacred vision hill, to an ancient Sun Dance circle, an old battleground, a place where something worth remembering happened. Mostly a death, a proud death or a drunken death. We are a great people for dying. "It's a good day to die!" that's our old battle cry. But the land with its tar paper shacks and outdoor privies, not one of them straight, but all leaning this way or that way, is also a land to live on, a land for good times and telling jokes and talking of great deeds done in the past. But you can't live forever off the deeds of Sitting Bull or Crazy Horse. You can't wear their eagle feathers, freeload off their legends. You have to make your own legends now. It isn't easy.

CHAPTER 2

Invisible Fathers

The father says so—E'yayo!
The father says so—E'yayo!
You shall see your grandfather!
You shall see your kindred—E'yayo!
The father says so.
A'te he'ye lo.

Child let me grasp your hand,
Child let me grasp your hand.
You shall live,
You shall live!
Says the father.
A'te he'ye lo.

—*Ghost Dance song*

Our people have always been known for their strong family ties, for people within one family group caring for each other, for the "helpless ones," the old folks and especially the children, the coming generation. Even now, among traditionals, as long as one person eats, all other relatives eat too. Nobody saves up money because there is always some poor relative saying, "Kanji, I need five bucks for food and gas," and he will not be refused as long as there is one single dollar left. Feeding every comer is still a sacred duty, and Sioux women seem always to be cooking from early morning until late at night. Fourth and fifth cousins still claim relationship and the privileges that go with it. Free enterprise has no future on the res.

At the center of the old Sioux society was the tiyospaye, the extended family group, the basic hunting band, which included grandparents, uncles, aunts, in-laws, and cousins. The tiyospaye was like a warm womb cradling all within it. Kids were never alone, always fussed over by not one but several mothers, watched and taught by several fathers. The real father, as a matter of fact, selected a second father, some well-thought-of relative with special skills as a hunter or medicine man, to help him bring up a boy, and such a person was called "Father" too. And the same was true for the girls. Grandparents in our tribe always held a special place in caring for the little ones, because they had more time to devote to them, when the father was out hunting, taking the mother with him to help with the skinning and butchering.

The whites destroyed the tiyospaye, not accidentally, but as a matter of policy. The close-knit clan, set in its old ways, was a stumbling block in the path of the missionary and government agent, its traditions and customs a barrier to what the white man called "progress" and "civilization." And so the government tore the tiyospaye apart and forced the Sioux into the kind of relationship now called the "nuclear family"—forced upon each couple their individually owned allotment of land, trying to teach them "the benefits of wholesome selfishness without which higher civilization is impossible." At least that is how one secretary of the interior put it. So the great brainwashing began, those who did not like to have their brains washed being pushed farther and farther into the back country into isolation and starvation. The civilizers did a good job on us, especially among the half-bloods, using the stick-and-carrot method, until now there is neither the tiyospaye nor a white-style nuclear family left, just Indian kids without parents. The only thing reminding one of the old Sioux family group is that the grandparents are playing a bigger role than ever. With often no mother or father around, it is the old folks who are bringing up the kids, which is not always a bad thing.

My father, Bill Moore, was part Indian, but mostly white, French with a little Spanish mixed in—Spanish not chicano. He was in the navy and later became a trucker. He lives in Omaha—I think. All that's left of him is his picture on the mantelpiece showing him in navy uniform, a lean-faced, sharp-eyed man. He stayed around just long enough until mom got pregnant with me. Then he split, telling my mother he was tired of all that baby shit. He just left. He was not interested in us, nor in the kids he had with another wife whom he did not want either and placed on welfare. I don't know what became of them. So there is just that one picture left to remind me that I, too, had a father like everybody else. My mother never talked of him; my grandfather—his own father—never talked of him. So all I know is that he wanted no part of me and liked to drink. That's the only things I was ever told about him.

I saw him twice in the flesh. He came back when I was eleven in order to ask his father for some money. The second time I saw him was when he came for his brother's funeral. He looked right through me as if I had not been there. His eyes were dead. He did not even ask who I was. As a matter of fact he did not talk at all, just grinned when some jokes were told and looked uncomfortable in his tight, new cowboy boots. After the funeral he just shook hands all around, without uttering a word, in a hurry to be off again. My mother divorced him in 1954 when I was one year old.

When I was nine or ten my mother married again. This stepfather was even worse than my real father, who at least was not around. My stepfather was. He was a wino and started us kids drinking when I was barely ten years old. After my mother married this man I did not want to be around. I did not like the way he stared at me. It made me uncomfortable. So I just kept away from my mother's place. I rather was on my own, took care of myself, hating myself for having allowed him to teach me to drink. On the rare occasions when I went home I always got into arguments with my mother, telling her, "Why did you marry that man? He's no dad. He doesn't love us. He does nothing for us."

So I and my mother did not get along then. I was a natural-born rebel. They were married and I could do nothing about it. So I drank and ripped off as I got older, living like a hobo, punishing my mother that way. I had to mature. My mother had to mature also. We get along now, really like and respect each other. I realize that I was very intolerant. My mother could not help herself. The little settlements we lived in—He-Dog, Upper Cut Meat, Parmelee, St. Francis, Belvidere—were places without hope where bodies and souls were being destroyed bit by bit. Schools left many of us almost illiterate. We were not taught any skills. The land was leased to white ranchers. Jobs were almost nonexistent on the reservation, and outside the res whites did not hire Indians if they could help it. There was nothing for the men to do in those days but hit the bottle. The men were psychologically crippled and thus my mother did not have much choice when it came to picking a husband. The men had nothing to live for, so they got drunk and drove off at ninety miles an hour in a car without lights, without brakes, and without destination, to die a warrior's death.

There were six of us kids. A seventh had died as a baby.

First, my oldest sister, Kathie, then my brother Robert, then Barbara, who is closest to me in life-style and has had experiences almost exactly like mine. Then came Sandra, and then myself, the youngest. After me came a little boy. We adopted him. This came about when my mother visited his parents for some reason or other. She found nobody at home except this baby boy, dirty, bawling with hunger, and soaking wet, in a box under the dresser. All alone. Everybody gone. Barhopping, most likely. It got my mother mad and somehow she worked it out so we could adopt the baby. He was very spoiled. Everything he wanted he got. So at least one kid in the family got pampered.

After father left, mother became our sole financial support. In order to earn a living she went to be trained as a nurse. When she had finished her training the only job she could find was in Pierre, some hundred miles away. There was nobody there to take care of us while she worked, so she had to leave us behind with our grandparents. We missed her at times. We would see her only rarely. She did not have many chances to come home because she had no transportation. She could not afford a car and it was impossible to get around without one. So she was not there when we needed her because she had to care for white patients. It was only after I was almost grown-up that I really became acquainted with her.

Like most reservation kids we wound up with our grandparents. We were lucky. Many Indian children are placed in foster homes. This happens even in some cases where parents or grandparents are willing and able to take care of them, but where the social workers say their homes are substandard, or where there are outhouses instead of flush toilets, or where the family is simply "too poor." A flush toilet to a white social worker is more important than a good grandmother. So the kids are given to wasičun strangers to be "acculturated in a sanitary environment." We are losing the coming generation that way and do not like it.

We were lucky, having good, warm-hearted grandparents until we, too, were taken away to a boarding school. My grandma was born Louise Flood and she was a Sioux. Her first husband's name was Brave Bird. I have tried to find out about this ancestor of mine. I looked in all the Lakota history books. There were Brave Bears, and Brave Bulls, and Brave Wolves, but no Brave Birds listed. I should have asked when grandma was still alive. They lived on their allotted land way out on the prairie. When grandma was young the whole tribe lived on commodities. Every head of household had a ration card, keeping this precious object in a small, beautifully beaded pouch around his neck, the kind which now costs collectors as much as three hundred dollars. Once a month everybody had to go for their supplies—coffee, sugar loaves, sacks of flour, bacon—mostly starch but filling enough while it lasted, and if we were not cheated out of part of it. Sometimes there was a beef issue of living cattle, the stringiest, skinniest beasts imaginable. This meat-on-the-hoof was driven into a huge corral and then our men were allowed to play buffalo hunters for a couple of hours and ride after them and shoot down those poor refugees from the glue factory and butcher them. This was always a big occasion, good entertainment one could talk about. One day, Grandfather Brave Bird hitched up his wagon and team to drive six hours to town to get his government issue. He went all by himself. On the way home he ran into a thunderstorm. Lightning spooked the horses. They raced off at a dead run, upsetting the wagon. The box seat got ripped off with Brave Bird still in it, entangled in the reins. The horses dragged him through the brush, over rocks, and finally for a couple of miles along a barbed-wire fence. He was dead when they found him.

At that time my grandmother had two girls and two boys. These uncles of mine got TB as they grew up, were taken to an institution, and died from this disease. Tuberculosis is still a problem with us, striking men more often than women. At least they died when they were grown-up, not as children as often happens. At least my grandmother thinks that is where and how they died. She never got any records. All she got was a box to bury.

There was a man called Noble Moore. He had a family and his wife died, and grandma had a family and her husband had died. So the widow and the widower got together and married. By this time my mom was already grown-up. Now Moore had a son of the same age called Bill. One thing led to another and mom married Bill, our absentee head of family, the ex-navy trucker in Omaha. Grandma had the father and my mother wound up with the son. In this kind of lottery grandma won the big prize, because the old man was as good and sober and caring as his son was the opposite.

Grandpa and Grandma Moore were good to us, raising us ever since we were small babies. Grandfather Noble Moore was the only father I knew. He took responsibility for us in his son's place. He gave us as good a home as he could. He worked as a janitor in the school and had little money to take care of a large family, his own and that of his son. Nine people in all plus always some poor relatives with no jobs. I don't know how he managed, but somehow he did.

The old couple raised us way out on the prairie near He-Dog in a sort of homemade shack. We had no electricity, no heating system, no plumbing. We got our water from the river. Some of the things which even poor white or black ghetto people take for granted we did not even know existed. We knew little about the outside world, having no radio and no TV. Maybe that was a blessing. Our biggest feast was Thanksgiving because then we had hamburgers. They had a wonderful taste to them which I still remember. Grandpa raised us on rabbits, deer meat, ground squirrels, even porcupines. They never seemed to have money to buy much food. Grandpa Moore and two of his brothers were hunting all the time. It was the only way to put some fresh, red meat on the table, and we Sioux are real tigers when it comes to meat. We can't do without it. A few times grandpa came back from fishing with a huge mud turtle and threw it in the pot. That was a feast for him. He said one could taste seven different kinds of meat flavors in a turtle stew—chicken, pork, beef, rabbit, deer, wild duck, antelope, all these. We also got the usual commodities after OEO came in.

Our cabin was small. It had only one room which served as our kitchen, living room, dining room, parlor, or whatever. At night we slept there, too. That was our home—one room. Grandma was the kind of woman who, when visitors dropped in, immediately started to feed them. She always told me: "Even if there's not much left, they gonna eat. These people came a long ways to visit us, so they gonna eat first. I don't care if they come at sunrise or at sundown, they gonna eat first. And whatever is left after they leave, even if it's only a small dried-up piece of fry bread, that's what we eat." This my grandmother taught me. She was Catholic and tried to raise us as whites, because she thought that was the only way for us to get ahead and lead a satisfying life, but when it came to basics she was all Sioux, in spite of the pictures of Holy Mary and the Sacred Heart on the wall. Whether she was aware of how very Indian she had remained, I cannot say. She also spoke the Sioux language, the real old-style Lakota, not the modern slang we have today. And she knew her herbs, showing us how to recognize the different kinds of Indian plants, telling us what each of them was good for. She took us to gather berries and a certain mint for tea. During the winter we took chokecherries, the skin and the branches. We boiled the inside layers and used the tea for various sorts of sicknesses. In the fall she took us to harvest chokecherries and wild grapes. These were the only sweets we had. I never discovered candy until much later when I was in school. We did not have the money for it and only very seldom went to town.

We had no shoes and went barefoot most of the time. I never had a new dress. Once a year we would persuade somebody to drive us to the Catholic mission for a basement rummage sale. Sometimes we found something there to put on our feet before it got cold, and maybe a secondhand blouse or skirt. That was all we could afford. We did not celebrate Christmas, at least not the kind of feast white people are used to. Grandma would save a little money and when the time came she bought some crystal sugar—it looked like small rocks of glass put on a string—some peanuts, apples, and oranges. And she got some kind of cotton material, sewing it together, making little pouches for us, and in each put one apple, one orange, a handful of peanuts, and some of that crystal sugar which took forever to melt in one's mouth. I loved it. That was Christmas and it never changed.

I was too small to know about racism then. When I was in third grade some relative took me to Pine Ridge and I went into a store. It was not very big, a small country grocery. One of my teachers was inside. I went right to the vegetable and fruit bins where I saw oranges just like the one I always got on Christmas. I sure wanted one of them. I picked the biggest one. An uncle had given me a nickel to go on a wild spree with and I wanted to use it paying for the orange. The store owner told me, "A nickel ain't enough to pay for one of them large Sunkist navel oranges, the only ones I got. Put it back." I still remember that. I had to put that damned orange back. Next to me, the wasičun teacher saw me do it and she made a face saying out loud, so that everyone in the store could hear it: "Why can't those dirty Indians keep their hands off this food? I was going to buy some oranges, but they put their dirty hands on them and now I must try to find some oranges elsewhere. How disgusting!" It made a big impression on me, even though I could not understand the full meaning of this incident.

Grandma told me: "Whatever you do, don't go into white people's homes. 'Cause when they come into our homes they make fun of us, because we are poor." When we were growing up at He-Dog there were a few Indian shacks and the garage for buses and the filling station and that was totally it. Then the government started to move us to Parmelee where they put up new OEO houses, small, matchstick structures without cellars which the people called "poverty houses." A school was also built and a few white teachers moved there. I made friends with a little white girl. She said, "Come to my house." I answered, "No, I ain't supposed to go to nobody's house." She said, "My ma ain't home. She's visiting neighbors. Just come!" So I sneaked over there without grandma knowing it. The white girl had many toys, dolls, a doll-house. All the things I used to admire in the *Sears, Roebuck Catalogue* which I always studied in the outhouse. She had everything. She said, "Sit down and play with my toys." I did. I thought she was my friend. Suddenly I heard the door banging, banging, banging. It was the little girl's mother and she was yelling, "You open this door! You got some nerve coming into my home. You locked me out." She was screaming and I was shaking. I did not know what to do. I told her, "I did not lock you out. I did not even know that door was locked." She yelled, "Where is my whip?" She went into the hallway and got hold of a big, thick leather belt. She said, "Get over here!"

I ran as fast as I could back to my grandmother's house. I told her, "That white woman is going to whip me."

"What did you do?"

"Nothing. I just went into her house and she wants to whip me. Her little girl got me into trouble. I didn't do nothing. Hide me, grandma!" I was so scared.

By about that time the lady was coming. Grandma told me, "You stay in here!" Then she got her big butcher knife. She went out standing in the doorway and told that woman, "You goddam white trash, you coming any closer and I'll chop your ears off." I never saw anybody run as fast as did that white lady.

In South Dakota white kids learn to be racists almost before they learn to walk. When I was about seven or eight years old, I fought with the school principal's daughter. We were in the playground. She was hanging on the monkey bar saying, "Come on, monkey, this thing is for you." She also told me that I smelled and looked like an Indian. I grabbed her by the hair and yanked her down from the monkey bar. I would have done more, but I saw the principal coming.

As I said, grandma spoke Sioux fluently. So does my mother. But we were not allowed to speak it and we were not taught. Many times I asked my grandmother, "Why don't you teach me the language?" Her answer always was: " 'Cause we want you to get an education, to live a good life. Not have a hard time. Not depend on nobody. Times coming up are going to be real hard. You need a white man's education to live in this world. Speaking Indian would only hold you back, turn you the wrong way."

She thought she was helping me by not teaching me Indian ways. Her being a staunch Catholic also had something to do with it. The missionaries had always been repeating over and over again: *You must kill the Indian in order to save the man!* " That was part of trying to escape the hard life. The

22

missions, going to church, dressing and behaving like a wasičun—that for her was the key which would magically unlock the door leading to the good life, the white life with a white-painted cottage, and a carpet on the floor, a shiny car in the garage, and an industrious, necktie-wearing husband who was not a wino. Examples abounded all around her that it was the wrong key to the wrong door, that it would not change the shape of my cheekbones, or the slant of my eyes, the color of my hair, or the feelings inside me. She had only to open her eyes to see, but could not or would not. Her little dream was nourished and protected by the isolation in which she lived.

Grandma had been to mission school and that had influenced her to abandon much of our traditional ways. She gave me love and a good home, but if I wanted to be an Indian I had to go elsewhere to learn how to become one. To grandma's older sister, Mary, for instance, the one who is married to Charlie Little Dog. I call them grandfather and grandmother, too, after the Sioux manner. He is a hundred and four years old now and grandma Little Dog about ninety-eight. They are very traditional people, faithful to the ancient rituals. They still carry their water from the river. They still chop wood. They still live like the Sioux of a hundred years ago. When Charlie Little Dog talks, he still uses the old words. You have to be at least sixty or seventy years old to understand what he is talking about—the language has changed that much. So I went to them if I wanted to hear the old tales of warriors and spirits, the oral history of our people.

I also went to grand-uncle Dick Fool Bull, the flute maker, who took me to my first peyote meeting, and to people like the Bear Necklaces, the Brave Birds, Iron Shells, Hollow Horn Bears, and Crow Dogs. One woman, Elsie Flood, a niece of grandma's, had a big influence upon me.

She was a turtle woman, a strong, self-reliant person, because a turtle stands for strength, resolution, and long life. A turtle heart beats and beats for days, long after the turtle itself is dead. It keeps on beating all by itself. In traditional families a beaded charm in the shape of a turtle is fastened to a newborn child's cradle. The baby's navel cord is put inside this turtle charm, which is believed to protect the infant from harm and bad spirits. The charm is also supposed to make the child live to a great old age. A turtle is a strength of mind, a communication with the thunder.

I loved to visit Aunt Elsie Flood to listen to her stories. With her high cheekbones she looked like grandma. She had a voice like water bubbling, talking with a deep, throaty sound. And she talked fast, mixing Indian and English together. I had to pay strict attention if I wanted to understand what she told me. She always paid her bills, earning a living by her arts and crafts, her beautiful work with beads and porcupine quills—what she called "Indian novelties." She was also a medicine woman. She was an old-time woman carrying her pack on her back. She would not let a man or younger woman carry her burden. She carried it herself. She neither asked nor accepted help from anybody, being proud of her turtle strength. She used turtles as her protection. Wherever she went, she always had some little live turtles with her and all kinds of things made out of tortoiseshell, little charms and boxes. She had a little place in Martin, halfway between Rosebud and Pine Ridge, and there she lived alone. She was very independent but always glad to have me visit her. Once she came to our home, trudging along as usual with the heavy pack on her back and two shopping bags full of herbs and strange things. She also brought a present for me—two tiny, very lively turtles. She had painted Indian designs on their shells and their bottoms. She communicated with them by name. One she called

"Come" and the other "Go." They always waddled over to her when she called them to get their food. She had a special kind of feed for them, leaving me whole bags of it. These small twin turtles stayed tiny. They never grew. One day the white principal's son came over and smashed them. Simply stomped them to death. When she heard it my aunt said that this was an evil sign for her.

The turtle woman was afraid of nothing. She was always hitchhiking, constantly on the road thumbing her way from one place to the other. She was a mystery to some. The Indians held her in great respect, saying that she was "wakan," that she was some sort of holy person to whom turtles had given their powers. In the summer of 1976 she was found beaten to death in her home. She was discovered under the bed, face down and naked, with weeds in her hair. She had never hurt anyone or done an unkindness to anybody, only helped people who needed it. No Indian would have touched a single hair on her head. She died that way. I still grieve for her. Her death has never been investigated. The life of an Indian is not held in great value in the State of South Dakota. There is no woman like her anymore.

So many of my relations and friends who were ever dear to me, or meant something to me, or meant something to the people, have either been killed or found dead on some out-of-the-way road. The good Indians die first. They do not grow old. This turtle aunt of mine was one of the traditionally strongest women of her generation. To bring back what knowledge she had is going to take time. It will take another generation or two to bring it back.

In spite of our grandparents trying so hard to be good Christians, some Indian beliefs rubbed off on them. I remember when I was little, if someone was sick, Grandfather Moore would fill one of the tubs used for watering the cattle and put live ducks in it, saying: "If those birds stay in and swim awhile, swim around, that sick person is gonna be all right. But if the ducks just jump out and leave, the sick one won't get better." He never explained it, just expected everybody to take it on faith. Much later, when my sister Barbara lost her baby, some relatives and friends held a peyote meeting for her. Barb asked our mother and grandmother to come and they actually did. They must have been a little uneasy among all these heathenish goings-on, but they lasted all night and behaved well, as if they had been doing it all their lives. I am sure they worried that the priest would hear about it. I also remember having been told that once, when a person living in a tent behind our shack fell ill, grandfather got a medicine man to doctor him and suck the evil poisons out of his system.

I lived the simple life at He-Dog until I had to go to boarding school. We kids did not suffer from being poor, because we were not aware of it. The few Indians nearby lived in the same kind of want, in the same kind of dilapidated shacks or one-room log cabins with dirt floors. We had nothing to compare our life to. We existed in a vacuum of our own. We were not angry because we did not know that somewhere there was a better, more comfortable life. To be angry, poverty has to rub shoulders with wealth, as for instance ghetto people in squalid tenements living next door to the rich in their luxury apartments as I have seen during my visits to New York. TV has destroyed the innocence, broken through the wall that separates the rich whites from the poor nonwhites. The "boob tube" brainwashes people, but if they are poor and nonwhite, it also makes them angry seeing all those things advertised that they can never hope to have—the fancy homes and cars, the dishwashers and microwaves, the whole costly junk of affluent America. I wonder whether the advertisers who spend a hundred thousand dollars on a commercial are aware of broadcasting a revolutionary message.

As we had no electricity we also had no "idiot box" and therefore felt no envy. Except for that one incident in the white lady's home, I had not yet encountered racism in its varied forms, and that one event I had not fully comprehended. It left me afraid of white people, though, that and some stories I had heard. As I hardly met any white people, they did not bother me. I liked the food I got; I did not know any other, and hunger is a good cook. I liked our shack. Its being overcrowded only meant womblike security to me. Again, except for that white lady's house, I only knew the kind that looked like ours, except for the filling station, but that was not a home. I had food, love, a place to sleep, and a warm, potbellied, wood-fed stove to sit near in the winter. I needed nothing more. Finally, I had something white kids don't usually have—horses to ride. No matter how poor we Sioux are, there are always a few ponies around. When I was a small girl you could buy a nice-looking pinto for ten dollars. So I was riding from as early an age as I can remember. I liked the feel of a horse under me, a feeling of mastery, of freedom, of wildness, of being Indian. It is a feeling shared by everybody on the reservation. Even the most white-manized Sioux is still half horse. I never particularly wished for anything during my earlier childhood except to own an Appaloosa, because I had seen a picture of one in a magazine and fell in love with it. Maybe one day, if I live, I'll get my wish.

Grandfather Moore died in 1972. He passed away peacefully in his sleep. I was glad he had such an easy death. He was a good, loving man, a hard-working janitor. I miss him. I miss grandma. They protected us as long as they were able, but they could not protect us from being taken away to boarding school.

CHAPTER 3

Civilize Them with a Stick

... Gathered from the cabin, the wickiup, and the tepee,
partly by cajolery and partly by threats;
partly by bribery and partly by force,
they are induced to leave their kindred
to enter these schools and take upon themselves
the outward appearance of civilized life.

—Annual report of the Department of Interior, 1901

It is almost impossible to explain to a sympathetic white person what a typical old Indian boarding school was like; how it affected the Indian child suddenly dumped into it like a small creature from another world, helpless, defenseless, bewildered, trying desperately and instinctively to survive and sometimes not surviving at all. I think such children were like the victims of Nazi concentration camps trying to tell average, middle-class Americans what their experience had been like. Even now, when these schools are much improved, when the buildings are new, all gleaming steel and glass, the food tolerable, the teachers well trained and well-intentioned, even trained in child psychology—unfortunately the psychology of white children, which is different from ours—the shock to the child upon arrival is still tremendous. Some just seem to shrivel up, don't speak for days on end, and have an empty look in their eyes. I know of an eleven-year-old on another reservation who hanged herself, and in our school, while I was there, a girl jumped out of the window, trying to kill herself to escape an unbearable situation. That first shock is always there.

Although the old tiyospaye has been destroyed, in the traditional Sioux families, especially in those where there is no drinking, the child is never left alone. It is always surrounded by relatives, carried around, enveloped in warmth. It is treated with the respect due to any human being, even a small one. It is seldom forced to do anything against its will, seldom screamed at, and never beaten. That much, at least, is left of the old family group among full-bloods. And then suddenly a bus or car arrives, full of strangers, usually white strangers, who yank the child out of the arms of those who love it, taking it screaming to the boarding school. The only word I can think of for what is done to these children is kidnapping.

Even now, in a good school, there is impersonality instead of close human contact; a sterile, cold atmosphere, an unfamiliar routine, language problems, and above all the mazaskan-skan, that damn clock—white man's time as opposed to Indian time, which is natural time. Like eating when you are hungry and sleeping when you are tired, not when that damn clock says you must. But I was not taken to one of the better, modern schools. I was taken to the old-fashioned mission school at St. Francis, run by the nuns and Catholic fathers, built sometime around the turn of the century and not improved a bit when I arrived, not improved as far as the buildings, the food, the teachers, or their methods were concerned.

In the old days, nature was our people's only school and they needed no other. Girls had their toy tipis and dolls, boys their toy bows and arrows. Both rode and swam and played the rough Indian games together. Kids watched their peers and elders and naturally grew from children into adults. Life in the tipi circle was harmonious—until the whiskey peddlers arrived with their wagons and barrels of "Injun whiskey." I often wished I could have grown up in the old, before-whiskey days.

Oddly enough, we owed our unspeakable boarding schools to the do-gooders, the white Indian-lovers. The schools were intended as an alternative to the outright extermination seriously advocated by generals Sherman and Sheridan, as well as by most settlers and prospectors overrunning our land. "You don't have to kill those poor benighted heathen," the do-gooders said, "in order to solve the Indian Problem. Just give us a chance to turn them into useful farmhands, laborers, and chambermaids who will break their backs for you at low wages." In that way the boarding schools were born. The kids were taken away from their villages and pueblos, in their blankets and moccasins, kept completely isolated from their families—sometimes for as long as ten years—suddenly coming back, their short hair slick with pomade, their necks raw from stiff, high collars, their thick jackets always short in the sleeves and pinching under the arms, their tight patent leather shoes giving them corns, the girls in starched white blouses and clumsy, high-buttoned boots—caricatures of white people. When they found out—and they found out quickly—that they were neither wanted by whites nor by Indians, they got good and drunk, many of them staying drunk for the rest of their lives.

I still have a poster I found among my grandfather's stuff, given to him by the missionaries to tack up on his wall. It reads:

1. Let Jesus save you.
2. Come out of your blanket, cut your hair, and dress like a white man.
3. Have a Christian family with one wife for life only.
4. Live in a house like your white brother. Work hard and wash often.
5. Learn the value of a hard-earned dollar. Do not waste your money on giveaways. Be punctual.
6. Believe that property and wealth are signs of divine approval.
7. Keep away from saloons and strong spirits.
8. Speak the language of your white brother. Send your children to school to do likewise.
9. Go to church often and regularly.
10. Do not go to Indian dances or to the medicine men.

The people who were stuck upon "solving the Indian Problem" by making us into whites retreated from this position only step by step in the wake of Indian protests.

The mission school at St. Francis was a curse for our family for generations. My grandmother went there, then my mother, then my sisters and I. At one time or other every one of us tried to run away. Grandma told me once about the bad times she had experienced at St. Francis. In those days they let students go home only for one week every year. Two days were used up for transportation, which meant spending just five days out of three hundred and sixty-five with her family. And that was an improvement. Before grandma's time, on many reservations they did not let the students go home at all until they had finished school. Anybody who disobeyed the nuns was severely punished. The building in which my grandmother stayed had three floors, for girls only. Way up in the attic were little cells, about five by five by ten feet. One time she was in church and instead of praying she was playing jacks. As punishment they took her to one of those little cubicles where she stayed in darkness because the windows had been boarded up. They left her there for a whole week with only bread and water for nourishment. After she came out she promptly ran away, together with three other girls. They were found and brought back. The nuns stripped them naked and whipped them. They used a horse buggy whip on my grandmother. Then she was put back into the attic—for two weeks.

My mother had much the same experiences but never wanted to talk about them, and then there I was, in the same place. The school is now run by the BIA—the Bureau of Indian Affairs—but only since about fifteen years ago. When I was there, during the 1960s, it was still run by the Church. The Jesuit fathers ran the boys' wing and the Sisters of the Sacred Heart ran us—with the help of the strap. Nothing had changed since my grandmother's days. I have been told recently that even in the '70s they were still beating children at that school. All I got out of school was being taught how to pray. I learned quickly that I would be beaten if I failed in my devotions or, God forbid, prayed the wrong way, especially prayed in Indian to Wakan Tanka, the Indian Creator.

The girls' wing was built like an F and was run like a penal institution. Every morning at five o'clock the sisters would come into our large dormitory to wake us up, and immediately we had to kneel down at the sides of our beds and recite the prayers. At six o'clock we were herded into the church for more of the same. I did not take kindly to the discipline and to marching by the clock, left-right, left-right. I was never one to like being forced to do something. I do something because I feel like doing it. I felt this way always, as far as I can remember, and my sister Barbara felt the same way. An old medicine man once told me: "Us Lakotas are not like dogs who can be trained, who can be beaten and keep on wagging their tails, licking the hand that whipped them. We are like cats, little cats, big cats, wildcats, bobcats, mountain lions. It doesn't matter what kind, but cats who can't be tamed, who scratch if you step on their tails." But I was only a kitten and my claws were still small.

Barbara was still in the school when I arrived and during my first year or two she could still protect me a little bit. When Barb was a seventh-grader she ran away together with five other girls, early in the morning before sunrise. They brought them back in the evening. The girls had to wait for two hours in front of the mother superior's office. They were hungry and cold, frozen through. It was wintertime and they had been running the whole day without food, trying to make good their escape. The mother superior asked each girl, "Would you do this again?" She told them that as punishment they would not be allowed to visit home for a month and that she'd keep them busy on work details until the skin on their knees and elbows had worn off. At the end of her speech she told each girl, "Get up from this chair and lean over it." She then lifted the girls' skirts and pulled down their underpants. Not little girls either, but teenagers. She had a leather strap about a foot long and four inches wide fastened to a stick, and beat the girls, one after another, until they cried. Barb did not give her that satisfaction but just clenched her teeth. There was one girl, Barb told me, the nun kept on beating and beating until her arm got tired.

I did not escape my share of the strap. Once, when I was thirteen years old, I refused to go to Mass. I did not want to go to church because I did not feel well. A nun grabbed me by the hair, dragged me upstairs, made me stoop over, pulled my dress up (we were not allowed at the time to wear jeans), pulled my panties down, and gave me what they called "swats"—twenty-five swats with a board around which Scotch tape had been wound. She hurt me badly.

My classroom was right next to the principal's office and almost every day I could hear him swatting the boys. Beating was the common punishment for not doing one's homework, or for being late to school. It had such a bad effect upon me that I hated and mistrusted every white person on sight, because I met only one kind. It was not until much later that I met sincere white people I could relate to and be friends with. Racism breeds racism in reverse.

The routine at St. Francis was dreary. Six A.M., kneeling in church for an hour or so; seven o'clock, breakfast; eight o'clock, scrub the floor, peel spuds, make classes. We had to mop the dining room twice every day and scrub the tables. If you were caught taking a rest, doodling on the bench with a fingernail or knife, or just rapping, the nun would come up with a dish towel and just slap it across your face, saying, "You're not supposed to be talking, you're supposed to be working!" Monday mornings we had cornmeal mush, Tuesday oatmeal, Wednesday rice and raisins, Thursday cornflakes, and Friday all the leftovers mixed together or sometimes fish. Frequently the food had bugs or rocks in it. We were eating hot dogs that were weeks old, while the nuns were dining on ham, whipped potatoes, sweet peas, and cranberry sauce. In winter our dorm was icy cold while the nuns' rooms were always warm.

I have seen little girls arrive at the school, first-graders, just fresh from home and totally unprepared for what awaited them, little girls with pretty braids, and the first thing the nuns did was chop their hair off and tie up what was left behind their ears. Next they would dump the children into tubs of alcohol, a sort of rubbing alcohol, "to get the germs off." Many of the nuns were German immigrants, some from Bavaria, so that we sometimes speculated whether Bavaria was some sort of Dracula country inhabited by monsters. For the sake of objectivity I ought to mention that two of the German fathers were great linguists and that the only Lakota-English dictionaries and grammars which are worth anything were put together by them.

At night some of the girls would huddle in bed together for comfort and reassurance. Then the nun in charge of the dorm would come in and say, "What are the two of you doing in bed together? I smell evil in this room. You girls are evil incarnate. You are sinning. You are going to hell and burn forever. You can act that way in the devil's frying pan." She would get them out of bed in the middle of the night, making them kneel and pray until morning. We had not the slightest idea what it was all about. At home we slept two and three in a bed for animal warmth and a feeling of security.

The nuns and the girls in the two top grades were constantly battling it out physically with fists, nails, and hair-pulling. I myself was growing from a kitten into an undersized cat. My claws were getting bigger and were itching for action. About 1969 or 1970 a strange young white girl appeared on the reservation. She looked about eighteen or twenty years old. She was pretty and had long, blond hair down to her waist, patched jeans, boots, and a backpack. She was different from any other white person we had met before. I think her name was Wise. I do not know how she managed to overcome our reluctance and distrust, getting us into a corner, making us listen to her, asking us how we were treated. She told us that she was from New York. She was the first real hippie or Yippie we had come across. She told us of people called the Black Panthers, Young Lords, and Weathermen. She said, "Black people are getting it on. In-

dians are getting it on in St. Paul and California. How about
you?" She also said, "Why don't you put out an underground paper, mimeograph it. It's easy. Tell it like it is. Let it
all hang out." She spoke a strange lingo but we caught on
fast.

Charlene Left Hand Bull and Gina One Star were two
full-blood girls I used to hang out with. We did everything
together. They were willing to join me in a Sioux uprising.
We put together a newspaper which we called the *Red Panther*. In it we wrote how bad the school was, what kind of
slop we had to eat—slimy, rotten, blackened potatoes for
two weeks—the way we were beaten. I think I was the one
who wrote the worst article about our principal of the moment, Father Keeler. I put all my anger and venom into it. I
called him a goddam wasičun son of a bitch. I wrote that he
knew nothing about Indians and should go back to where he
came from, teaching white children whom he could relate to.
I wrote that we knew which priests slept with which nuns
and that all they ever could think about was filling their
bellies and buying a new car. It was the kind of writing
which foamed at the mouth, but which also lifted a great
deal of weight from one's soul.

On Saint Patrick's Day, when everybody was at the big
powwow, we distributed our newspapers. We put them on
windshields and bulletin boards, in desks and pews, in
dorms and toilets. But someone saw us and snitched on us.
The shit hit the fan. The three of us were taken before a
board meeting. Our parents, in my case my mother, had to
come. They were told that ours was a most serious matter,
the worst thing that had ever happened in the school's long
history. One of the nuns told my mother, "Your daughter
really needs to be talked to." "What's wrong with my daughter?" my mother asked. She was given one of our *Red Panther*
newspapers. The nun pointed out its name to her and then

my piece, waiting for mom's reaction. After a while she asked, "Well, what have you got to say to this? What do you think?"

My mother said, "Well, when I went to school here, some years back, I was treated a lot worse than these kids are. I really can't see how they can have any complaints, because we was treated a lot stricter. We could not even wear skirts halfway up our knees. These girls have it made. But you should forgive them because they are young. And it's supposed to be a free country, free speech and all that. I don't believe what they done is wrong." So all I got out of it was scrubbing six flights of stairs on my hands and knees, every day. And no boy-side privileges.

The boys and girls were still pretty much separated. The only time one could meet a member of the opposite sex was during free time, between four and five-thirty, in the study hall or on benches or the volleyball court outside, and that was strictly supervised. One day Charlene and I went over to the boys' side. We were on the ball team and they had to let us practice. We played three extra minutes, only three minutes more than we were supposed to. Here was the nuns' opportunity for revenge. We got twenty-five swats. I told Charlene, "We are getting too old to have our bare asses whipped that way. We are old enough to have babies. Enough of this shit. Next time we fight back." Charlene only said, "Hoka-hay!"

We had to take showers every evening. One little girl did not want to take her panties off and one of the nuns told her, "You take those underpants off—or else!" But the child was ashamed to do it. The nun was getting her swat to threaten the girl. I went up to the sister, pushed her veil off, and knocked her down. I told her that if she wanted to hit a little girl she should pick on me, pick one her own size. She got herself transferred out of the dorm a week later.

In a school like this there is always a lot of favoritism. At St. Francis it was strongly tinged with racism. Girls who were near-white, who came from what the nuns called "nice families," got preferential treatment. They waited on the faculty and got to eat ham or eggs and bacon in the morning. They got the easy jobs while the skins, who did not have the right kind of background—myself among them—always wound up in the laundry room sorting out ten bushel baskets of dirty boys' socks every day. Or we wound up scrubbing the floors and doing all the dishes. The school therefore fostered fights and antagonism between whites and breeds, and between breeds and skins. At one time Charlene and I had to iron all the robes and vestments the priests wore when saying Mass. We had to fold them up and put them into a chest in the back of the church. In a corner, looking over our shoulders, was a statue of the crucified Savior, all bloody and beaten up. Charlene looked up and said, "Look at that poor Indian. The pigs sure worked him over." That was the closest I ever came to seeing Jesus.

I was held up as a bad example and didn't mind. I was old enough to have a boyfriend and promptly got one. At the school we had an hour and a half for ourselves. Between the boys' and the girls' wings were some benches where one could sit. My boyfriend and I used to go there just to hold hands and talk. The nuns were very uptight about any boy-girl stuff. They had an exaggerated fear of anything having even the faintest connection with sex. One day in religion class, an all-girl class, Sister Bernard singled me out for some remarks, pointing me out as a bad example, an example that should be shown. She said that I was too free with my body. That I was holding hands which meant that I was not a good example to follow. She also said that I wore unchaste dresses, skirts which were too short, too suggestive, shorter than regulations permitted, and for that I would be punished. She dressed me down before the whole class, carrying on and on about my unchastity.

I stood up and told her, "You shouldn't say any of those things, miss. You people are a lot worse than us Indians. I know all about you, because my grandmother and my aunt told me about you. Maybe twelve, thirteen years ago you had a water stoppage here in St. Francis. No water could get through the pipes. There are water lines right under the mission, underground tunnels and passages where in my grandmother's time only the nuns and priests could go, which were off-limits to everybody else. When the water backed up they had to go through all the water lines and clean them out. And in those huge pipes they found the bodies of newborn babies. And they were white babies. They weren't Indian babies. At least when our girls have babies, they don't do away with them that way, like flushing them down the toilet, almost.

"And that priest they sent here from Holy Rosary in Pine Ridge because he molested a little girl. You couldn't think of anything better than dump him on us. All he does is watch young women and girls with that funny smile on his face. Why don't you point him out for an example?"

Charlene and I worked on the school newspaper. After all we had some practice. Every day we went down to Publications. One of the priests acted as the photographer, doing the enlarging and developing. He smelled of chemicals which had stained his hands yellow. One day he invited Charlene into the darkroom. He was going to teach her developing. She was developed already. She was a big girl compared to him, taller too. Charlene was nicely built, not fat, just rounded. No sharp edges anywhere. All of a sudden she rushed out of the darkroom, yelling to me, "Let's get out of here! He's trying to feel me up. That priest is nasty." So there was this too to contend with—sexual harassment. We complained to the student body. The nuns said we just had a dirty mind.

We got a new priest in English. During one of his first classes he asked one of the boys a certain question. The boy was shy. He spoke poor English, but he had the right answer. The priest told him, "You did not say it right. Correct yourself. Say it over again." The boy got flustered and stammered. He could hardly get out a word. But the priest kept after him: "Didn't you hear? I told you to do the whole thing over. Get it right this time." He kept on and on.

I stood up and said, "Father, don't be doing that. If you go into an Indian's home and try to talk Indian, they might laugh at you and say, 'Do it over correctly. Get it right this time!' "

He shouted at me, "Mary, you stay after class. Sit down right now!"

I stayed after class, until after the bell. He told me, "Get over here!" He grabbed me by the arm, pushing me against the blackboard, shouting, "Why are you always mocking us? You have no reason to do this."

I said, "Sure I do. You were making fun of him. You embarrassed him. He needs strengthening, not weakening. You hurt him. I did not hurt you."

He twisted my arm and pushed real hard. I turned around and hit him in the face, giving him a bloody nose. After that I ran out of the room, slamming the door behind me. He and I went to Sister Bernard's office. I told her, "Today I quit school. I'm not taking any more of this, none of this shit anymore. None of this treatment. Better give me my diploma. I can't waste any more time on you people."

Sister Bernard looked at me for a long, long time. She said, "All right, Mary Ellen, go home today. Come back in a few days and get your diploma." And that was that. Oddly enough, that priest turned out okay. He taught a class in grammar, orthography, composition, things like that. I think he wanted more respect in class. He was still young and unsure of himself. But I was in there too long. I didn't feel like hearing it. Later he became a good friend of the Indians, a personal friend of myself and my husband. He stood up for us during Wounded Knee and after. He stood up to his superiors, stuck his neck way out, became a real people's priest. He even learned our language. He died prematurely of cancer. It is not only the good Indians who die young, but the good whites, too. It is the timid ones who know how to take care of themselves who grow old. I am still grateful to that priest for what he did for us later and for the quarrel he picked with me—or did I pick it with him?—because it ended a situation which had become unendurable for me. The day of my fight with him was my last day in school.

CHAPTER 4

Drinking and Fighting

Got them real bad relocation blues,
Got them long-haired Injun big city woes.
One drunk Indian yells 'cause he's being mugged,
Some young Indian complains his phone is bugged,
But nobody is getting hugged.
Passerby says: "How, big chief,
What's your beef?"
Ugh, ugh, big chief, how, how.
Hio, yana-yanay, hi-oh.

Got them sweet muscatel relocation blues,
Got them lemon-vodka big city woes.
Something rubs my leg. "Hi there, pussycat."
Has a pink and naked tail, some big rat!
Home sweet home!
Hear the police whistle blow,
Someone pissing in the snow,
Tweet, tweet, ugh, ugh, clank, clank.
Hio, yana-yanay, hi-oh.

—Forty-niner song

S t. Francis, Parmelee, Mission, were the towns I hung out in after I quit school, reservation towns without hope. Towns that show how a people can be ground under the boot, ground into nothing. The houses are made of tar paper and almost anything that can be scrounged. Take a rusty house trailer, a small, old one which is falling apart. Build onto it a cube made of orange crates. That will be the kitchen. Tack on to that a crumbling auto body. That will be the bedroom. Add a rotting wall tent for a nursery. That will make a typical home, larger than average. Then the out-house, about fifty feet away. With a blizzard going and the usual bowel troubles, a trip to the privy at night is high adventure. A big joke among drunks was to wait for some-body to be in the outhouse and then for a few guys to root it up, lift it clear off the ground, and turn it upside down with whoever was inside hollering like crazy. This was one of the amusements Parmelee had to offer.

Parmelee, St. Francis, and Mission were drunk towns full of hang-around-the-fort Indians. On weekends the lease money and ADC checks were drunk up with white light-ning, muscatel—mustn't tell, purple Jesus, lemon vodka, Jim Beam, car varnish, paint remover—anything that would go down and stay down for five minutes. And, of course, beer by the carload. Some people would do just about anything for a jug of wine, of mni-sha, and would not give a damn about the welfare of their families. They would fight con-stantly over whatever little money they had left, whether to buy food or alcohol. The alcohol usually won out. Because there was nobody else, the staggering shapes took out their misery on each other. There was hardly a weekend when somebody did not have an eye gouged out or a skull cracked. "Them's eyeballs, not grapes you're seeing on the floor," was the standing joke.

When a good time was had by all and everybody got slaphappy and mellow—lila itomni, as they said—they all piled into their cars and started making the rounds, all over the three million acres of Rosebud and Pine Ridge, from Mission Town to Winner, to Upper Cut Meat, to White River, to He-Dog. To Porcupine, Valentine, Wanblee, Oglala, Murdo, Kadokah, Scenic, Ghost Hawk Park—you name it. From one saloon to the other—the Idle Hour, Arlo's, the Crazy Horse Cafe, the Long Horn Saloon, the Sagebrush, the Dew-Drop Inn, singing forty-niner songs:

> Heyah-heya, weyah-weya,
> give me whiskey, honey,
> Suta, mni wakan,
> I do love you,
> Heya, heyah.

Those cars! It was incredible how many people they could cram into one of their jalopies, five of them side by side and one or two on their laps, little kids and all. The brakes were all gone, usually, and one had to pump them like crazy about a mile before coming to a crossing. There were no windshield wipers. They were not needed because there were no windshields either. If one headlight was working, that was cool. Often doors were missing, too, or even a tire. That did not matter because one could drive on the rim. There were always two cases of beer in the back and a few gallons of the cheapest California wine. The babies got some of that too. So they took off amid a shower of beer cans, doing ninety miles with faulty brakes and forty cans of beer sloshing in their bellies. A great way to end it all.

At age twelve I could drink a quart of the hard stuff and not show it. I used to be a heavy drinker and I came close to being an out-and-out alcoholic—very close. But I got tired of drinking. I felt it was all right to drink, but every morning

I woke up sick, feeling terrible, with a first-class hangover. I did not like the feeling at all but still kept hitting the bottle. Then I stopped. I haven't touched a drop of liquor for years, ever since I felt there was a purpose to my life, learned to accept myself for what I was. I have to thank the Indian movement for that, and Grandfather Peyote, and the pipe. Having children played a big role too, though I stopped drinking even before I had my first baby.

Barb and I have a lot of friends. Most of them are drinkers and I tell them I don't booze anymore. When I go with them I drink 7UP. They keep asking me, "Are you too good for us, or what?" And I tell them, "I just don't find that alcohol is doing you any good. And if you feel that I'm acting too good for you, then that's up to you. You can have that feeling. If you want to drink, go ahead, don't mind me." I do not preach to them. In their drunken state they ask Barb or me what to do. Sometimes we feel like mother hens. They come and tell me their problems. So I try to talk to them in a way that peyote would want me to advise them. They listen to me and tell me that I am right and that they will stop, but they are not strong enough to do it. They say I am right, but the next day they just go out and get full again. I do not judge them. I am the last person in the world to have a right to do that, and I know where they are coming from. I tell them, "Enjoy your Budweiser, I'll stay with my 7UP or Pepsi."

I started drinking because it was the natural way of life. My father drank, my stepfather drank, my mother drank— not too much, but she used to get tipsy once in a while. My older sisters drank, Barbara starting four years before me, because she is that much older. I think I grew up with the idea that everybody was doing it. Which was nearly true, even with some of the old traditionals who always pour a few drops out of their bottles and glasses, sprinkle it on the floor or into corners for the spirits of their departed drinking companions, saying in Sioux, "Here, cousin, here is a little mni-sha for you, savor it!"

I started drinking when I was ten, when my mother married that man. He was always drinking, so I would sneak in and help myself to some of his stuff. Vodka mostly—that's what he liked. In school I crept into the vestry and drank the church wine, Christ's blood. He must have understood, hanging out with people like us. At any rate no lightning struck me. The first time I got drunk was when some grown-up relatives had a drinking party. One woman asked me, "Do you want some lemonade?" I said yes and she gave me a big, tall glass of lemonade and put some of that stuff in it. That was my first time. I was trying to walk across the room and could not, just kept falling down, while everybody laughed at me.

Liquor is forbidden on the reservation, which is something of a joke, and drinking it is illegal. But towns like Winner, St. Francis, and Mission have a population which is almost half white and the wasičuns want to have their legal booze. So they incorporated these towns, which are within the reservation, putting them under white man's law. Which means that you have bars there and package stores. Also all around the reservation are the white cow towns with their saloons. Even if you are stuck in the back country, you can always find a bootlegger. My sister Barb was my best friend, the one who really loved me. She was the one who got me up in the morning and put clothes on me, watched over me. One day a boy took me to a John Wayne movie. Afterward we went "uptown" to hustle some hard stuff. The town hardly had four or five streets, two of them paved, and maybe two dozen shacks and mobile homes sprinkled around, but it had an "uptown," and a "downtown." So uptown we went to the cabin of a half-blood bootlegger, getting ourselves a pint of moonshine, the kind they call "liquid TNT, guaranteed to blow your head off," and a small bottle of rum. As we were coming out of the door we collided with Barb, who had come to get her ration of wet goods. She made a face as if she couldn't believe her eyes and said, "What in hell are you doing here?"

I answered, "What are *you* doing here? I didn't know you patronized this place."

She got really mad. "It's all right for me. I am seventeen. But you are not supposed to be doing that. You are too young!" She took the bottles away from us, threatening to crack the head of the boy if he dared to interfere. In her excitement she smashed the bottles against the corner of the log cabin instead of saving them for herself and her friends.

Another time, after a school dance, I was sitting with a boy I liked, smoking a cigarette, and out of nowhere suddenly there was Barbara yanking the cigarette out of my mouth. She threw it on the floor and stomped on it right in front of everybody. I hit her, yelling, "But you do it." And again she said, "Yeah, but I'm older." We used to fight a lot, out of love and desperation.

After I quit school the situation at home got worse and worse. I had nothing but endless arguments with my mother and fights with my stepfather. So I ran away. At first only for two weeks to a place that was not very far, just a few miles, then I stayed away for months, and in the end, altogether. I drank and smoked grass all the time. At age seventeen that was just about all I did. Whiskey, straight whiskey, and not Johnny Walker or Cutty Sark either. Then I changed over to gin because I liked the taste. How I survived the wild, drunken rides which are such an integral part of the reservation scene, I don't know. One time we were coming back from Murdo at the usual eighty miles an hour. The car was bursting at the seams, it was so full of people. In the front seat were two couples kissing, one of the kissers being the driver. One tire blew out. The doors flew open and the two couples fell out arm in arm. The girls were screaming, especially the one at the bottom who was bleeding, but nobody was seriously hurt. I must have lost more than two dozen relatives and friends in such accidents. One of those winos was out in his car getting a load on. He had a woman with him. His old lady was in another car, also getting smashed. Somebody told her he was making it with that other woman. So she started chasing them all over Pine Ridge. In the end she caught up with them. I do not think they were lovers. He was at that stage where the bottle was his only mistress. His wife shook her fists at them, screaming, "I smash you up! I total you!" All the other drivers on the road who watched those cars drunkenly lurching about scrambled to get out of the way, running their cars off the highway into the sagebrush. Well, the wife succeeded in bringing about a head-on collision at full speed and all three of them were killed.

Supposedly you drink to forget. The trouble is you don't forget, you remember—all the old insults and hatreds, real and imagined. As a result there are always fights. One of the nicest, gentlest men I knew killed his wife in a drunken rage. One uncle had both his eyes put out while he was lying senseless. My sister-in-law Delphine's husband lost one eye. She herself was beaten to death by a drunken tribal policeman. Such things are not even considered worth an investigation.

I fight too. During my barhopping days I went into a Rapid City saloon for a beer. Among Sioux people, Rapid City has a reputation for being the most racist town in the whole country as far as Indians are concerned. In the old days many South Dakota saloons had a sign over the door reading NO INDIANS AND DOGS ALLOWED! I sat down next to an old honky lady. Actually she looked about thirty, but when you are seventeen that seems old. She gave me a dirty look, moving to another stool away from me, saying, "Goddam, dirty Injun. You get out into the streets and the gutter where you belong."

I came back, "What did you say?"

"You heard me. This place ain't for Indians. Dammit, isn't there a place left where a white man (I remember, she actually said "man") can drink in peace without having to put up with you people?"

I felt the blood pounding in my head. In front of me where I was sitting was a glass ashtray. I broke it on the counter and cut her face with the jagged edge. In my insane drunken rage I felt good doing it. Possibly I would have felt good even had I been sober.

One time I was in Cedar Rapids, Iowa, visiting a girl friend among the Sac and Fox Indians. She is poor but always cleans out her whole icebox to feed me. Her tribe happened to be having a powwow with a lot of young people participating, over sixty of them young men. The full-bloods were all standing or sitting around a drum, drinking beer. A lot were dancing with roaches or war bonnets on their heads, feather bustles on their butts, and bells on their ankles. The songs were militant. Some of the white boys and breeds were catching on to that and started hassling the skins. I should make clear that being a full-blood or breed is not a matter of bloodline, or how Indian you look, or how black your hair is. The general rule is that whoever thinks, sings, acts, and speaks Indian is a skin, a full-blood, and whoever acts and thinks like a white man is a half-blood or breed, no matter how Indian he looks. So the full-bloods told the others, "If you are ready to get it on with us, so get it on!" The half-bloods and white boys had white or cowboy shirts on while the skins wore ribbon shirts and chokers. They wore their hair long, often in braids. The others wore it short. It was easy to tell friend from foe. They got it on. It was one of the biggest drunken free-for-alls I was ever involved in. It lasted about half an hour, but already after five minutes the breeds had three casualties. One man got his face knocked in, the others had concussions. In the end there were about nine of these white shirts lying on the ground under a big tree, bloody and knocked out. One had a broken arm. It's something you can't stop once it starts. If somebody in that fighting mood yells at you, "Go, get 'em!" you can't tell that person, who has been fucked over for so many years, that he is wrong, that he should be a pacifist.

In Seattle I went with my Blackfoot girl friend Bonnie to a little bar on skid row, I think it was called the Tugboat Cafe. This was in a neighborhood frequented by Indians. It was Christmastime and the stores and bars were hung with blinking red and green lights. We wanted to buy booze for a Christmas and New Year's party. My friend said, "I'm gonna call my folks to wish them happy holidays." We found a phone booth on a street corner. Bonnie was making her long-distance call when a drunk white guy tried to force his way in, yelling at Bonnie to get out, that he wanted to use the phone, saying, "What's so important for an Indian to make a phone call? I bet you don't even know how to dial. Use a tom-tom!"

Bonnie said, "You goddam honky, leave me alone!" She was trying to fight him off. He had a beer bottle and he busted it on her head and face. She staggered out of the booth dripping blood. I rushed to her aid and we tried to fight him, but the blood was running down into her eyes so that she could not see. He hit her again, knocking her sprawling into the gutter. She was lying there, looking up at me but not seeing a thing, calling my name. I yelled for the cops, but the white winos hid that guy and the police made no effort to find him. People were milling around me— white, black, and Indian. One white lady pushed me aside, shouting, "Get out of the way, I'm trained as a nurse, what you're doing is all wrong."

I told her, "Don't push me. This is my friend." But she still insisted: "Get out of the way. Can you believe that? Those Indians are really something!" I threw her against the car and she fell on her ass. The cops promptly arrested me. If you are an Indian woman, especially in a ghetto, you have to fight all the time against brutalization and sexual advances. After a while you yourself begin to strike out blindly, anticipating attacks even when none are intended. Many of these brawls are connected with drinking, but many occur just because you are an Indian. Also in Seattle I saw a white man kicking a passed-out Indian in the head with his boots, screaming, *"This is for Wounded Knee!"*

By nature I am not a violent person. When I get mad, I start shaking, my blood starts to heat up, and I am afraid I might hurt somebody fighting or get hurt myself. So I try to cool off and stay out of it. But if I see an Indian sister being abused, harassed, getting beaten or raped, I have to take up for her. Once I am in the middle of a fight, though, I enjoy it. I have often thought that given an extreme situation, I'd have it in me to kill, if that was the only way. I think if one gets into an "either me or you" situation, that feeling is instinctive. The average white person seldom gets into such a corner, but that corner is where the Indian lives, whether he wants to or not.

Nowadays I have learned better to control myself and situations as they arise, or if I cannot control them, avoid getting sucked into them. Barbara tells me that she prefers to sit back and watch a fight, rather than join in. She told me, "There is nothing sweeter than revenge, but don't do it physically. Revenge yourself with mind power, let your mind do the fighting." But when it comes down to the nitty-gritty, Barb's mind is often in her fists. I have seen it.

One night, at Rosebud, Barb had a date with a boy called Poor Bear. She was sober, but he had a load on and the liquor had roused his fighting spirit. They were driving past the tribal office when Poor Bear suddenly stopped the car, saying, "That's where all our trouble comes from, from inside that building!" He had a shotgun in his trunk, took it out, and methodically busted every window in the building. Then he drove to the top of a hill overlooking Rosebud where he parked the car to admire his handiwork. The tribal police were there in no time. "We're just checking," they said. They found a half-empty gallon jug of wine and some whiskey under the seat that Barb had not known about, and finally the gun and some spent shells. They said, "So you're the ones who've been shooting up the tribal building, huh?" They took Poor Bear in and Barb had to bail him out. He only got a year's probation for this stunt. Down where I live they are rather relaxed about this kind of thing because it happens all the time.

I am a wife and mother now and my husband is a medicine man. I have my baby with me nearly all the time. I don't drink anymore. So it stands to reason that I try very hard not to get into fights. But no matter how hard I try, I sometimes still find myself in the middle of an uproar. There seems to be no escape. One evening, early in 1975, we were on an Indian reservation in Washington State where my husband had to run some ceremonies—Leonard, myself, my little boy Pedro, another Sioux leader, and my friend Annie Mae. We had taken rooms in a motel inside a border town inhabited mostly by whites, half in and half outside the reservation. We were just leaving to drive back home. Leonard, as always, had his long braids wrapped in strips of red trade cloth. As we were putting our things into the car we noticed that the gas tank was leaking. It had been okay before. As we were standing around, trying to figure out how to fix it, two rednecks came up. They started making offensive remarks: "Look at those Indians, look at their long hair. How long since you've been to a barber?" They just stood there, staring at us and laughing. Leonard told them, "We did not come here to fight. We came here on business. What do you want? This is an Indian reservation, do you know that? Let's not have any trouble."

The honkies laughed, grabbed Leonard's braids, and yanked them hard. Then they jumped him. At that moment two Indian friends came out of a barn, Russ and Iron Shell, and they joined in the fight. I had my baby to protect. Then another carload of rednecks came onto the scene. One guy had a sawed-off shotgun, the others were armed with baseball bats. I tried to head them off, pleading with them to leave us alone, but they just kept going after our men. I heard later that beating up Indians was a regular pastime among the white lumberjacks and fishery workers in that area. Suddenly I saw that a police car was parked across the street. I told Annie Mae, "Take Pedro. Watch over him," and I ran over to the police. There were two of them, state troopers. I told them, "Look what's going on. We didn't do anything. They're hurting our men. Why don't you do something?" The troopers said nothing, just started up their car and drove off. They stopped about fifty yards away and sat there, watching and grinning. By then the hoodlums were demolishing our car with their bats, busting all the windows. I ran over to an Indian friend's house and she gave me her car for a getaway, to make it possible for us to escape. When I got back a few more skins had joined our men. The street was full of honkies with shotguns and baseball bats. As I drove up I heard gunshots. Pedro was in the front seat of our car and one shot just missed his leg. Two more police cars drove up. The troopers told the honkies, "Break it up, fellows, go home to the little woman. Call it a day!" Then they started arresting the Indians.

It was the usual sequence. Honkies, be so kind, and go

home! Then arrest the Indians for "disturbing the peace."
Put them in jail. Charge them. Let them get bailed out. Drag
them into court. Collect the fine. I got scars in my face from
this incident, barely an inch from my eye. I kicked one of the
honkies in the head, between the legs, wherever I could kick
him. Alcohol was not involved in that fracas, except among
the honkies. It gets tiresome, almost boring. These things
remind me of an old joke: One Indian tells his white neighbor: "You've stolen my land, shot my father, raped my wife,
got my daughter with child, turned my son on to whiskey.
One day I'm gonna lose my patience. Better watch that
shit!"

It seemed that my early life, before I met Leonard and
before I went to Wounded Knee, was just one endless,
vicious circle of drinking and fighting, drinking and fighting. Barb was caught up in the same circle, except that she
was running with a different crowd most of the time. She
was unusual in that she could drink just one beer or one glass
of wine and then stop if she wanted to. Most of us at that
stage could not do that.

I had not been drinking for years, but when I heard that
one of my closest friends had been found dead with a bullet
through her head I broke down completely and felt a sudden
need for a drink. I happened to be in New York at the time.
Shaking, and with tears streaming down my face, I blindly
staggered to the nearest bar and downed four margaritas,
one after the other. It had no effect on me. I remained totally
sober. And it did not help my sadness. That was the last
time.

People talk about the "Indian drinking problem," but we
say that it is a white problem. White men invented whiskey
and brought it to America. They manufacture, advertise,
and sell it to us. They make the profit on it and cause the
conditions that make Indians drink in the first place.

CHAPTER 5

Aimlessness

I am roaming,
Roaming,
Restless,
Aimless.
In the snow I see
My ancestors'
Bloody footprints,
Moccasin prints.
My old boots are worn
And down at the heels.
On what road am I?
The white man's road,
Or the Indians'?
There are no signposts.
The road is uphill,
And the wind in my face.
Still I go on.

—*Yellow Bird*

I was a loner, always. I was not interested in dresses, makeup, or perfume, the kinds of things some girls are keen on. I was scared of white people and uneasy in their company, so I did not socialize with them. I could not relate to half-bloods and was afraid that full-bloods would not accept me. I could not share the values my mother lived by. For friends I had only a few girls who were like me and shared my thoughts. I had no place to go, but a great restlessness came over me, an urge to get away, no matter where. Nowhere was better than the place I was in. So I did what many of my friends had already done—I ran away. Barbara, being older, had already set the precedent. A clash with my mother had sent Barb on her way. My mother was, at that time, hard to live with. From her point of view, I guess, we were not easy to get along with either. We didn't have a generation gap, we had a generation Grand Canyon. Mother's values were Puritan. She was uptight. I remember when Barbara was about to have her baby, mom cussed her out. Barb was still in high school and my mother was cursing her, calling her a no-good whore, which really shook my sister up. Barb said, "I'm going to have your grandchild, I thought you'd be happy," but my mother was just terrible, telling Barb that she was not her daughter anymore. My sister lost her baby. She had a miscarriage working in a kitchen detail one morning. They gave her a big, heavy dishpan full of cereal to carry and that caused it right there. She lost the baby. She could not get over mother's attitude.

My other sister, Sandra, when she was going to have her eldest boy, Jeff, my mother did the same thing to her, saying, "What the hell are you trying to do to me? I can't hold up my head among my friends!" She was more concerned about her neighbors' attitude than about us. Barb told her, "Mom, if you don't want us around, if you are ashamed of your own grandchildren, then, okay, we'll leave."

I understood how mom was feeling. She was wrapped up in a different culture altogether. We spoke a different language. Words did not mean to her what they meant to us. I felt sorry for her, but we were hurting each other. After Barbara lost her baby she brooded. It seemed as if in her mind she blamed mother for it, as if mother had willed that baby to die. It was irrational, but it was there all the same. Once mother told us after a particularly emotional confrontation, "If you ever need any help, don't come to me!" Of course she did not mean it. She will stick up for us, always, but looking over her shoulder in case her friends should disapprove. To be able to hold up your head among what is called "the right kind of people," that is important to her. She has a home, she has a car. She has TV and curtains at the windows. That's where her head is. She is a good, hardworking woman, but she won't go and find out what is really happening. For instance, a girl who worked with mother told her she couldn't reach Barbara at work by phone. Immediately mom jumped to the conclusion that Barb had quit her job. So when my sister got home, she got on her case right away: "I just don't give a damn about you kids! Quitting your job!" continuing in that vein.

Barb just rang up her boss and handed the phone to mom, let her know from the horse's mouth that she had not quit. Then she told mother: "Next time find out and make sure of the facts before you get on my case like that. And don't be so concerned about jobs. There are more important things in life than punching a time clock."

There was that wall of misunderstanding between my mother and us, and I have to admit I did not help in breaking it down. I had little inclination to join the hang-around-the-fort Indians, so one day I just up and left, without saying good-bye. Joining up with other kids in patched Levi's jackets and chokers, our long hair trailing behind us. We traveled and did not give a damn where to.

One or two kids acted like a magnet. We formed groups. I traveled with ten of those new or sometimes old acquaintances in one car all summer long. We had our bedrolls and cooking utensils, and if we ran out of something the pros among us would go and rip off the food. Rip off whatever we needed. We just drifted from place to place, meeting new people, having a good time. Looking back, a lot was based on drinking and drugs. If you had a lot of dope you were everybody's friend, everybody wanted to know you. If you had a car and good grass, then you were about one of the best guys anybody ever knew.

It took me a while to see the emptiness underneath all this frenzied wandering. I liked pot. Barb was an acid freak. She told me she once dropped eight hits of LSD at a time. "It all depends on your mood, on your state of mind," she told me. "If you have a stable mind, it's going to be good. But if you are in a depressed mood, or your friend isn't going to be able to handle it for you, then everything is distorted and you have a very hard time as that drug shakes you up."

Once Barb took some acid in a girl friend's bedroom. There was a huge flag on the wall upside down. The Stars and Stripes hanging upside down used to be an international signal of distress. It was also the American Indian's sign of distress. The Ghost Dancers used to wrap themselves in upside-down flags, dancing that way, crying for a vision until they fell down in a trance. When they came to, they always said that they had been in another world, the world as it was before the white man came, the prairie covered with herds of buffalo and tipi circles full of people who had been killed long ago. The flags which the dancers wore like blankets did not prevent the soldiers from shooting them down. Barb was lying on the bed and the upside-down flag began to work on her mind. She was watching it and it was just rippling up the wall like waves; the stripes and the stars would fall from the flag onto the floor and would scatter into thousands of sprays of light, exploding all over the room. She told me she did not quite know whether it was an old-fashioned vision or just a caricature of one, but she liked it.

After a while of roaming and dropping acid she felt burned out, her brain empty. She said she got tired of it, just one trip after the other. She was waiting, waiting for something, for a sign, but she did not know what she was waiting for. And like her, all the other roaming Indian kids were waiting, just as the Ghost Dancers had waited for the drumbeat, the message the eagle was to bring. I was waiting, too. In the meantime I kept traveling.

I was not into LSD but smoked a lot of pot. People have the idea that reservations are isolated, that what happens elsewhere does not touch them, but it does. We might not share in all the things America has to offer some of its citizens, but some things got to us, all right. The urban Indians from L.A., Rapid City, St. Paul, and Denver brought them to us on their visits. For instance, around 1969 or 1970 many half-grown boys in Rosebud were suddenly sniffing glue. If the ghetto Indians brought the city with them to the reservation, so we runaways dragged the res and its problems around with us in our bedrolls. Wherever we went we formed tiny reservations.

"You are an interesting subculture," an anthropologist in Chicago told me during that time. I didn't know whether that was an insult or a compliment. We both spoke English but could not understand each other. To him I was an interesting zoological specimen to be filed away someplace; to me he was merely ridiculous. But anthropologists are a story in themselves.

It is hard being forever on the move and not having any money. We supported ourselves by shoplifting, "liberating" a lot of stuff. Many of us became real experts at this game. I was very good at it. We did not think that what we were doing was wrong. On the contrary, ripping off gave us a great deal of satisfaction, moral satisfaction. We were meting out justice in reverse. We had always been stolen from by white shopkeepers and government agents. In the 1880s and '90s a white agent on the reservation had a salary of fifteen hundred dollars a year. From this salary he managed to save within five or six years some fifty thousand dollars to retire. He simply stole the government goods and rations he was supposed to distribute among the Indians. On some reservations people were starving to death waiting for rations which never arrived because they had been stolen. In Minnesota the Sioux died like flies. When they complained to their head agent, he told them to eat grass. This set off the so-called Great Sioux Uprising of the 1860s, during which the Indians killed that agent by stuffing earth and grass down his throat.

Then the peddlers arrived with their horse-drawn wagons full of pins and needles, beads and calico, always with a barrel of Injun whiskey under the seat. In no time the wagons became log-cabin stores, the stores shopping emporiums which, over the years, blossomed into combination supermarkets-cafeterias-tourist traps-Indian antiques shops-craft centers-filling stations. The trading post at Wounded Knee which started with almost nothing was, after one short generation, worth millions of dollars.

It did not take a genius to get rich in this business. There was always only one store in any given area. You got your stuff there or you did not get it at all. Even now, trading posts charge much higher prices than stores in the cities charge for the same articles. The trading posts have no competition. They sell beads to Indian craftworkers at six times the price of what they buy them for in New York and pay the Indian artists in cans of beans, also at a big markup.

They give Indians credit against lease money coming in months later—at outrageous interest rates. I have seen traders take Indian jewelry and old beadwork in pawn for five dollars' worth of food and then sell it for hundreds of dollars to a collector when the Indian owner could not redeem the article within a given time. For this reason we looked upon shoplifting as just getting a little of our own back, like counting coup in the old days by raiding the enemy's camp for horses.

I was built just right for the job. I looked much younger than I really was, and being so small I could pretend that I was a kid looking for her mother. If my friends were hungry and wanted something to eat, they would often send me to steal it. Once, early in the game, I was caught with a package of ham, cheese, bread, and sausages under my sweater. Suddenly there was this white guard grabbing me by the arm: "Come this way, come this way!" He was big and I was scared, shaking like a leaf. He was walking down the aisle ordering me to follow him, looking over his shoulder every two or three seconds to make sure that I was still behind him. Whenever he was not looking at me I threw the stuff back into the bins as I was passing them. Just threw them to both sides. So when I finally got to the back they searched me and found nothing. I said: "You goddam redneck. Just because I'm an Indian you are doing this to me. I'm going to sue you people for slander, for making a false arrest." They had to apologize, telling me it had been a case of mistaken identity. I was fifteen at the time.

There was a further reason for our shoplifting. The store owners provoked it. They expected us to steal. Being Indian, if you went into a store, the proprietor or salesperson would watch you like a hawk. They'd stand next to you, two feet away, with their arms crossed, watching, watching. They didn't do that with white customers. If you took a little time choosing an item they'd be at your elbow at once, hovering over you, asking, "May I help you?" Helping you was the furthest from their mind.

I'd say, "No, I'm just looking." Then if they kept standing there, breathing down my neck, I'd say, "Hey, do you want something from me?" And they answer, "No, just watching."

"Watching what? You think I'm gonna steal something?"

"No. Just watching."

"Well, don't stare at me." But still they were standing there, following every move you made. By then the white customers would be staring, too. I didn't mind, because I and the store owners were in an open, undeclared war, a war at first sight. But they treated even elderly, white-haired, and very respectable Indians the same way. In such situations even the most honest, law-abiding person will experience a mighty urge to pocket some article or other right under their noses. I knew a young teacher, a college graduate, who showed me a carton of cigarettes and a package of Tampax with that incredulous look on her face, saying, "Imagine, I stole this! I can't believe it myself, but they made it impossible for me not to steal it. It was a challenge. What do I do now? I don't even smoke." I took it as a challenge, too.

While I was roving, an Indian couple in Seattle took me in, giving me food and shelter, treating me nice as if they had been my parents. The woman's name was Bonnie and we became close friends in no time. I managed to rip off the credit card of a very elegant-looking lady—the wife of an admiral. Ship ahoy! I at once took my friend to a fancy store and told her to take anything she wanted. I "bought" her about two hundred dollars' worth of clothes, courtesy of the navy. Another time I pointed out a similarly well-dressed woman to a store manager, saying, "I work for that lady over there. I'm supposed to take these packages to the car. She'll pay you." While the manager argued with the lady, I took off with the packages down the road and into the bushes.

Once I got a nice Indian turquoise ring, a bracelet, and a pin. I always admired the beautiful work of Indian artists, getting mad whenever I saw imitations made in Hong Kong or Taiwan. I learned to watch the storekeepers' eyes. As long as their eyes are not on you, you are safe. As long as they are not watching your hands. You can also tell by the manner in which they talk to you. If they concentrate too much on your hands, then they won't know what they are saying. It helps if you have a small baby with you, even a borrowed one. For some reason that relaxes their suspicions. I had no special technique except studying them, their gestures, their eyes, their lips, the signs that their bodies made.

I was caught only twice. The second time I happened to be in Dubuque, Iowa. That was after the occupation of Alcatraz, when the Indian civil rights movement started to get under way, with confrontations taking place between Indians and whites in many places. I had attached myself to a caravan of young militant skins traveling in a number of cars and vans. While the caravan stopped in Dubuque to eat and wash up, I went to a shopping mall, saw a sweater I liked, and quickly stuffed it under my Levi's jacket.

I got out of the store all right, and walked across the parking lot where the caravan was waiting. Before I could join it, two security guards nabbed me. One of them said, "I want that sweater." I told him, "But I don't have no sweater." He just opened my jacket and took the sweater from under my arm. They took me back to the office, going through my ID, putting down my name, all that kind of thing. They had a radio in the office going full blast and I could hear the announcer describing the citizens' concern over a huge caravan of renegade Indians heading their way. One of the guards suddenly looked up at me and asked, "Are you by any chance one of those people?"

"Yeah," I told him. "They're just half a mile behind me and they'll be here soon, looking for me."

He said, "You don't have to sign your name here. Just go. You can take that damn sweater too. Just get out of here!" The incident made me realize that ripping off was not worth the risks I took. It also occurred to me there were better, more mature ways to fight for my rights.

Barb was less lucky. During the riots at Custer, South Dakota, she spent two days in the Rapid City jail. She was pulled in for third-degree burglary. It was the usual liberating of some food for which they were arrested, Barb and an Indian boy, but when she went before the judge and he told her that she was facing fifteen years, it made her sit up. She too started to reflect that if you had to go to jail it shouldn't be for a Saran-Wrapped chicken worth two bucks.

Most of the arrests occurred not for what we did, but for what we were and represented—for being skins. For instance once, near Martin, South Dakota, we had a flat tire and pulled off the road to fix it. It was late at night, dark, and very cold. While the boys were attending to the car, we girls built a good-sized fire to warm our backsides and make some coffee, coffee—pejuta sapa—being what keeps a roaming skin going. A fire truck went by. We did not pay any attention to it. A little while later the truck came back followed by two police cars. The police stared at us but kept on going, but pretty soon they made a U-turn and came back.

Across the road stood a farmhouse. The owner had called the police saying that Indians were about to burn his house down. All we were doing was fixing the tire and making coffee. The farmer had us arrested on a charge of attempted arson, trespassing, disturbing the peace, and destroying private property—the latter because in building our fire we had used one of his rotten fence posts. We spent two days in jail and then were found not guilty.

Little by little, those days in jail began adding up. We took such things in stride because they happened all the time, but subconsciously, I think, they had an effect upon us. During the years I am describing, in some Western states, the mere fact of being Indian and dressing in a certain way provoked the attention of the police. It resulted in having one's car stopped for no particular reason, in being pulled off the street on the flimsiest excuse, in being constantly shadowed and harassed. It works subtly on your mind until you start to think that if they keep on arresting you anyway you should at least give them a good reason for it.

I kept on moving, letting the stream carry me. It got to a point where I always looked forward to my next joint, my next bottle of gin. Even when the friends around me seemed to cool down I could not stop. Once I got hold of fifty white cross tablets—speed—and started taking them. The people I saw in the streets were doing it, why shouldn't I do it also? It gave me a bad case of the shakes and made me conclude that roving was not that much fun anymore. But I knew of no other way to exist.

Sexually our roaming bands, even after we had been politically sensitized and joined AIM, were free, very free and wild. If some boy saw you and liked you, then right away that was it. "If you don't come to bed with me, wincincala, I got somebody else who's willing to." The boys had that kind of attitude and it caused a lot of trouble for Barb and myself, because we were not that free. If we got involved we always took it seriously. Possibly our grandparents' and mother's staunch Christianity and their acceptance of the missionaries' moral code had something to do with it. They certainly tried hard to implant it in us, and though we furiously rejected it, a little residue remained.

There is a curious contradiction in Sioux society. The men pay great lip service to the status women hold in the tribe. Their rhetoric on the subject is beautiful. They speak of Grandmother Earth and how they honor her. Our great-est culture hero—or rather heroine—is the White Buffalo Woman, sent to us by the Buffalo nation, who brought us the sacred pipe and taught us how to use it. According to the legend, two young hunters were the first humans to meet her. One of them desired her physically and tried to make love to her, for which he was immediately punished by lightning reducing him to a heap of bones and ashes.

We had warrior women in our history. Formerly, when a young girl had her first period, it was announced to the whole village by the herald, and her family gave her a big feast in honor of the event, giving away valuable presents and horses to celebrate her having become a woman. Just as men competed for war honors, so women had quilling and bead-ing contests. The woman who made the most beautiful fully beaded cradleboard won honors equivalent to a warrior's coup. The men kept telling us, "See how we are honoring you . . ." Honoring us for what? For being good beaders, quillers, tanners, moccasin makers, and child-bearers. That is fine, but . . . In the governor's office at Pierre hangs a big poster put up by Indians. It reads:

> WHEN THE WHITE MAN
> DISCOVERED THIS COUNTRY
> INDIANS WERE RUNNING IT—
> NO TAXES OR TELEPHONES.
> WOMEN DID ALL THE WORK—
> THE WHITE MAN THOUGHT
> HE COULD IMPROVE UPON
> A SYSTEM LIKE THAT.

If you talk to a young Sioux about it he might explain: "Our tradition comes from being warriors. We always had to have our bow arms free so that we could protect you. That was our job. Every moment a Pawnee, or Crow, or white soldier could appear to attack you. Even on the daily hunt a man might be killed, ripped up by a bear or gored by a buffalo. We had to keep our hands free for that. That is our tradition."

"So, go already," I tell them. "Be traditional. Get me a buffalo!"

They are still traditional enough to want no menstruating women around. But the big honoring feast at a girl's first period they dispense with. For that they are too modern. I did not know about menstruating until my first time. When it happened I ran to my grandmother crying, telling her, "Something is wrong. I'm bleeding!" She told me not to cry, nothing was wrong. And that was all the explanation I got. They did not comfort me, or give horses away in my honor, or throw the red ball, or carry me from the menstruation hut to the tipi on a blanket in a new white buckskin outfit. The whole subject was distasteful to them. The feast is gone, only the distaste has remained.

It is not that a woman during her "moontime" is considered unclean, but she is looked upon as being "too powerful." According to our old traditions a woman during her period possesses a strange force which could render a healing ceremony ineffective. For this reason it is expected that we stay away from all rituals while menstruating. One old man once told me, "Woman on her moon is so strong that if she spits on a rattlesnake, that snake dies." To tell the truth I never felt particularly powerful while being "on my moon."

I was forcefully raped when I was fourteen or fifteen. A good-looking young man said, "Come over here, kid, let me buy you a soda"—and I fell for it. He was about twice my weight and a foot taller than I am. He just threw me on the ground and pinned me down. I do not want to remember the details. I kicked and scratched and bit but he came on like a steamroller. Ripped my clothes apart, ripped me apart. I was too embarrassed and ashamed to tell anyone what had happened to me. I think I worked off my rage by slashing a man's tires.

Rapes on the reservations are a big scandal. The victims are mostly full-blood girls, too shy and afraid to complain. A few years back the favorite sport of white state troopers and cops was to arrest young Indian girls on a drunk-and-disorderly, even if the girls were sober, take them to the drunk tanks in their jails, and there rape them. Sometimes they took the girls in their squad cars out into the prairie to "show you what a white man can do. I'm really doin' you a favor, kid." After they had done with them, they often kicked the girls out of their cars and drove off. Then the girl who had been raped had to walk five or ten miles home on top of everything else. Indian girls accusing white cops are seldom taken seriously in South Dakota. "You know how they are," the courts are told, "they're always asking for it." Thus there were few complaints for rapes or, as a matter of fact, for forced sterilizations. Luckily this is changing as our women are less reluctant to bring these things into the open.

I like men as friends, like to socialize with them, to know them. But going to bed with one is a commitment. You take responsibility for each other. But responsibility in a relationship was not what our young men wanted, some ninety percent of them. They just wanted to hop in the sack with us. Then they'd be friends. If you didn't cooperate then they were no longer interested in you as a person. With some of them, their whole courtship consists in pointing at you and then back at their tent, sleeping bag, or bedroll, saying, "Woman, come!" I won't come that easily. So I was a lot by myself and happy that way.

Once I played a joke on one of our great macho warriors, a good-looking guy, a lady's man. Women were always swarming over him, especially white groupies. One night, during a confrontation in California, I was lying in my sleeping bag when the great warrior (and he is a great warrior, I don't call him that facetiously) suddenly came up: "I had a little fight with my old lady. Can I share your sleeping bag?"

He did not wait for an answer but at once wedged himself in. This happened before Wounded Knee when I was in my eighth month. He put his hand upon my breast. I did not say anything. Then his hand wandered farther down, coming to a sudden stop atop that big balloon of a belly. "What in hell is this?" I smiled at him very sweetly. "Oh, I'm just about to have my baby. I think I feel my birth pangs coming on right now!" He got out of the sleeping bag even faster than he had crept in.

One Sioux girl whose lover had left her for a Crow woman was making up forty-niner songs about him. Forty-niners are songs which are half English and half Indian, common to all tribes, often having to do with love and sometimes funny or biting. We were always singing them while we were on the move. So that girl made up this one:

> Honey, you left me for to go,
> Crow Fair and Indian Rodeo,
> Hope you get the diarrhea,
> Heya—heya—heya.

It became a great favorite with us, though I don't remember all of it. One song was all Indian except for the refrain: "Sorry, no pizza today." But to sum up: our men were magnificent and mean at the same time. You had to admire them. They had to fight their own men's lib battles. They were incredibly brave in protecting us, they would literally die for us, and they always stood up for our rights—*against outsiders!*

Sexual harassment causes a lot of fights between Indians and whites. Our boys really try to protect us against this. At Pierre, South Dakota's state capital, during a trial of AIM Indians, a lot of us came to lend our moral support, filling the motel, eight to ten people in a room. Barb was with a group occupying three rooms on the ground floor. On her way out to go to the car for some stuff, she passed three cowboy-type white boys leaning against a wall drinking beer and wine. Barb said she could smell the liquor on their breath from some ways off. They at once hemmed her in, making their usual remarks: "Look at the tits on that squaw. Watch her shaking her ass at us. I bet we could show that Injun squaw a good time," speculating aloud how it would be having her. My sister tried to ignore them, but in the end just turned around and ran back into the motel. The only one she could find there was Tom Poor Bear, an Oglala boy from Pine Ridge. Barb told him that some honkies had been harassing her outside. Tom at once went out with her and these cowboys again started with the same kind of shit, the same sort of sexual harassment. When they noticed Poor Bear they slowly began walking off. Tom called to them, "Hey, you guys come back and apologize."

The cowboy who had made the most offensive remarks turned around and fingered Poor Bear. He was grinning. "I don't apologize to her kind ever. She's nothing but a squaw."

Poor Bear told him, "You motherfucker, I'll show you who's nothing!" Then the fight started, all three of them jumping Tom, stomping him, three wasičuns against one skin. So again Barb scrambled back into the motel and in the lobby ran into Bobby Leader Charge, a Rosebud boy who was only fifteen years old at the time. Young as he was, Bobby just came out of that lobby like a thunderbolt, according to Barb, and joined the fight. By that time the cowboys had been reinforced by three more friends and again we were badly outnumbered. They were beating up on Poor Bear and Leader Charge, really hurting them, kicking them in the groin, going after their eyes. So once again Barbara was trying to round up more help. Luckily, at that moment Russel with the Means brothers and Coke Millard appeared at the motel. The whole sling of them rushed out. The honkies tried to get away, but were not fast enough. Coke Millard knocked one of them right over the top of a parked car. One cowboy got knocked out, just lying there. Another tried crawling away on his hands and knees. The others had run for it. This finished the incident as far as our men were concerned, and all went back to the motel.

But it was not finished. In no time the whole motel was lit up with searchlights as about half a dozen squad cars pulled up in front of it with their red lights flashing and sirens howling. Out of each car stepped two troopers with riot guns, helmets, and plastic shields, positioning themselves at both sides of each car. Already the loudspeaker was blaring: "This is the sheriff speaking. You Indians in there, you are wanted for assault and battery. We know you're in there. Come on out with your hands on your heads or we'll come in shooting!" Barb and the others peeked out from behind their window shades. Seeing the muzzles of all those riot guns and sawed-off shotguns pointing at them, they had little desire to come out. South Dakota police are notoriously trigger-happy when dealing with Indians, especially AIM people. One of the Means brothers went to the telephone and called up a white friend of ours who was in an upstairs room with one of the lawyers, helping with the trials. He told him to get his ass down to their room double quick, to bring the lawyer, and please, not to ask any foolish questions, just to hurry up.

It was two o'clock in the morning and very cold. Somehow it is always exceedingly hot or very, very cold in South Dakota. So, looking down from my room on the second floor

I saw the two of them shivering, none too happy walking between the motel wall and the row of squad cars and troopers pointing their guns. Then I saw two pairs of hands reaching for them out of Room 108 and yanking them inside. I did not know at the time what it was all about. Barbara told me later that the two of them started negotiating by phone with the sheriff saying, "Our Indian friends and clients have been assaulted by a bunch of vicious, white, drunken, would-be rapists, but they are willing to withdraw these charges if your cowboys withdraw theirs."

While they were arguing back and forth on the phone, the others had a little problem with Coke, who had consumed a few beers and was singing his death song: "It's a good day to die! Let me out of here! I want to die a warrior's death. Let me count coup on them pigs! Hoka-hay!" They had to hold him back, literally sitting on him in order to keep him from going outside and getting himself killed. In the end both sides agreed to withdraw charges and call it quits to prevent a massacre. The squad cars drove off and all was quiet again, but it had been a near thing. There is always the danger for us that one little incident will set off a major confrontation.

Looking back upon my roving days, it is hard to say whether they were good or bad, or whether I accomplished or learned anything by being endlessly, restlessly on the move. If nothing else, my roaming gave me a larger outlook and made me more Indian, made me realize what being an Indian within a white world meant. My aimlessness ended when I encountered AIM.

CHAPTER 6

We AIM Not to Please

They call us the New Indians.
Hell, we are the Old Indians,
the landlords of this continent,
coming to collect the rent.

—*Dennis Banks*

T he American Indian Movement hit our reservation like
a tornado, like a new wind blowing out of nowhere, a
drumbeat from far off getting louder and louder. It was
almost like the Ghost Dance fever that had hit the tribes in
1890, old uncle Dick Fool Bull said, spreading like a prairie
fire. It even was like the old Ghost Dance song Uncle Dick
was humming:

> Maka sitomniya teca ukiye
> Oyate ukiye, oyate ukiye . . .
> A new world is coming,

A nation is coming,
The eagle brought the message.

I could feel this new thing, almost hear it, smell it, touch it. Meeting up with AIM for the first time loosened a sort of earthquake inside me. Old Black Elk in recounting his life often used the expression "As I look down from the high hill of my great old age . . ." Well, as I am looking from the hill of my old age—I am thirty-seven now but feel as if I have lived for a long time—I can see things in perspective, not subjectively, no, but in perspective. Old Black Elk had a good way of saying it. You really look back upon ten years gone past as from a hill—you have a sort of bird's-eye view. I recognize now that movements get used up and the leaders get burned out quickly. Some of our men and women got themselves killed and thereby avoided reaching the dangerous age of thirty and becoming "elder statesmen." Some leaders turned into college professors, founded alternative schools, or even took jobs as tribal officials. A few live on in the past, refusing to recognize that the dreams of the past must give way to the dreams of the future. I, that wild, rebellious teenager of ten years ago, am nursing a baby, changing diapers, and making breakfast for my somewhat extended family. And yet it was great while it lasted and I still feel that old excitement merely talking about it. Some people loved AIM, some hated it, but nobody ignored it.

I loved it. My first encounter with AIM was at a powwow held in 1971 at Crow Dog's place after the Sun Dance. Pointing at Leonard Crow Dog, I asked a young woman, "Who is that man?"

"That's Crow Dog," she said. I was looking at his long, shining braids. Wearing one's hair long at the time was still something of a novelty on the res. I asked, "Is that his real hair?"

"Yes, that's his real hair."

I noticed that almost all of the young men wore their hair long, some with eagle feathers tied to it. They all had on ribbon shirts. They had a new look about them, not that hangdog reservation look I was used to. They moved in a different way, too, confident and swaggering, the girls as well as the boys. Belonging to many tribes, they had come in a dilapidated truck covered with slogans and paintings. They had traveled to the Sun Dance all the way from California, where they had taken part in the occupation of Alcatraz Island.

One man, a Chippewa, stood up and made a speech. I had never heard anybody talk like that. He spoke about genocide and sovereignty, about tribal leaders selling out and kissing ass—white man's ass. He talked about giving up the necktie for the choker, the briefcase for the bedroll, the missionary's church for the sacred pipe. He talked about not celebrating Thanksgiving, because that would be celebrating one's own destruction. He said that white people, after stealing our land and massacring us for three hundred years, could not come to us now saying, "Celebrate Thanksgiving with us, drop in for a slice of turkey." He had himself wrapped up in an upside-down American flag, telling us that every star in this flag represented a state stolen from Indians.

Then Leonard Crow Dog spoke, saying that we had talked to the white man for generations with our lips, but that he had no ears to hear, no eyes to see, no heart to feel. Crow Dog said that now we must speak with our bodies and that he was not afraid to die for his people. It was a very emotional speech. Some people wept. An old man turned to me and said, "These are the words I always wanted to speak, but had kept shut up within me."

I asked one of the young men, "What kind of Indians are you?" "We are AIM," he told me, "American Indian Movement. We're going to change things."

AIM was born in 1968. Its fathers were mostly men doing

time in Minnesota prisons, Ojibways. It got its start in the slums of St. Paul taking care of Indian ghetto problems. It was an Indian woman who gave it its name. She told me, "At first we called ourselves 'Concerned Indian Americans' until somebody discovered that the initials spelled CIA. That didn't sound so good. Then I spoke up: 'You guys all aim to do this, or you aim to do that. Why don't you call yourselves AIM, American Indian Movement?' And that was that."

In the beginning AIM was mainly confined to St. Paul and Minneapolis. The early AIM people were mostly ghetto Indians, often from tribes which had lost much of their language, traditions, and ceremonies. It was when they came to us on the Sioux reservations that they began to learn about the old ways. We had to learn from them, too. We Sioux had lived very isolated behind what some people called the "Buckskin Curtain." AIM opened a window for us through which the wind of the 1960s and early '70s could blow, and it was no gentle breeze but a hurricane that whirled us around. It was after the traditional reservation Indians and the ghetto kids had gotten together that AIM became a force nationwide. It was flint striking flint, lighting a spark which grew into a flame at which we could warm ourselves after a long, long winter.

After I joined AIM I stopped drinking. Others put away their roach clips and airplane glue bottles. There were a lot of things wrong with AIM. We did not see these things, or did not want to see them. At the time these things were unimportant. What was important was getting it on. We kids became AIM's spearheads and the Sioux set the style. The AIM uniform was Sioux all the way, the black "angry hats" with the feathers stuck in the hatband, the bone chokers, the medicine pouches worn on our breasts, the Levi's jackets on which we embroidered our battle honors—Alcatraz, Trail of Broken Treaties, Wounded Knee. Some dudes wore a third, extra-thin braid as a scalp lock. We made up our own songs—forty-niners, honoring songs, songs for a warrior behind bars in the slammer. The AIM song was made up by a fourteen-year-old Sioux boy. The Ojibways say it was made up by one of their own kids, but we know better.

We all had a good mouth, were good speakers and wrote a lot of poetry, though we were all dropouts who could not spell. We took some of our rhetoric from the blacks, who had started their movements before we did. Like them we were minorities, poor and discriminated against, but there were differences. I think it significant that in many Indian languages a black is called a "black white man." The blacks want what the whites have, which is understandable. They want *in*. We Indians want *out*! That is the main difference.

At first we hated all whites because we knew only one kind—the John Wayne kind. It took time before we met whites to whom we could relate and whose friendships we could accept. One of our young men met a pretty girl. She said she was Indian and looked it. She told him, "Sleep with me." In bed, in the middle of the night, he somehow found out that she was Puerto Rican. He got so mad that she was not a real skin that he beat up on her. He wanted to have to do only with Indian girls and felt tricked. He had run away from a real bad foster home, seeking refuge among his own kind. Later he felt ashamed for what he had done and apologized. Eventually we were joined by a number of Chicano brothers and sisters and learned to love and respect them, but it took time. We lived in a strange, narrow world of our own, suspicious of all outsiders. Later, we found ourselves making speeches on campuses, in churches, and on street corners talking to prominent supporters such as Marlon Brando, Dick Gregory, Rip Torn, Jane Fonda, and Angela Davis. It was a long-drawn-out process of learning and experiencing, this widening of our horizons.

We formed relationships among ourselves and with outsiders. We had girls who would go to bed with any warrior
who had done something brave. Other girls loved one boy
only. Usually a boy would say to a girl, "Be my old lady,"
and she might answer, "Ohan, you are my old man." They
would go find a medicine man to feather and cedar them, to
smoke the pipe with them, to put a red blanket around their
shoulders. That made them man and wife Indian style.
Then they slept under the same blanket. The white law did
not recognize such a marriage, but we would respect it. It
might last only a few days. Either of them could have a run-
in with the law and wind up in jail or be blown away by the
goons. We did not exactly lead stable lives, but some of these
marriages lasted for years. Short or long, it was good while it
lasted. The girl had somebody to protect and take care of
her; the boy had a wincincala to cook his beans or sew him a
ribbon shirt. They inspired each other to the point where
they would put their bodies on the line together. It gave
them something precious to remember all their lives. One
seventeen-year-old boy had a twenty-two-year-old girl-
friend. He called her "grandma." He had a T-shirt made for
her with the word GRANDMA on it, and one for himself with
the legend I LOVE GRANDMA. He was heartbroken when she
left him for an "older man." Some of the AIM leaders
attracted quite a number of "wives." We called them "wives
of the month."

I got into one of these marriages myself. It lasted just long
enough for me to get pregnant. Birth control went against
our beliefs. We felt that there were not enough Indians left to
suit us. The more future warriors we brought into the
world, the better. My older sister Barbara got pregnant too.
She went to the BIA hospital where the doctors told her she
needed a cesarean. When she came to, the doctors informed
her that they had taken her womb out. In their opinion, at

that time, there were already too many little red bastards for the taxpayers to take care of. No use to mollycoddle those happy-go-lucky, irresponsible, oversexed AIM women. Barb's child lived for two hours. With better care, it might have made it. For a number of years BIA doctors performed thousands of forced sterilizations on Indian and Chicano women without their knowledge or consent. For this reason I was happy at the thought of having a baby, not only for myself but for Barbara, too. I was determined not to have my child in a white hospital.

In the meantime I had nine months to move around, still going from confrontation to confrontation. Wherever anthros were digging up human remains from Indian sites, we were there threatening to dig up white graves to display white men's skulls and bones in glass cases. Wherever there was an Indian political trial, we showed up before the courthouse with our drums. Wherever we saw a bar with a sign NO INDIANS ALLOWED, we sensitized the owners, sometimes quite forcefully. Somehow we always found old jalopies to travel in, painted all over with Red Power slogans, and always found native people to take us in, treating us to meat soup, fry bread, and thick, black coffee. We existed entirely without money, yet we ate, traveled, and usually found a roof over our heads.

Something strange happened then. The traditional old, full-blood medicine men joined in with us kids. Not the middle-aged adults. They were of a lost generation which had given up all hope, necktie-wearers waiting for the Great White Father to do for them. It was the real old folks who had spirit and wisdom to give us. The grandfathers and grandmothers who still remembered a time when Indians were Indians, whose own grandparents or even parents had fought Custer gun in hand, people who for us were living links with a great past. They had a lot of strength and power, enough to give some of it to us. They still knew all the old legends and the right way to put on a ritual, and we were eager to learn from them. Soon they had us young girls making flesh offerings or piercing our wrists at the Sun Dance, while young warriors again put the skewers through their breast and found out the hard way where they came from. Even those who had grown up in cities, who had never been on a horse or heard an owl hoot, were suddenly getting it together. I am not bragging, but I am proud that we Lakotas started this.

The old grandmothers especially made a deep impression upon me. Women like Lizzy Fast Horse, a great-grandmother, who scrambled up all the way to the top of Mount Rushmore, standing right on the top of those gigantic bald pates, reclaiming the Black Hills for their rightful owners. Lizzy who was dragged down the mountain by the troopers, handcuffed to her nine-year-old great-granddaughter until their wrists were cut, their blood falling in drops on the snow. It is really true, the old Cheyenne saying: "A nation is not dead until the hearts of its women are on the ground." Well, the hearts of our old full-blood women were not on the ground. They were way up high and they could still encourage us with their trilling, spine-tingling brave-heart cry which always made the hairs on my back stand up and my flesh break out in goose pimples whenever I heard it, no matter how often.

We did freak out the honkies. We were feared throughout the Dakotas. I could never figure out why this should have been so. We were always the victims. We never maimed or killed. It was we who died or got crippled. Aside from ripping off a few trading posts, we were not really bad. We were loud-mouthed, made a lot of noise, and got on some people's nerves. We made Mr. White Man realize that there were other Indians besides the poor human wrecks who posed for him for a quarter—but that should not have made them kill us or hide from us under their beds. "The AIMs is coming, the AIMs is coming" was the cry that went up whenever a couple of fourteen-year-old skins in Uncle Joe hats showed up. The ranchers and the police spread the most fantastic rumors about us. The media said that we were about to stage bank robberies, storm prisons, set fire to the state capitol, blow up Mount Rushmore, and assassinate the governor. The least we were accused of was that we were planning to paint the noses of the giant Mount Rushmore heads red. Worst of all we were scaring the tourists away. The concessionaires at Rushmore and in all the Black Hills tourist traps were losing money. It was only right to kill us for that.

I think it was their bad conscience which made the local whites hate us so much. Bill Kunstler, the movement lawyer who defended us in a number of trials, once said: "You hate those most whom you have injured most." The whites near the reservations were all living on land stolen from us— stolen not in the distant past, but by their fathers and grand-fathers. They all made their living in some way by exploit-ing us, by using Indians as cheap labor, by running their cattle on reservation land for a mere pittance in lease money, by using us as colorful props to attract the Eastern tourists. They could only relate to the stereotyped song-and-dance Indian, locking their doors and cowering behind their cur-tains whenever we came to town, crying: "The AIMs is coming, get the police." Always a day or two after we made our appearance all the gun shops in the place were sold out. White folks took to toting guns again. They carried revolvers wherever they went, slept with loaded .38s under their pillows, drove around with high-powered rifles in racks be-hind the seats of their pickups. It was rumored that the then governor of South Dakota, who once vowed to put every

AIM member behind bars or six feet underground, had imported a special, quick-firing, newly invented type of machine gun from West Germany and installed it in the dome of the state capitol, where he spent hours, training the gun on Indians who happened to walk by, zeroing in, moving the gun silently back and forth, back and forth. It may be only a story, but knowing the man, I am prepared to believe it. I did not mind their being afraid of us. It was better than being given a quarter and asked to pose smilingly for their cameras.

We were not angels. Some things were done by AIM, or rather by people who *called* themselves AIM, that I am not proud of. But AIM gave us a lift badly needed at the time. It defined our goals and expressed our innermost yearnings. It set a style for Indians to imitate. Even those Native Americans who maintained that they wanted to have nothing to do with AIM, that it ran counter to their tribal ways of life, began to dress and talk in the AIM manner. I have had some conflicts with the American Indian Movement at some time or another. I don't know whether it will live or die. Some people say that a movement dies the moment it becomes acceptable. In this case there should be some life left in its body, at least in the Dakotas. But whatever happens, one can't take away from AIM that it fulfilled its function and did what had to be done at a time which was decisive in the development of Indian America.

The Sun Dance at Rosebud in the late summer of 1972 will forever remain in my memory. Many of the AIM leaders came to Crow Dog's place to dance, to make flesh offerings, to endure the self-torture of this, our most sacred rite, gazing at the sun, blowing on their eagle-bone whistles, praying with the pipe. It was like a rebirth, like some of the prophesies of the Ghost Dancers coming true. The strange thing was seeing men undergoing the ordeal of the Sun Dance who came from tribes which had never practiced this ritual. I felt it was their way of saying, "I am an Indian again."

This Sun Dance was also an occasion for getting to know each other, for a lot of serious talk. I was happy watching the women taking a big part in these discussions. One of the AIM men laughingly said, "For years we couldn't get the women to speak up, and now we can't get them to shut up." I just listened. I was still too shy and too young to do anything else but stay in the background.

The people were tensed up. Everything was in ferment. The mood was bitter. News reached us after the Sun Dance that Richard Oaks, from the Mohawk tribe, a much loved and respected leader at Alcatraz, had been murdered by a white man. Not long before that a Sioux, Raymond Yellow Thunder, a humble, hard-working man, had been stripped naked and forced at gunpoint to dance in an American Legion hall at Gordon, Nebraska. Later he was beaten to death—just for the fun of it. Before that a millionaire rancher had shot and killed an unarmed Indian from Pine Ridge, Norman Little Brave, and gone unpunished. Norman had been a sober-minded churchgoer, but that had not saved him. It was open season on Indians again and the people were saying, "Enough of this shit!" It was out of these feelings of anger, hope, and despair that the "Trail of Broken Treaties" was born.

I am still proud that it was born at Rosebud, among my people. That is probably bad. The feeling of pride in one's particular tribe is standing in the way of Indian unity. Still it is there and it is not all bad. The man who first thought of having caravans of Indians converging upon Washington from all directions was Bob Burnette. He had been tribal chairman at Rosebud and he was not an AIM member. Other Indian leaders of this caravan, such as Hank Adams, Reuben Snake, and Sid Mills—Sid and Hank from the

Northwest, where they had been fighting for native fishing rights—were not AIM. Neither were the Six Nation people from upstate New York or the representatives of some Southwestern tribes, but though they had not started it, it was the AIM leaders who dominated this march in the end.

The Trail of Broken Treaties was the greatest action taken by Indians since the Battle of the Little Big Horn. As Eddie Benton, the Ojibway medicine man, told us: "There is a prophecy in our tribe's religion that one day we would all stand together. All tribes would hook arms in brotherhood and unite. I am elated because I lived to see this happen. Brothers and sisters from all over this continent united in a single cause. That is the greatest significance to Indian people . . . not what happened or what may yet happen as a result of our actions."

Each caravan was led by a spiritual leader or medicine man with his sacred pipe. The Oklahoma caravan followed the Cherokees' "Trail of Tears," retracing the steps of dying Indians driven from their homes by President Andrew Jackson. Our caravan started from Wounded Knee. This had a special symbolic meaning for us Sioux, making us feel as if the ghosts of all the women and children murdered there by the Seventh Cavalry were rising out of their mass grave to go with us.

I traveled among friends from Rosebud and Pine Ridge. My brother and my sister Barbara were among this group. I did not know what to expect. A huge protest march like this was new to me. When we arrived in Washington we got lost. We had been promised food and accommodation, but due to government pressure many church groups which had offered to put us up and feed us got scared and backed off. It was almost dawn and still we were stumbling around looking for a place to bed down. I could hardly keep my eyes open. One thing we did accomplish: in the predawn light we drove around the White House, honking our horns and beating our drums to let President Nixon know that we had arrived.

We were finally given a place to sleep in, an old, dilapidated, and abandoned church. I had just crawled into my bedroll when I saw what I thought to be a fair-sized cat walking over it. I put my glasses on and discovered that it was a big rat, the biggest and ugliest I had ever seen. The church was in an uproar. Women screamed. Mine was not the only rat in the place, as it turned out. An old lady who had hitchhiked two thousand miles from Cheyenne River to get to Washington complained that the toilets were broken. It was the first week of November and there was no heat. An elderly Canadian Indian dragged himself around on crutches. His legs were crippled and he could find no soft place to rest. A young girl shouted that there were not only rats but also millions of cockroaches. A young Ojibway man said that he had not left the slums of St. Paul for this kind of facility. I told him that I had expected nothing else. Did he think Nixon would put him up at the Holiday Inn with wall-to-wall carpeting and color TV? Everywhere groups were standing huddled together in their blankets. People were saying, "They promised us decent housing. Look how they're treating us. We ain't gonna stand for this."

Somebody suggested, "Let's all go to the BIA." It seemed the natural thing to do, to go to the Bureau of Indian Affairs building on Constitution Avenue. They would have to put us up. It was "our" building after all. Besides, that was what we had come for, to complain about the treatment the bureau was dishing out to us. Everybody suddenly seemed to be possessed by the urge to hurry to the BIA. Next thing I knew we were in it. We spilled into the building like a great avalanche. Some people put up a tipi on the front lawn. Security guards were appointed. They put on red armbands or fastened rainbow-colored bits of cloth to their ribbon shirts or denim jackets. They watched the doors. Tribal groups took over this or that room, the Iroquois on one floor, the Sioux on another. The Oklahoma Indians, the North-west Coast people, all made themselves a place to stay. Children were playing while old ladies got comfortable on couches in the foyer. A drum was roaring. I could smell kinnikinnick—Indian tobacco. Someone put up a sign over the front gate reading INDIAN COUNTRY. The building fi-nally belonged to us and we lost no time turning it into a tribal village.

My little group settled down in one room on the second floor. It was nice—thick carpets, subdued light, soft couches, and easy chairs. The bureaucrats sure knew how to live. They had marble stairs, wrought-iron banisters, fine statues and paintings depicting the Noble Savage, valuable artifacts. I heard somebody speaking Sioux. I opened a door and there was Leonard Crow Dog talking to some young men, telling them why we were here, explaining what it all meant. Somebody motioned to me: "Quiet! Crow Dog is talking!" Young as I was, Crow Dog seemed an old man to me, old with responsibilities, but he was only thirty-two then. It did not occur to me that one day I would bear his children.

The takeover of the BIA building had not been planned. We honestly thought that arrangements for our stay had been made. When the promises turned out to be the same old buffalo shit, as one of the leaders put it, we simply occupied the BIA. It was a typical spontaneous Indian hap-pening. Nobody had ordered us to do it. We were not very amenable to orders anyhow. It's not our style. The various tribal groups caucussed in their rooms, deciding what pro-posals to make. From time to time everybody would go down into the great hall and thrash out the proposals. The assembly hall had a stage, many chairs, and loudspeakers.

Always discussions opened with one of the medicine men performing a ceremony. I think it was a black civil rights organization which brought in the first truckload of food. Later various church groups and other sympathizers donated food and money. The building had a kitchen and cafeteria and we quickly organized cooking, dishwashing, and garbage details. Some women were appointed to watch the children, old people were cared for, and a medical team was set up. Contrary to what some white people believe, Indians are very good at improvising this sort of self-government with no one in particular telling them what to do. They don't wait to be told. I guess there were altogether six to eight hundred people crammed into the building, but it did not feel crowded.

The original caravan leaders had planned a peaceful and dignified protest. There had even been talk of singing and dancing for the senators and inviting the lawmakers to an Indian fry bread and corn soup feast. It might have worked out that way if somebody had been willing to listen to us. But the word had been passed to ignore us. The people who mattered, from the president down, would not talk to us. We were not wanted. It was said that we were hoodlums who did not speak for the Indian people. The half-blood tribal chairmen with their salaries and expense accounts condemned us almost to a man. Nixon sent some no-account underling to tell us that he had done more for the American Indian than any predecessor and that he saw no reason for our coming to Washington, that he had more important things to do than to talk with us—presumably surreptitiously taping his visitors and planning Watergate. We wondered what all these good things were that he had done for us.

We had planned to have Crow Dog conduct a ceremony at the grave of Ira Hayes, the Pima Indian who had won the Congressional Medal of Honor at Iwo Jima, and who had died drunk and forgotten in a ditch. The army, which was in charge of Arlington Cemetery, forbade this ceremony "because it would be political, not religious." Slowly our mood changed. There was less talk of dancing and singing for the senators and more talk about getting it on. Dennis Banks said that AIM was against violence, but that it might take another Watts to bring home to the public the plight of Native Americans. Russel Means remarked to some reporters that the media were ignoring us: "What do we have to do to get some attention? Scalp somebody?" It was on this occasion that I learned that as long as we "behaved nicely" nobody gave a damn about us, but as soon as we became rowdy we got all the support and media coverage we could wish for.

We obliged them. We pushed the police and guards out of the building. Some did not wait to be pushed but jumped out of the ground-floor windows like so many frogs. We had formulated twenty Indian demands. These were all rejected by the few bureaucrats sent to negotiate with us. The most we got out of these talks was one white official holding up an Indian baby for a snapshot, saying, "Isn't she sweet?" We had not come for baby-kissing nor for kissing ass. The moderate leaders lost credibility. It was not their fault. Soon we listened to other voices as the occupation turned into a siege. I heard somebody yelling, "The pigs are here." I could see from the window that it was true. The whole building was surrounded by helmeted police armed with all kinds of guns. A fight broke out between the police and our security. Some of our young men got hit over the head with police clubs and we saw the blood streaming down their faces. There was a rumor, which turned out to be true, that we had received an ultimatum: "Clear out—or else!"

I felt the tension rise within the building, felt it rising within me, an ant heap somebody was plunging a stick into,

stirring it up. I heard a woman screaming, "They are coming, they are going to kill us all!" Men started shouting,
"Women and children upstairs! Get upstairs!" But I went
downstairs. I saw the riot squad outside. They had just
beaten up two Indians and were hauling them off to jail. We
barricaded all doors and the lowest windows with document
boxes, Xerox machines, tables, file cabinets, anything we
could lay our hands on. Some brothers piled up heavy type-
writers on windowsills to hurl down on the police in case
they tried to storm the building. Young men were singing
and yelling, "It's a good day to die!" We started making
weapons for ourselves. Two or three guys discovered some
archery sets and were ready to defend themselves with bow
and arrows. Others were swinging golf clubs, getting the
feel of them. Still others were tying pen knives to fishing
rods. A letter opener taped to a table leg became a toma-
hawk. Floyd Young Horse, a Sioux from Cherry Creek, was
the first to put war paint on his face in the ancient manner.
Soon a lot of young men did the same. Many wrapped
themselves in upside-down American flags—like the Ghost
Dancers of old.

I took apart a pair of scissors and taped one half to a
broken-off chair leg and went outside to join the security.
My brother was one of the guards. He saw me and laughed.
He had been four years in the marines and had taught me to
take apart, clean, and fire a .38. Seeing me with my measly
weapon broke him up. "What are you going to do with that
thing?" "Get them in the balls before they can hit me!"

At last the police were withdrawn and we were told that
they had given us another twenty-four hours to evacuate the
building. This was not the end of the confrontation. From
then on, every morning we were given a court order to get
out by six P.M. Came six o'clock and we would be standing
there ready to join battle. I think many brothers and sisters

were prepared to die right on the steps of the BIA building. When one of the AIM leaders was asked by a reporter whether the Indians were not afraid that their women and children could get hurt, he said, "Our women and children have taken this risk for four hundred years and accept it," and we all shouted "Right on!" I don't think I slept more than five or six hours during the whole week I was inside the BIA.

Every morning and evening was crisis time. In between, the negotiations went on. Groups of supporters arrived, good people as well as weirdos. The Indian commissioner Lewis Bruce stayed one night in the building to show his sympathy. So did LaDonna Harris, a Kiowa-Comanche and a senator's wife. One guy who called himself Wavy Gravy, who came from a place in California called the Hog Farm and who wore a single enormous earring, arrived in a psychedelically decorated bus and set up a loudspeaker system for us. At the same time the police cut all our telephone wires except the one connecting us with the Department of the Interior. A certain Reverend McIntire came with a bunch of followers waving signs and singing Christian hymns. He was known to us as a racist and Vietnam War hawk. Why he wanted to support us was a big mystery. Cameramen and reporters swarmed through the building; tourists took snapshots of our guards. It was as if all these white people around the BIA were hoping for some sort of Buffalo Bill Wild West show.

For me the high point came not with our men arming themselves, but with Martha Grass, a simple middle-aged Cherokee woman from Oklahoma, standing up to Interior Secretary Morton and giving him a piece of her mind, speaking from the heart, speaking for all of us. She talked about everyday things, women's things, children's problems, getting down to the nitty-gritty. She shook her fists in Morton's face, saying, "Enough of your bullshit!" It was good to see an Indian mother stand up to one of Washington's highest officials. "This is our building!" she told him. Then she gave him the finger.

In the end a compromise was reached. The government said they could not go on negotiating during Election Week, but they would appoint two high administration officials to seriously consider our twenty demands. Our expenses to get home would be paid. Nobody would be prosecuted. Of course, our twenty points were never gone into afterward. From the practical point of view, nothing had been achieved. As usual we had bickered among ourselves. But morally it had been a great victory. We had faced White America collectively, not as individual tribes. We had stood up to the government and gone through our baptism of fire. We had not run. As Russel Means put it, it had been "a helluva smoke signal!"

CHAPTER 7

Crying for a Dream

The white man's reality are his streets with their
banks, shops, neon lights, and traffic, streets full of
policemen, whores, and sad-faced people in a hurry
to punch a time clock.
    But this is unreal. The real reality is underneath
all this. Grandfather Peyote helps you find it.

—*Crow Dog*

You should know that the movement for Indian rights
was first of all a spiritual movement and that our ancient religion was at the heart of it. Up to the time of
Franklin D. Roosevelt, Indian religion was forbidden. Children were punished for praying Indian, men were jailed for
taking a sweat bath. Our sacred pipes were broken, our
medicine bundles burned or given to museums. Christian-
izing us was one way of making us white, that is, of making
us forget that we were Indians. Holding on to our old reli-

gion was one way of resisting this kind of slow death. As long as people prayed with the pipe or beat the little water drum, Indians would not vanish, would continue to exist as Indians. For this reason our struggles for Indian rights over the past hundred years came out of our ancient beliefs. And so, under the impact of AIM and other movements, more and more native people abandoned the missionaries and went back to the medicine men and peyote road men.

I went that way, too. Hand in hand with my radicalization went my going back to Indian traditions. To white people this may seem contradictory, but for me and for my friends it was the most natural thing in the world. This process had already begun when I was still a child. I felt that the kind of Christianity the priests and nuns of St. Francis dished out was not good for my digestion. Jesus would have been all right except that I felt he had been coopted by white American society to serve its purpose. The men who had brought us whiskey and the smallpox had come with the cross in one hand and the gun in the other. In the name of all-merciful Jesus they had used that gun on us. Our sacred pipe and Grandfather Peyote had not been coopted and so I was instinctively drawn to them. Not that I could have put it in these words at the time.

To be an Indian I had to go to the full-bloods. My mother and grandmother were Indians, but I am a half-breed and I could not accept this. The half-breeds, the iyeskas, I thought, never really cared for anybody but themselves, having learned that "wholesome selfishness" alone brought the blessings of civilization. The full-bloods have a heart. They are humble. They are willing to share whatever happiness they have. They sit on their land which has a sacred meaning for them, even if it brings them no income. The iyeskas have no land because they sold theirs long ago. Whenever some white businessmen come to the res trying to make a deal to dig for coal or uranium, the iyeskas always say, "Let's do it. Let's get that money. Buy a new car and a color TV." The full-bloods say nothing. They just sit on their little patches of land and don't budge. It is because of them that there are still some Indians left. I felt drawn to my stubborn old full-blood relatives, men like my Uncle Fool Bull who always spoke of a sacred herb, a holy medicine which was the Creator's special gift to the Indian people. He told me the legend of an old woman and her granddaughter who were lost in the desert and on the point of dying when they heard a little voice calling to them, a voice coming out of a tiny herb which saved their lives, and how the women brought this sacred medicine to their tribe and to all the native people of this hemisphere. I listened to these stories and one day I told my mother, "I'm gonna grow up to be an Indian!"

She did not like it. She was upset because she was a Catholic and was having me brought up in her faith. She even had me confirmed. I sometimes try to imagine how I must have looked in my white outfit, with veil and candle, and it always makes me smile. I was then white outside and red inside, just the opposite of an apple. It was old Grandpa Dick Fool Bull who took me to my first peyote meeting. It was not until I was grown-up that I really got to know him and found out that he was a close relative. The last peyote meeting I had with him he was already over a hundred years old. He stood up and he talked for nearly three hours. He was preparing himself for his death. He was talking about going into the happy hunting grounds, the Milky Way, the great ultimate road to meet with all his old friends, with Carl Iron Shell and Good Lance. He talked about being with them again and being again with his kind of people, the sort who have all died out, the people who themselves had been a hundred years old when Grandpa Fool Bull was still young,

who would be waiting for him with a drum and, maybe, a
kettle full of steaming buffalo hump. He was really anxious
to go. And he remembered and recalled all kinds of things,
like being in an old-style saloon one time, leaning against the
bar behind which there was a wall with just kegs and kegs of
beer and whiskey stacked up to the ceiling. And these two
white men came in. They got into a fight and started shooting at each other. Grandpa Fool Bull managed to crawl
behind a barrel of Old Crow. He barely got himself settled
when a bullet came in and it landed right close to his head,
knocking a hole in that keg, and all the good red-eye started
pouring out and his open mouth was right underneath that
hole and he was having himself a high old time in his hiding
place going on a happy drunk while those crazy white sons of
bitches took a full hour to kill each other. And he talked
about how he wanted to be buried in the old Indian way,
wrapped in his star blanket with Crow Dog praying for him
and burning sweetgrass. He was not sad at all. He was even
joking about it and he still had all his wits about him. He was
not feeble or sickly either. He just thought that it was about
time for him to travel that road. And a short while later he
died. I wished I had made an effort to know him better while
I still had the chance. He was the last man among us who
knew how to make and play the siyotanka, the old Sioux
courting flute. A year ago as I was walking near the tribal
office I had a vision. It was very real. I saw Fool Bull standing
there with one of his flutes in his hand. I wanted to go up to
him and say, "How wonderful, Grandpa Fool Bull, you
aren't dead after all," and then he changed into somebody
else and was just another idle old man leaning against the
wall of the tribal office waiting for God knows what.

Well, Grandpa Fool Bull took me to my first peyote meeting and I sat close by him the whole night. Even though I
was a young girl I took a lot of medicine. I saw a lot of good

things, and I suddenly understood. I understood the reality contained in this medicine, understood that this herb was our heritage, our tradition, that it spoke our language. I became part of the earth because peyote comes from the earth, even tastes like earth sometimes. And so the earth was in me and I in it, Indian earth making me more Indian. And to me Peyote was people, was alive, was a remembrance of things long forgotten.

The medicine was brought to me four times during the night by a man I did not know. It came to me before it came to Grandpa Fool Bull because I was sitting on his right. The man said something to me in Indian, very fast. I could not speak Sioux at the time, but it seemed to me that I could understand what he said, take in the meaning of his words. I was in the power. I heard my long-dead relatives talking to me. It was a feeling, a message coming to me with the voice of the drum, coming down the staff, speaking in the whirr of the feathers, breathing in the smoke of the fire, the smell of the burning cedar. I felt the drumbeat in my heart. My heart became the drum, both beating and beating and beating. I heard things. I did not know whether to believe what the voice told me, what Grandfather Peyote told me. Even now I cannot explain it.

When the sun rose, after we had eaten our morning food and drunk the ice-cold water from the stream, I felt as I had never felt before. I felt so happy, so good. When I got home I blurted out to my mother that I had been to a Native American Church meeting. Mom was hurt. In the end she shrugged her shoulders: "Well, it's up to you. I can't tell you what to do!" But she also added something that I liked: "Remember, whatever, the Indian is closest to God." I understood what she meant.

Two weeks later I was staying at my grandmother's and a dream came to me. It was in the nighttime, toward morning.

I tried to wake up but could not. I was awake and not awake. I could not move. I was crying. I opened my eyes once and saw my grandmother sitting by my bed. She was asking whether I was all right, but I could not answer her. In my dream I had been going back into another life. I saw tipis and Indians camping, huddling around a fire, smiling and cooking buffalo meat, and then, suddenly, I saw white soldiers riding into camp, killing women and children, raping, cutting throats. It was so real, much more real than a movie— sights and sounds and smells: sights I did not want to see, but had to see against my will; the screaming of children that I did not want to hear, but had to all the same. And the only thing I could do was cry. There was an old woman in my dream. She had a pack on her back—I could see that it was heavy. She was singing an ancient song. It sounded so sad, it seemed to have another dimension to it, beautiful but not of this earth, and she was moaning while she was singing it. And the soldiers came up and killed her. Her blood was soaked up by the grass which was turning red. All the Indians lay dead on the ground and the soldiers left. I could hear the wind and the hoofbeats of the soldiers' horses, and the voices of the spirits of the dead trying to tell me something. I must have dreamed for hours. I do not know why I dreamed this but I think that the knowledge will come to me some day. I truly believe that this dream came to me through the spiritual power of peyote.

For a long time after that dream I felt depressed, as if all life had been drained from me. I was still going to school, too young to bear such dreams. And I grieved because we had to live a life that we were not put on this earth for. I asked myself why things were so bad for us, why Indians suffered as they did. I could find no answer.

Crow Dog always says: "Grandfather Peyote, he has no mouth, but he speaks; no eyes, but he sees; no ears, but he hears and he makes you listen." Leonard does not read or write. He tells me: "Grandfather Peyote, he is my teacher, my educator." When he was in jail for having been at Wounded Knee, the prison psychiatrist visited him in his "house"—that's what they call their tiny cells. Crow Dog told him: "I don't need you. Peyote, he is my psychiatrist. With the power of this holy herb I could analyze you." The shrink did not know what to make of it. To a judge, Leonard said: "Peyote is my lawyer."

Crow Dog is a peyote road man. He is showing the people the road of life. Only after I married Crow Dog did I really come to understand this medicine. Leonard has the peyote, which we call peyuta or unkcela, and he has his sacred pipe. He is a peyote priest, but also a traditional Lakota medicine man, a yuwipi, and a Sun Dancer. Some people criticize him, or rather all of us who take part in Crow Dog's ceremonies. They say we should be one or the other, believe in the peyote or in the pipe, not in both. But Leonard cannot put his beliefs into separate little cubbyholes. He looks upon all ancient Indian religions as different aspects of one great overall power, part of the same creative force. Grandfather Peyote is just one of the many forms Wakan Tanka, Tunkashila, the Great Spirit, takes. The peyote button, the pipe, a deer, a bird, a butterfly, a pebble—they are all part of the Spirit. He is in them, and they are in him.

Dreams and visions are very important to us, maybe more important than any other aspect of Indian religion. I have met Indians from South and Central America, from Mexico and from the Arctic Circle. They all pray for visions, they are all "crying for a dream," as the Sioux call it. Some get their visions from fasting for four days and nights in a vision pit on a lonely hilltop. Others get their visions fasting and suffering during the long days of the Sun Dance, gazing at the blinding light in the sky. The Ghost Dancers went around and around in a circle, chanting until they fell down in a swoon, leaving their own bodies, leaving the earth, wandering along the Milky Way and among the stars. When they woke up they related what they had seen. Some found "star flesh" in their clenched fists, and moon rocks, so it is said. Still others receive their dreams out of the flash of lightning and the roar of thunder. Some tribes get their visions with the help of sacred mushrooms or jimsonweed. Not a few experience insight in the searing steam of the sweat lodge. Crow Dog receives what for lack of a better term I call sudden flashes of revelation during a vision quest as well as during a peyote meeting.

The Aztec word for the sacred herb was *peyotl*, meaning caterpillar, because this cactus is fuzzy like the hairs on a caterpillar. Our Sioux word for medicine is pejuta. Peyote, pejuta, that sounds very close. Maybe it is just a coincidence. It is certain that peyote came to us out of Mexico. In the 1870s the Kiowas and Comanches prayed with this medicine and established what they called the Native American Church. By now the peyote religion is common among most tribes all the way up to Alaska. Since peyote does not grow farther north than the Rio Grande, we must get our medicine from the border region. It is in the Southwest that we have our "peyote garden."

Peyote came to the Plains Indians just when they needed it most, at a time when the last of the buffalo were being killed and the tribes driven into fenced-in reservations, literally starving and dying of the white man's diseases, deprived of everything that had given meaning to their lives. The Native American Church became the religion of the poorest of the poor, the conquered, the despoiled. Peyote made them understand what was happening and made them endure. It was the only thing that gave them strength in those, our darkest days. Our only fear is that the whites will take this from us, too, as they have taken everything else. I am sure there are some people at this moment saying, "This is too good for those dumb Indians. Let us take it away from them and get high." Sometimes whites come to Leonard to "see the medicine man," like somebody at a country fair come to see the calf with two heads, and often the first words they say are, "Hey, got any peyote, chief?" Already I have seen white people misusing peyote, using it just like another drug to get stoned on. Already our sacred medicine is getting scarce.

It is perfectly legal for Indians to buy and use peyote as a sacrament in a religious ceremony—to buy it at a price, that is. As peyote is being fenced in, like us Indians, and as it is getting harder to come by, all along the Texas border dealers are selling it at exorbitant prices to the Native American Church people. For the sellers it is something like a gold rush. Peyote has been hit by inflation. It has been subjected to the rule of supply and demand, and selling it has become a business—can you imagine, an herb which grows wild in abundance, which nature has put on this earth for the use of the native peoples since the beginning of time.

Peyote makes me understand myself and the world around me. It lets me see the royalness of my people, the royalness of peyote, how good it can be. It is so good, and yet it can be dangerous if a person misuses it. You have to be in the right mind, approach it in the right way. If people have the wrong thoughts about it, it could hurt them. But peyote has never hurt me, it has always treated me well. It helped me when nothing else could. Grandfather Peyote knows you; you can't hide from him. He makes the unborn baby dance inside its mother's womb. He has that power. When you partake of this medicine in the right way, you feel strength surging through you, you "get into the power," other-world power given specially to you and no one else.

This also is common to all Indians whether or not they use peyote, this concept of power.

Peyote is a unifier, that is one of its chief blessings. This unifying force brought tribes together in friendship who had been enemies before, and it helped us in our struggle. I took the peyote road because I took the AIM road. For me they became one path. I have visited many tribes. They have different cultures and speak different languages. They may even have different rituals when partaking of this medicine. They may be jealous of each other, saying, "We are the better tribe. Our men used to fight better than yours. We do things better." But once they meet inside the peyote tipi, all differences are forgotten. Then they are no longer Navajos, or Poncas, Apaches, or Sioux, but just Indians. They learn each others' songs and find out that they are really the same. Peyote is making many tribes into just one tribe. And it is the same with the Sun Dance which also serves to unite the different Indian nations.

The words we put into our songs are an echo of the sacred root, the voices of the little pebbles inside the gourd rattle, the voices of the magpie and scissortail feathers which make up the peyote fan, the voice from inside the water drum, the cry of the water bird. Peyote will give you a voice, a song of understanding, a prayer for good health or for your people's survival. Once I saw a star shining through the opening on top of the tipi. It shone upon the sacred altar and it gave me a song. Many songs have no words, but you can put in words if you want to. It's up to the peyote to put words into your song. Women always took part in peyote meetings but for a long time they were not supposed to sing. They were not supposed to pray with the staff, because the staff is a man and women should not try to be men. I was one of the first women to sing during meetings. I have a very high voice, and I am told that I sound like a sad little girl. Leonard's sisters are all fine singers, especially Christine with her deep, strong voice. Now many women sing while holding the staff and shaking the gourd.

Leonard is the best of all peyote singers in the whole country and I am not saying this just because I am his wife. He knows literally hundreds and hundreds of different songs from many tribes. He must have made up at least a hundred songs himself. While his songs are traditional, he puts something new and special into them which is hard to define. At times his voice does not seem to belong to an ordinary human being. At other times it sounds as if two or three people were singing together, not just he alone. He puts birdcalls into his songs. He has made up a few roadrunner songs and while you hear him singing in Sioux, at the same time you can also hear the call of the roadrunner, very fast. You'd swear there was a roadrunner racing through the tipi, around and around, but it exists only in the song.

When I sit in the circle with Poncas, Otos, Winnebagos, or Cheyennes, I feel as if I am among my own people. We cannot understand each other except by talking English, but through peyote we speak one tongue, spiritually. The ceremony might change a little from tribe to tribe, but not much. Essentially it is always the same. The Navajos might use cornhusk cigarettes during their ritual, while we use the pipe and can-shasha, Indian willow bark tobacco. The Navajos form their main altar in the shape of a half-moon; another tribe may shape it another way. In some places they have their meetings inside the house in an ordinary room, cleared and purified for the purpose. Somewhere else they prefer to meet in a tipi. When Navajo people visit Leonard, he runs his ceremony Navajo style. If we go down to Arizona, the Navajos might put up a meeting for us in the Sioux manner. The differences are minor. Always the meeting lasts from sundown to sunup, always you have the songs, the staff, the gourd, the fan, the drum, the smoking, the fire, the drink of cold water. It is only when you travel below the border that peyote is worshiped in a markedly different way. In 1975 Leonard held a Ghost Dance at his place and to our great surprise a couple of Mexican Indians showed up— Yaqui, Huichol, and Nahuatl. How they knew about the Ghost Dance and what exactly had made them travel this long distance to Crow Dog's place was something of a mystery. One, a guy from Oaxaca, came in his typical Mexican Indian outfit and told us that his Nahua name was Warm Southwind. The Sioux, with their peculiar kind of Lakota humor, immediately named him "Mild Disturbance." We found out that these Indian brothers from Aztec and Maya country also were peyote people, but from what they told us their rituals were not at all like ours, going back to the dawn of history.

The peyote staff is a man. It is alive. It is, as my husband says, a "hot line" to the Great Spirit. Thoughts travel up the staff, and messages travel down. The gourd is a brain, a skull, a spirit voice. The water drum is the water of life. It is the Indians' heartbeat. Its skin is our skin. It talks in two voices—one high and clear, the other deep and reverberating. The drum is round like the sacred hoop which has no beginning and no end. The cedar's smoke is the breath of all green, living things, and it purifies, making everything it touches holy. The fire, too, is alive and eternal. It is the flame passed from one generation to the next. The feather fan is a war bonnet. It catches songs out of the air. Crow Dog's father, Henry, had a fan of magpie feathers and the magpie taught him a song. Magpie feathers are for doctoring. Water bird feathers are the road man's companions. The water bird is the chief symbol of the peyote religion. A fan made from its feathers is used by the road man to bless the water. Hawk feathers are for good understanding. A scissortail fan represents the Indian mothers, Indian maidens with black hair wearing white buckskin dresses. Everybody would like to own a macaw feather fan, but these are hard to come by. The macaw speaks all tongues and unifies the tribes. You can see good things in a macaw parrot fan. The strange thing is that in prehistoric Indian ruins going back a thousand years, in New Mexico, Arizona, and Colorado, the feathers and remains of macaws have been found. I have also seen many centuries-old rock paintings depicting parrots. The feathers, mummies, and paintings of these macaws are found some fifteen hundred to two thousand miles north from the nearest place where these huge parrots occur in the wild. It proves that the North American pueblos were in communication with the Aztecs and Toltecs. I often wonder whether the prehistoric Anasazi were peyote people and imported their macaws to use the feathers during their rituals. Maybe someday I will find out.

The first adherents of the Native American Church were harassed by missionaries and government agents, not because they used peyote as a sacrament, but because all Indian rituals were outlawed as standing in the way of "whitemanizing" the native peoples. In many states, until fairly recently, many who prayed with the sacred medicine had to go to jail. My husband's family were early victims of this sort of harassment. The Crow Dogs were among the first on our reservation to join the Peyote Church. That was about 1918 or 1920. Leonard's father, Henry, had a little boy before my husband was born. During the early thirties the family was living in St. Francis, a town dominated by Catholic priests who have their big mission and parochial boarding school there. One winter night one of the priests heard the sound of the peyote drum. It was traced to Henry Crow Dog's place where a ceremony was in progress. The BIA police received orders to drive Crow Dog from the town. He was the heathen rotten apple who spoiled the barrel of good Christian, submissive apples. The police piled Crow Dog's belongings, his wife, and children onto his old, horse-drawn buggy and told him to get out of St. Francis or go to jail. A blizzard was raging, and South Dakota blizzards are beyond anything an Eastern city dweller could imagine. Henry drove his buggy to his piece of allotted land some ten miles away. From his own land, he thought, nobody could drive him away. He was traveling in the face of the storm all the way, sometimes through deep snowdrifts. It took him all night. When he reached his land in the wee hours of the morning, they all had to sleep in the wagon. It was the only shelter they had against the icy winds. There was no house there at the time. Shortly after it got light the little boy died from exposure. He was two years old—a big brother whom Leonard never knew. A faith you have suffered for becomes more precious. The more the Crow Dogs and other traditional families were persecuted for their beliefs, the more stubbornly they held on to them.

After Wounded Knee, when I became Crow Dog's wife, I started to go down south with him to what he called his "peyote gardens." This always involved a round trip of some three thousand miles and staying with various tribes along the way. I have to admit that in the beginning I had the typical Sioux prejudice against some of the southern tribes. To me they seemed at first to be too peaceful and self-contented, not "committed to the struggle," the Pueblos especially. They did not have the Plains tribes' aversion to farming and were growing their corn and squash on fields which they had tended for hundreds of years before the first white man set foot on this continent. In time I recognized that they had an inner strength that we Plains people lacked, strength without macho, without bragging about what great warriors they were, or had been. I had to admire the way they kept the government at arm's length, kept tourists and photographers out, and managed to hold on to their old ways without theatricals or confrontations. They worked and kept themselves busy. They had, on the whole, fewer problems with alcoholism than we did. Of course, they had been farmers since the dawn of history, great potters, and nowadays also jewelry makers. Through their farming and craftwork they had been able to adapt to the system without being overrun by it.

They lived a lot better than we northern tribes. Their beautiful traditional adobe houses were comfortable, with modern bathrooms and kitchens. They sat by cozy fireplaces. Fine Indian rugs covered their floors; strings of red chilis hung from their rafters. Outside, the family car was always new and shiny, not like our old Sioux jalopies with one headlight out and a window smashed. I could not help noticing the great role women played in Pueblo society. Women owned the houses and actually built them. Children often got their mother's last name, not their father's. Sons joined their mothers' clans. It made me a little jealous. Of course, the Pueblos were lucky. Unlike us poor Sioux who were driven into fenced-in reservations, they still lived in their ancient villages which had already been old when the Spaniards came. Even so the Pueblos have many of the same problems facing us Sioux. They have to protect their land and water from developers, strip miners, uranium seekers, and dam builders. I sometimes think that in their quiet way they might be doing a better job at this than we flamboyant Lakotas. Traveling and meeting many tribes we learned a lot. At least I did.

Having our certificates and other documents proving that we are acting on behalf of all the Native American Church people in the Dakotas, and that Leonard is an official as well as priest of that church, it is now legal for us to go down into Texas and Mexico to harvest our medicine. Leonard only has to show his papers to get all the peyote he wants—if he has the money to pay for it. It took some tough court battles to bring this about. One of the funniest court cases he won arose from an incident on the Navajo reservation. Leonard had been invited to a peyote meeting by some Navajo friends. It was run by a Navajo, but they gave Leonard the job of fire chief. At the beginning an Indian woman came in with a white man. She explained, "He is my husband. That makes it all right for him to partake." This white guy was dressed like a hippie. He had long hair and beads all over him. He was dressed like an Indian. He took some medicine and seemed to be affected by it. He acted drunk. Halfway through the meeting he suddenly got up to take a leak outside. As he stumbled back into the tipi he did not bend down low enough to clear the entrance hole. His long hair got caught and came off. It was a wig. Underneath he had a crew cut. At once he said, "I am the sheriff of Holbrook, and I arrest the whole bunch of you." All the Indians burst into laughter, it was so grotesque.

When the trial came up, one of the charges was that the Indians had let a white man participate. Of course, Leonard had only been a guest. It had not been up to him to let or not let the white man participate. When it was Leonard's turn to speak, he said: "Judge, if it is illegal for a white man to take this medicine, then the sheriff has broken his own law. We did not break it, because we have been allowed to use this herb as a sacrament for a long, long time. But I think the sheriff has not broken any law, because this was a religious meeting and even a white man has the right to participate— if we let him—as long as it is a strictly conducted ceremony. Freedom of religion doesn't stop at the door of a peyote tipi. Also, the sheriff had no jurisdiction on Indian land in the first place. Inside the reservation he was just a tourist. Only the tribal police would have had the right to make an arrest. This is all I have to say." We won that case and it was a landmark decision in favor of the peyote church.

When we go down to the peyote gardens we usually travel in four or five cars or trucks. It takes a good number of people to do the harvesting. They have "distributors" on the border, peyote dealers. The last time we had to pay over a hundred dollars for a thousand buttons. Five years ago it was twenty-five dollars. That's inflation for you. But on the last few trips we did not go to a dealer; we did the harvesting on our own. It is not only cheaper, but a lot more fitting to get the medicine in the right, sacred way, than just to buy it like aspirin or cough drops.

We found a place where we saw the desert sprinkled with peyote. It is a kind of cactus plant. We got up at sunrise and Leonard performed a prayer ceremony that he said would make us find plenty of medicine, that the prayer would help us go to the right spots. We all spread out and looked around. The whole area was covered with cactus, Joshua trees, chapparal, and creosote bushes. Some of the cactuses were gigantic, up to twenty feet high. The peyote was sitting there between all those thorns, prickles, and spikes. It was really hard to get at. I felt that it was good that we had to work for it and got scratched up. It gave the harvest a special meaning for me.

On one occasion Barbara found the chief peyote. It was large, divided into sixteen segments, four times the sacred number of the four directions. When you find a chief peyote you pray for him, to him, with him. We think that every person or family in the Native American Church should have a chief peyote in their home. So when somebody finds him, someone who doesn't have one yet, we dig him out with the whole root and a lot of his natural soil and take him back with us. Barb did not have a chief peyote yet, so Leonard helped to dig it out and gave it to her, saying, "Just take this peyote and pray with him whenever you need help." The plant thrived. Barb kept it watered and it grew. Every week she had a little flower on her chief peyote. Every time I saw it, it seemed to have grown. When Barb was not at home, grandmother watered it and made sure that it had enough sunlight. One day my mother visited her and said, "Why don't you just throw that thing out?" But grandma told her, "Mary and Barb think a lot of this plant and I'm gonna take care of it when they are not here." It showed that grandma was more Indian than mom, and it also showed the cultural and generation gap between our mother and us.

Some people take the whole peyote plant, but we decided to take only the tops and leave the roots so that the peyote could grow again. It took us a little more than two weeks to harvest about thirty-five thousand peyotes, enough for the whole tribe and for a whole year. While we were gathering our medicine, the rancher who owned the land came up and asked what we were doing on his property. When we explained, he smiled and said we were welcome any time. If we had been forced to pay for them all at the price the dealers were charging just then, it would have meant no shoes for the kids. We would have had to save on food and everything else for the rest of the year. Thirty-five thousand buttons! Maybe all that medicine on his land had influenced the man's thinking, "sensitized" him, as the AIM guys would say. The first harvesting was a new experience for me. It made me want to go back and do a little better each time, do the gathering in an ever more sacred way, more knowingly.

Once we went harvesting in Old Mexico. As we drove back to the States we had little peyotes lying all over the car, all those little buttons on the dashboard. Somebody said, "Jesus! It's illegal to bring it across the border. They'll arrest us and take our medicine away." I did not want to throw our medicine out the window. So I and another girl decided to eat it. It seemed more respectful. When we got back to our motel in Texas we were all peyoted up. My head was spinning. When you take medicine in a ceremonial context it does not affect you that way. There I was sitting on the carpet in our room and I sure was in the power. Later we found out that the customs inspectors had known all about us, had seen Crow Dog's certificate, and had waved the other cars ahead of us through with a smile—buttons and all. And there I had struggled getting a record amount of our medicine down into my stomach in record time; for nothing. But later, in the motel, it felt so nice!

Rosebud Sioux reservation, South Dakota. A typical house.

Leonard Crow Dog at Wounded Knee in 1973.

The church at Wounded Knee, April 1973. (Photo by Owen C. Luck.)

Saloon at Scenit, South Dakota, with sign "No Indians Allowed."

Mary Crow Dog's son Pedro, who was born at Wounded Knee during the siege in 1973.

Clash with police at Custer, North Carolina, where demonstrators were manhandled when they protested the murder of Bad Heart Bull, a Sioux. (Photo by Ken Norgar.)

Leonard Crow Dog and friend in front of the Bureau of Indian Affairs building in Washington, D.C., during the takeover in 1972.

Mary Ellen Crow Dog catching a nap during her husband's trial in 1976.

Leonard Crow Dog talking to Mary's son Pedro during visiting hours in jail.

Rally for Leonard Crow Dog in 1976.

Leonard Crow Dog, with Mary and her son Pedro, after his release from Lewisburg, Pennsylvania, prison in 1977.

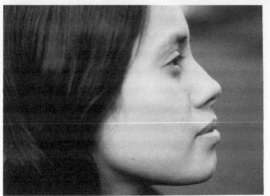

"The Longest Walk" in Washington, D.C., in July 1977.

Mary Ellen Crow Dog, née Brave Bird, 1976.

Leonard Crow Dog praying.

Ina Crow Dog being cured in a curing ceremony.

Revival of the Ghost Dance at Rosebud Reservation in 1974.

Piercing during the Sun Dance ceremony at Leonard Crow Dog's place.

Henry Crow Dog in sweat lodge, 1969.

Henry Crow Dog before vision quest.

Leonard Crow Dog preparing for vision quest in 1973.

Leonard Crow Dog in Sun Dance regalia, 1973.

Sun Dancer Merle Left Hand Bull blowing on eaglebone whistle during Sun Dance

CHAPTER 8

Cankpe Opi Wakpala

I knew when I brought my body here,
it might become food for the
worms and magpies.
I threw my body away before
I came here.

—*Young man from Eagle Butte*

I do not consider myself a radical or revolutionary. It is
white people who put such labels on us. All we ever
wanted was to be left alone, to live our lives as we see fit. To
govern ourselves in reality and not just on paper. To have our
rights respected. If that is revolutionary, then I sure fit that
description. Actually, I have a great yearning to lead a normal, peaceful life—normal in the Sioux sense. I could have
accepted our flimsy shack, our smelly outhouse, and our
poverty—but only on my terms. Yes, I would have accepted
poverty, dignified, uninterfered-with poverty, but not the

drunken, degrading, and humiliating poverty we had to endure. But normality was a long time in coming. Even now I don't have the peace I crave.

When my husband was in a maximum-security prison in Lewisburg, Pennsylvania, I spent many months in New York with white friends in order to be near him. For the first time I lived a life which white Americans consider "normal." I have to admit that I developed a certain taste for it. It was a new, comfortable, exciting life for a young Indian hobo girl like me. I became quite a New Yorker. I took my little boy Pedro down to the Village to Pancho's, buying wonderful-tasting nachos for him and virgin coladas for myself. I liked to go window-shopping. Everything was so much cheaper than on the reservation where the trading posts have no competition and charge what they please. Everything is more expensive if you are poor. I went down to Greene's on 38th Street in the millinery district and bought beads at one-sixth the price Indian craftworkers are charged by the white dealer in Rosebud. They had many more beads to choose from, the kinds of beads I had not seen for years, indis-tinguishable from the old, nineteenth-century ones, like tiny, sweaty green and yellow beads, and cut-glass beads of the type Kiowas use in beading peyote staffs and gourds. I learned to like spicy Szechuan and Hunan food, learned to accept and talk with white friends, and lost some of my shyness to the extent of making public speeches on behalf of my imprisoned husband. I luxuriated in bathtubs with hot and cold running water and admitted that modern flush toilets were suiting me a lot better than our Leaning Tower of Pisa privies, even though they were products of white American technology which I usually condemned. Once, in a fit of total irresponsibility, I blew $99.99 on an imitation Persian rug on special sale at Macy's. I took this thing home and spread it on the floor of our shack, feeling smugly middle-class. The rug didn't last long, what with the dogs, the kids, and many people dropping in constantly with their problems. Once even a horse forced its way in through the unlocked door and relieved itself on this proud possession of mine. This rug was a symbol of the good little housewife I could have been. It is the government which made me into a militant. If you approach them hat in hand as a "responsible, respectable" apple, red outside, white inside, you get no-where. If you approach them as a militant you get nowhere either, except giving them an excuse to waste you, but at least you don't feel so shitty. Wounded Knee was not the brainchild of wild, foaming-at-the-mouth militants, but of patient and totally unpolitical, traditional Sioux, mostly old Sioux ladies.

The trouble started with Dicky Wilson, or rather it started long ago with the Indian Reorganization Act of 1934. At that time a government lawyer decided to do something for "Lo, the poor Indian," and wrote a constitution for all the tribes. Indians were to have their own little governments patterned after that of the Great White Father in Washington. Every Indian nation was to have an elected tribal president and council. Poor benighted Mr. Lo was to have the blessings of democracy bestowed upon him by all-wise white benefactors. The people who thought it all up probably really meant to do well by us. Sometimes I think that the do-gooders do us more harm than the General Custer types. There were two things very wrong with this sudden gift of democracy. The most important was that the Reorganization Act destroyed the old, traditional form of Indian self-government. The Sioux always had their ancient council of chiefs; other tribes were guided by their clan mothers or, as among the Pueblos, by their caciques and kikmongwis, who were priests. All traditional Indian government was founded on religion. The Reorganization Act brought into being a class of half- and quarter-blood politicians whose allegiance was mainly to Washington. The full-blood traditionals never took to these puppet regimes, looking upon them as the work of white men, installed for white men's advantage. They would have nothing to do with them and often refused to take part in tribal elections. As a result, in many tribes, the chairmen were voted into power by a small minority of half-breed Uncle Tomahawks who did not represent the grass-roots people but only the educated, well-off, landless part-Indians. A great number of tribes were split by the Reorganization Act into "cooperating friendlies" and "recalcitrant hostiles." The first usually occupied a tribe's administrative center, the latter the outlying backwoods settlements. This rift created in 1934 has lasted in many places to this day.

The second thing wrong with the whole scheme was that the tribal governments, such as they were, had very little real power. Power remained always in the hands of the white superintendent and the white BIA bureaucrats. It was the superintendent who held the purse strings and gave out what few jobs there were. He had the support of Washington. In a conflict between the tribal president and the superintendent, it was always the white superintendent who came out on top. It was the same with the tribal courts, which were allowed to handle only minor offenses—wife-beating, speeding, drunk and disorderly, and such stuff. The so-called ten major crimes, which included everything but simple misdemeanors, were handled by federal courts outside the reservation before white juries. There were some good tribal chairmen, but many of them were corrupt. The typical bad tribal chairman practiced nepotism, filling up all available positions with his relatives. His brother became the chief of police, his nephews tribal policemen, his brothers-in-law tribal judges, his uncle head of the election board.

You get the idea. Once such a guy had settled in, it was impossible to get rid of him.

Dicky Wilson at Pine Ridge was about the worst tribal president of this type. Pine Ridge is our neighbor reservation. Together with our own, Rosebud, it forms a very big chunk of land, some two, three million acres. Both are Sioux reservations. The people speak the same language, have the same rituals and customs, and intermarry all the time. Most Rosebud people have Pine Ridge relatives. Pine Ridge Sioux are Oglalas—Red Cloud's and Crazy Horse's people. In the early 1960s, Wilson and his wife had to leave the reservation after being accused of conflict-of-interest abuses while he was a plumber for the Pine Ridge housing authority. A few years later he came back and was accused, together with another man, of illegally converting tribal funds. When he became tribal president he abolished freedom of speech and assembly on the reservation. He distributed John Birch Society literature and was showing John Birch Society–made hate films. He misused tribal moneys. He took tribal ballot boxes into his basement and there "counted" the votes. Worst of all, he maintained his rule with the help of his private army, known and feared under the name of the goons. Opponents of his regime had their houses fire-bombed, their cars and windows riddled with bullets. People were beaten and shot. Pine Ridge experienced a rash of violent deaths, unexplained and uninvestigated. People were afraid to leave their homes. A small girl had her eye shot out. Most of the victims were people who had stood up against Wilson or had otherwise offended him. He had people stomped and beaten in his presence. Things got so out of hand that even the long-suffering back-country full-bloods, known for their capacity to endure in silence, began to grumble. The old treaty chiefs, medicine men, tribal interpreters, and traditionalists finally formed an organization known as OSCRO, Oglala Sioux Civil Rights Organization. Its head was Pedro Bissonette, a close friend who was later killed under mysterious circumstances by Wilson's goons. While a sort of undeclared civil war raged on the Pine Ridge Reservation, AIM had come in force to nearby Rapid City, which some Indians called the "most racist town in the United States." The AIM people were demonstrating against prevailing housing conditions in Indian slums, against discrimination and police brutality. While fights between Indians and whites broke out in Rapid City streets and bars, a Sioux by the name of Wesley Bad Heart Bull was stabbed to death by a white man in front of a saloon in Buffalo Gap, a small hamlet not far from Rapid City. The case was tried in Custer, situated deep inside the Paha Sapa—our sacred Black Hills—and upon Custer converged the AIM people as well as many Sioux from Pine Ridge, Rosebud, and Cheyenne River, with the AIM and OSCRO people mingling together. Among the AIM leaders was Russel Means, himself a Pine Ridge Sioux, born and enrolled in the Oglala tribe. His family's home was at Porcupine, some ten miles from Wounded Knee. Wilson had promised to "personally cut off Russel Means's braids if he ever set foot on the reservation." He forbade Means to speak at Pine Ridge. Russel went there anyway and Wilson had him beaten up. Russel wound up in the hospital with a hairline skull fracture, but was soon released. In that explosive situation, OSCRO asked AIM for help against the goons. Thus the stage was set.

For me, Wounded Knee started in Rapid City. This is John Wayne country. Everybody tries to look like the guy in the Marlboro ads. At that time I was not yet Crow Dog's woman. I had been in love with a young boy who was not cut out to be a husband, much less a father. He had disappeared from my life, but he left me pregnant. I was in my eighth month and very big. My smallness only emphasized my enormous belly. It seemed as if the whole Sioux Nation, all the Seven Campfires, had come to Rapid City to demonstrate against the racism for which the city had become notorious. My brother was there, and Barb. So naturally I was there, too. We all stayed at the Mother Butler Seminary, a hangout for Indian activists. One night I was trying to sleep when a girl called Toony came in, all excited. She was a good friend of mine. She told me, "This whole goddam town is going to blow up any minute!" All business, she put down her bag, pulled out a knife, and stuck it in her boot. Her cowboy boots were tipped with metal. She was showing them off: "These are my special shitkickers. I'm putting on war paint."

I asked, "What's going on? Can I come?" "No," she said, "not you. No way. Not in your condition."

Outside, Russel and Dennis were drilling some guys in nonviolent tactics. They would blow a whistle and everybody would run into the street. Another whistle and they all would run back into Mother Butler's. Most of the guys took it as a big joke. Indians are not very good at being drilled—even by their own leaders.

The bars in Rapid City were known to be tough on Indians. The unspoken rule was "Indians enter at their own risk." Groups of skins were forming to sensitize the saloons. Nobody wanted me around, but I went along anyhow. We trooped from bar to bar, and wherever we went we caused a riot. One redneck told me, "We're goin' to make good Injuns out of you!" I kicked him in the shin and he hit me hard in the chest. I charged blindly and we both wound up on the floor. It was sure no way for a lady in my interesting condition to behave. A kind of insane rage seemed to possess, not only me, but everybody. Rapid City had been a bad scene for us ever since the town was founded on land stolen from us after Custer had found gold in the Black Hills. There was not one single Sioux from Rosebud, Pine Ridge, Standing Rock, Cheyenne River, or Oak Creek who did not bear the scars of humiliations, undeserved arrests, or beatings received in this town whose main sport has always been Indian-baiting. The resentment that had been smoldering for eighty years finally boiled over in one wild night. The police went berserk, going on a rampage with their nightsticks, busting the head of anybody who looked Indian. They arrested skins at random, stuffing them into a big, old Greyhound bus, carting about two hundred of us off to the small, cramped, and decrepit Pennington County Jail. Those of us who had not been arrested snake-danced around the jail, drumming and singing war songs.

It was then that Dennis Banks told us that Wesley Bad Heart Bull had been stabbed to death by a white man and that the trial was about to start at Custer, inside the Black Hills, forty-five miles from Rapid City. Custer! The name itself was a provocation. Custer, a town built on a spot which our legends told us was the home of the sacred thunderbirds, desecrated by tourist traps such as a phony Indian village with a big sign: SEE HOW THEY LIVE!

A couple hundred of us formed up a thirty-car caravan to drive to Custer. It was early February 1973 and it was cold, below freezing. It was snowing heavily. When we arrived the first thing I saw was a huge sign: WELCOME TO CUSTER—THE TOWN WITH THE GUNSMOKE FLAVOR, and another billboard: SEE THE PAGEANT, HOW THE WEST WAS WON! Soon the smoke flavor would be stronger. We had come not to make a riot, but to see justice done. In South Dakota the killing of an Indian was usually treated as a mere misdemeanor and went unpunished, but if an Indian killed a white man he was condemned to death and was lucky to have it bargained down to a life sentence. We were fed up with this kind of judicial double standard.

We gathered before the courthouse. At first everything was dignified, even jolly. A delegation of four or five of our spokesmen (or should I say "spokespersons"? But they were all men; we were not in the spokesperson stage yet) entered the courthouse. A short while later the district attorney came out on the court steps with a smile in order to address us. As I remember, it went like this: "My Indian *ffrrrriends*. I promise you, justice will be done. Depend on it. The man who killed Wesley Bad Heart Bull will be prosecuted to the full extent of the law—for *second-degree manslaughter.*"

At the words "second-degree manslaughter" a deep growl went up. They were like a knife stuck into our bellies. It meant another Indian-killer would go free. Dennis, Russel, and Crow Dog argued with the DA, telling him not to specify the charge, but to let the jury decide whether it was murder or manslaughter. The DA refused. After that things were neither dignified nor jolly. The state highway patrolmen tried to keep the Sioux out of the courthouse. A scuffle broke out. The troopers had been waiting for this—with visored helmets, guns, and long riot sticks. They clubbed down the mother of the murdered Indian, Sarah Bad Heart Bull, and choked her by pressing a riot stick against her throat. Our delegation inside the courthouse was also attacked. I saw Russel being dragged out, sitting on the pavement, handcuffed, dazed, and bleeding, telling the police, "We're fighting for our lives. You are only fighting for your paychecks." Crow Dog was jumping out of a broken first-floor courthouse window. Dennis jumped out after him with a big grin: "I'm following my spiritual leader."

Then all hell broke loose. The police used tear gas, smoke bombs, and fire hoses to drive us away from the courthouse. A few older men and women were still trying to reason with them: "All this isn't necessary. We just want to be heard." But it was no good. The troopers and Indians began fighting for possession of the main street in front of the courthouse. A young Indian girl had her clothes torn off in the struggle. I saw two helmeted pigs with huge sticks dragging her almost naked through the snow. She was bleeding. A man in front of Barb was clubbed senseless, lying like a heap of old rags in the middle of the road. One of the pigs yelled at us, "You damn Indians have raised enough cain around here and we're goin' to kick your ass. We're not goin' to give you a chance to wreck this place. We're goin' to crack your goddam heads first."

Then the Sioux let out a big war whoop and charged. They started trashing a police car parked in the street. In their frustration they jumped on it, kicked it, beat it with their fists. Somebody lit a match and threw it into the gas tank. It wouldn't light. Somebody else poured gas around it and tried to set it on fire. His matches wouldn't light. The snow had made everything wet. The guys then tried to tip the squad car over, rocking it back and forth. It did not budge. Everybody vented their fury upon it, but the thing seemed invulnerable. Barb was laughing: "All these Indians and they can't total one lousy pig car!"

People were scampering in and out of stores, ripping everything out, breaking windows. Two young men came running with a trash can full of gasoline. They ran up the steps of the courthouse, doused the door with gas, and poured some of it inside through a broken window. Some other boys were racing up from the gas station with burning flares, the kind one sets out on the road if one has to fix a flat at night. They chucked the flares at the entrance door where the gas had formed a puddle, but they missed. The flares were hissing harmlessly on the steps. More flares. A sheriff who looked as if he had come out of a Grade B western movie aimed his rifle at one of our men: "If you throw that flare I'll kill you, so help me!" The sisters were screaming, "Do it, do it, do it! AIM, AIM, AIM, make every aim count!" I was screaming, too. One of the girls had a candle, another a kerosene lamp. Young men were making molotov cocktails and throwing them. The troopers were yelling back, "We'll kill any man who throws a flare!"

Suddenly a great roar went up, "*Aaaaaahhhhhhh!*"—the old bear sound the Sioux make when they are killing mad. The gasoline had caught fire. A fire truck came careering around the corner. While firemen and police tried to keep the court-house from burning down, we set fire to the Chamber of Commerce—an imitation pioneer log cabin. It went up in flames, making a huge fire with sparks flying in all direction. The sign WELCOME TO CUSTER—THE TOWN WITH THE GUNSMOKE FLAVOR was burning brightly. All the women made the spine-tingling brave-heart cry. Out of nowhere a gasoline truck appeared and stopped right in front of the burning Chamber of Commerce. The driver was completely freaked out. He couldn't figure out what the hell was going on. He was sitting in his cab, bug-eyed and petrified with fear, not knowing what to do. He just kept staring open-mouthed at the flames. We waved him on, but he just sat there. One of our boys stuck his head inside the cab and yelled at him, "Get your ass out of here. What do you want to do, blow us all up?" He was so scared we almost felt sorry for him. At the same time we had to laugh, it was so ludi-crous. Finally he woke up and got the hell out of there as fast as his truck would go.

The fighting lasted from morning until midafternoon, luckily without shooting, just rocks, fists, and clubs. Many Indians were arrested and some were later tried. Sarah Bad Heart Bull was indicted on several counts of rioting and arson, and faced a possible maximum sentence of forty years. Her son's murderer was acquitted without doing any time at all, while Sarah actually spent a few weeks in jail for having made a nuisance of herself over her son's death. Barb was arrested and told she was facing ten years, but nothing came of it and she was let go. I was not arrested at all. I left Custer in a car which had an old bumper sticker on its rear fender: CUSTER HAD IT COMING! It made me laugh. That same night, back in Rapid City, we could see ourselves on TV. It had been quite a day.

We had little time to catch our breath. Already the OSCRO people at Pine Ridge were sending out urgent calls for us to help them. Wilson's goons were on the rampage, maiming and killing people. The Oglala elders thought that we all had been wasting our time and energies in Rapid City and Custer when the knife was at our throats at home. And so, finally and inevitably, our caravan started rolling toward Pine Ridge. Wilson was expecting us. His heavily armed goons had been reinforced by a number of rednecks with Remingtons and Winchesters on gun racks behind their driver's seats, eager to bag themselves an Injun. The marshals and FBI had come too, with some thirty armored cars equipped with machine guns and rocket launchers. These were called APCs, Armored Personnel Carriers. The tribal office had been sandbagged and a machine gun installed on its roof. The Indians called it "Fort Wilson." Our movements were kept under observation and reported several times a day. Still we came on.

To tell the truth, I had not joined the caravan with the notion that I would perform what some people later called "that great symbolic act." I did not even know that we would wind up at Wounded Knee. Nobody did. I went because everybody went, because I was young and it was my life-style to go along. It would not have occurred to me not to go. At this time the community hall at Calico, five miles north of Pine Ridge, was the meeting place of OSCRO and all those who opposed Wilson's regime. Now they were being joined by AIM. People had had a powwow there for a few days, dancing and singing, though Wilson had forbidden it.

The scene upon our arrival was peaceful enough. Kids were playing frisbee. Elders were drinking coffee out of paper cups. An old man was telling me, "What are we to do? If you are with AIM you're a no-good renegade. If you are with Dickie Wilson you're a goddam goon. If you are with the government, you're no Indian at all." All the old chiefs with the historic great names were there and all the medicine men, people like Fools Crow, Wallace Black Elk, Crow Dog, Chips, and Pete Catches. Only one important traditional man was missing who was too old and sick to attend. Even some tribal judges were there. One of them said to the AIM and OSCRO guys, commenting on what had happened at Custer, "In my job I really have to be against any destruction of private property, but privately I enjoyed what you did. You should have burned that whole goddam town down." Contrary to what some of the media said later, the overwhelming majority of those present were Sioux, born and bred on the reservation. Russel Means said a few words which I still remember, though I can't quote them exactly. The drift of his speech was: "If I have to die, I don't want to die in some barroom brawl, or in a stupid car accident, but want my death to have some meaning. Maybe the time has come when we need some Indian martyrs." One old man said something to the effect that he had lived all his life in Pine Ridge in darkness. That the whites and men like Wilson had thrown a blanket over the whole reservation and that he hoped we would be the ones to yank this blanket off and let some sunshine in.

It began to dawn upon me that what was about to happen, and what I personally would be involved in, would be unlike anything I had witnessed before. I think everybody who was there felt the same way—an excitement that was choking our throats. But there was still no definite plan for what to do. We had all assumed that we would go to Pine Ridge town, the administrative center of the reservation, the seat of

Wilson's and the government's power. We had always thought that the fate of the Oglalas would be settled there. But as the talks progressed it became clear that nobody wanted us to storm Pine Ridge, garrisoned as it was by the goons, the marshals, and the FBI. We did not want to be slaughtered. There had been too many massacred Indians already in our history. But if not Pine Ridge, then what? As I remember, it was the older women like Ellen Moves Camp and Gladys Bissonette who first pronounced the magic words "Wounded Knee," who said, "Go ahead and make your stand at Wounded Knee. If you men won't do it, you can stay here and talk for all eternity and we women will do it."

When I heard the words "Wounded Knee" I became very, very serious. Wounded Knee—Cankpe Opi in our language—has a special meaning for our people. There is the long ditch into which the frozen bodies of almost three hundred of our people, mostly women and children, were thrown like so much cordwood. And the bodies are still there in their mass grave, unmarked except for a cement border. Next to the ditch, on a hill, stands the white-painted Catholic church, gleaming in the sunlight, the monument of an alien faith imposed upon the landscape. And below it flows Cankpe Opi Wakpala, the creek along which the women and children were hunted down like animals by Custer's old Seventh, out to avenge themselves for their defeat by butchering the helpless ones. That happened long ago, but no Sioux ever forgot it.

Wounded Knee is part of our family's history. Leonard's great-grandfather, the first Crow Dog, had been one of the leaders of the Ghost Dancers. He and his group had held out in the icy ravines of the Badlands all winter, but when the soldiers came in force to kill all the Ghost Dancers he had surrendered his band to avoid having his people killed. Old accounts describe how Crow Dog simply sat down between the rows of soldiers on one side, and the Indians on the other, all ready and eager to start shooting. He had covered himself with a blanket and was just sitting there. Nobody knew what to make of it. The leaders on both sides were so puzzled that they just did not get around to opening fire. They went to Crow Dog, lifted the blanket, and asked him what he meant to do. He told them that sitting there with the blanket over him was the only thing he could think of to make all the hotheads, white and red, curious enough to forget fighting. Then he persuaded his people to lay down their arms. Thus he saved his people just a few miles away from where Big Foot and his band were massacred. And old Uncle Dick Fool Bull, a relative of both the Crow Dogs and my own family, often described to me how he himself heard the rifle and cannon shots that mowed our people down when he was a little boy camping only two miles away. He had seen the bodies, too, and described to me how he had found the body of a dead baby girl with an American flag beaded on her tiny bonnet.

Before we set out for Wounded Knee, Leonard and Wallace Black Elk prayed for all of us with their pipe. I counted some fifty cars full of people. We went right through Pine Ridge. The half-bloods and goons, the marshals and the government snipers on their rooftop, were watching us, expecting us to stop and start a confrontation, but our caravan drove right by them, leaving them wondering. From Pine Ridge it was only eighteen miles more to our destination. Leonard was in the first car and I was way in the back.

Finally, on February 27, 1973, we stood on the hill where the fate of the old Sioux Nation, Sitting Bull's and Crazy Horse's nation, had been decided, and where we, ourselves, came face to face with our fate. We stood silently, some of us wrapped in our blankets, separated by our personal thoughts and feelings, and yet united, shivering a little with excitement and the chill of a fading winter. You could almost hear our heartbeats.

It was not cold on this next-to-last day of February—not for a South Dakota February anyway. Most of us had not even bothered to wear gloves. I could feel a light wind stirring my hair, blowing it gently about my face. There were a few snowflakes in the air. We all felt the presence of the spirits of those lying close by in the long ditch, wondering whether we were about to join them, wondering when the marshals would arrive. We knew that we would not have to wait long for them to make their appearance.

The young men tied eagle feathers to their braids, no longer unemployed kids, juvenile delinquents, or winos, but warriors. I thought of our old warrior societies—the Kit Foxes, the Strong Hearts, the Badgers, the Dog Soldiers. The Kit Foxes—the Tokalas—used to wear long sashes. In the midst of battle, a Tokala would sometimes dismount and pin the end of his sash to the earth. By this he signified his determination to stay and fight on his chosen spot until he was dead, or until a friend rode up and unpinned him, or until victory. Young or old, men or women, we had all become Kit Foxes, and Wounded Knee had become the spot upon which we had pinned ourselves. Soon we would be encircled and there could be no retreat. I could not think of anybody or anything that would "unpin" us. Somewhere, out on the prairie surrounding us, the forces of the government were gathering, the forces of the greatest power on earth. Then and there I decided that I would have my baby at Wounded Knee, no matter what.

Suddenly the spell was broken. Everybody got busy. The men were digging trenches and making bunkers, putting up low walls of cinder blocks, establishing a last-resort defense perimeter around the Sacred Heart Church. Those few who had weapons were checking them, mostly small-bore .22s and old hunting rifles. We had only one automatic weapon, an AK-47 that one Oklahoma boy had brought back from Vietnam as a souvenir. Altogether we had twenty-six firearms—not much compared to what the other side would bring up against us. None of us had any illusions that we could take over Wounded Knee unopposed. Our message to the government was: "Come and discuss our demands or kill us!" Somebody called someone on the outside from a telephone inside the trading post. I could hear him yelling proudly again and again, *"We hold the Knee!"*

CHAPTER 9

The Siege

Coming to Wounded Knee was just the most
natural thing in the world to do.

—*Chief Frank Fools Crow*

I am not afraid to die.
If I die at Wounded Knee,
I will go where Crazy Horse
and Sitting Bull
and our grandfathers are.

—*Crow Dog*

The three main centers around which the seventy-one-
days-long siege of Wounded Knee revolved were the
Sacred Heart Church, the Gildersleeve Trading Post, and
the museum. The most important for us was the store,
which was really a little empire by itself. It consisted of an
Indian arts and crafts and artifact store, a Western curio

shoppe, a supermarket, a cafeteria which had on its menu the worst frozen, factory-made pizzas I ever tasted, a filling station, and private quarters for the manager's family—a jumble of additions piled upon additions. The circular museum was part of the trading post, but a separate building a little ways off. Gildersleeve had always tried to exploit the site of our greatest tragedy, making it into a tourist attraction. For seventy-five miles around he had put up billboards: SEE THE WOUNDED KNEE MASSACRE SITE, VISIT THE MASS GRAVE. POSTCARDS, CURIOS, DON'T MISS IT! Some of the postcards advertised showed our slaughtered men and women frozen stiff in grotesque attitudes. Others showed grinning soldiers posing with the corpses. We had always resented Gildersleeve and his empire built dollar by dollar out of our poverty.

I spent my first night in the church under the eyes of Holy Mary and some plaster-cast saints. Some of the young people had pushed the pews aside, brought out a drum, and begun to dance in Indian fashion. The elderly priest could not understand what was happening. Somebody told him, "You're a prisoner of war." He started to tremble. "Naw," one of the men told him, "we just want you to go over there, in back, in case there should be some shooting. We don't want you to get hurt." He was led away in a daze. He was mumbling that our dance and drum had desecrated his church. One woman told him that he had got it wrong, that his church was a desecration of the grave of our slaughtered people who had not been Christians. In the ravines coyotes were howling.

In the morning everybody was milling around. Stan Holder was named head of security, Bod Free chief of engineers to keep the electricity running and so forth. Crow Dog was the spiritual leader. The rifles were counted. Somebody was measuring the amount of gasoline left in the tanks of the filling station. Some of us women went down to the store to take inventory of the groceries and tinned goods. On the way we met a whole safari bringing up foodstuffs from the cafeteria to give breakfast to the crowd in the church and the warriors in the bunkers. A car full of goons appeared on the horizon. Some men fired upon it and it took off in a hurry. I could see an FBI car coming up the road, but it stayed at a respectful distance. We were being watched.

Dennis Banks had told us, "Don't take anything from the store." He could have saved himself the trouble. The place was already pretty well stripped. A young man seemed happy with a 30–30 rifle he had "liberated." Already groups of Indians had staked out their territory, making themselves at home in cubbyholes, putting up partitions—Sioux here, Oklahoma boys over there, AIM guys next door. Tables and beds were being made out of odd pieces of lumber. Some people put up Indian posters. A boy was painting slogans on the wall. One sign read: !!!REWARD!!! BRAIDS OF RUSSEL MEANS. ONE BRAID—$50.00. TWO BRAIDS—$300.00. WITH MEANS' HEAD—$1,000.00. COLLECT AT TRIBAL OFFICE. This was a reference to Wilson's promise to personally cut off Russel Means's braids—a promise he did not keep. Another sign promised two packages of Bull Durham for Wilson's entire body—pickled.

Shortly after I ate lunch—baked beans out of a can warmed over a sterno—airplanes were flying low over the hamlet. Some had photographers in them. By late afternoon three hundred marshals and FBI agents had formed a loose ring around us, their armored vehicles blocking the few roads in and out of Wounded Knee. In answer we were establishing roadblocks of our own. Already we had our first casualty. A young boy, unfamiliar with firearms, shot one of his fingers off.

Wounded Knee lasted seventy-one long days. These days

were not all passed performing heroic deeds or putting up media shows for the reporters. Most of the time was spent in boredom, just trying to keep warm and finding something to eat. Wounded Knee was a place one got scared in occasionally, a place in which people made love, got married Indian style, gave birth, and died. The oldest occupants were over eighty, the youngest under eight. It was a heyoka place, a place of sacred clowns who laughed while they wept. A young warrior standing up in the middle of a fire-fight to pose for the press; Russel Means telling the photographers, "Be sure to get my good side."

We organized ourselves. The biggest room in the store became the community hall. A white man's home, the only house with heat and tap water, became the hospital, and women were running it. The museum became the security office. We all took turns doing the cooking, sewing shirts, and making sleeping bags for the men in bunkers. We embroidered the words "Wounded Knee" on rainbow-colored strips of cloth. Everybody got one of those as a badge of honor, "to show your grandchildren sometime," as Dennis said. We shared. We did things for each other. At one time a white volunteer nurse berated us for doing the slave work while the men got all the glory. We were betraying the cause of womankind, was the way she put it. We told her that her kind of women's lib was a white, middle-class thing, and that at this critical stage we had other priorities. Once our men had gotten their rights and their balls back, we might start arguing with them about who should do the dishes. But not before.

Actually, our women played a major part at Wounded Knee. We had two or three pistol-packing mamas swaggering around with six-shooters dangling at their hips, taking their turns on the firing line, swapping lead with the feds. The Indian nurses bringing in the wounded under a hail of fire were braver than many warriors. The men also did their share of the dirty work. Bob Free, our first chief of engineers, had a crew which built twelve fortified bunkers, made an apartment house out of the trading post, dug latrines and constructed wooden privies, kept the juice going, repaired cars, operated the forklift and an earth-moving bulldozer. The men also formed a sanitary squad, picking up garbage and digging trenches to bury all that crap. One day Bob laid down the law: "Okay, that's it. The only electricity we keep is for the freezers to store the meat, for the gas pumps and three lights. That's all!" And he enforced it.

For a while I stayed at the trading post. But it was too much for me. Too many people and too little privacy. I figured that I would have my baby within two weeks. I moved into a trailer house at the edge of Wounded Knee. By then daily exchanges of fire had become commonplace. The bullets were flying as I got bigger and bigger. One day the government declared a cease-fire so that the women and children could leave. One of the AIM leaders came up to me: "You're leaving. You're pregnant, so you've got to go." I told him, "No, I won't. If I'm going to die, I'm going to die here. All that means anything to me is right here. I have nothing to live for out there."

"It doesn't matter whether you want to or not, you've got to go. All the women and children are going."

But we were not going. I stayed, all the older women stayed, most of the young mothers with children stayed, the sweethearts of the warriors stayed. Only a handful took advantage of the cease-fire and left. The deadline passed. The firing started again. Heavy MGs, automatic rifles, trip-wire flares, single shots from the government sniper experts. Some of our men burned the wooden bridge over the creek so the feds couldn't sneak up on us across it. Somebody said, "Now we've burned our bridge behind us."

One morning I got up early to bring coffee to the security in their bunkers and the feds opened up on me. A young Apache boy named Carlos rushed up, pushed me down, and covered me with his body. I am short, but he was even smaller than me. Some of the shots barely missed us. When the shooting eased up he dragged me into the bunker. He got after me: "Are you crazy? You should stay indoors. You have no business out there." I laughed at him: "I'm about to be a mother and you're just a kid. You want to tell me what to do?" But I was touched. I was not really that much older than he. All the men were overprotective, worrying about me. We were down to dry beans and a little flour. No coffee, no sugar, no cigarettes. The head of the marshals had announced publicly, "We're gonna change their diets!"

Dennis was keeping an eye on our dwindling supplies. For Easter Sunday he had been saving some ham and potatoes. So we had something close to a feast in the second, smaller church on the other side of Wounded Knee. I walked down there with some feed on my back in a heavy knapsack. Stan Holder came up to me: "What's wrong with you? Don't you know better?" Some friends joined in: "Get that backpack off you! We're responsible if you hurt yourself."

I told them, "You get off my back! You're not responsible for me. The only person responsible for me is myself." I continued doing my chores, cooking, bringing coffee to the bunkers. Pedro Bissonette was always teasing me whenever we met, pointing at my belly: "That little warrior in there is hungry. Here is a little something for him," forcing me to accept a morsel of food that I knew came from his own meager ration. Or he would come up and ask whether I wanted to play basketball. That always got a big laugh because I was so huge. We actually laughed and kidded each other a lot. It helped us to last as long as we did.

When the food situation got out of hand we sent out a

party of young hunters to bring in some "slow elk," that is, some of the white ranchers' cattle which were grazing in the vicinity. "Get a young, juicy cow," Dennis had told them. Instead they brought in a tough old bull. That poor old bull didn't want to die. They had to shoot him about twenty times before he finally lay down and gave up the ghost. Then it turned out that our young men did not know how to butcher. Some hunters! They were all city kids from St. Paul, Denver, or Rapid City. One of the white reporters had to show them how to do it. The women pounded and pounded that meat. They boiled it for hours. It remained as hard as stone. It was like chewing on a rope when I tried my teeth on it. After that Dennis put up a large poster. It showed the rear end of a bull with huge balls and underneath the words: THIS IS A BULL. Next to it was drawn a cow's ass with the udder and the legend: THIS IS A COW. And above the whole thing, very big: COW—SI, BULL—NO!

The three hundred feds, the goons, and the BIA police were never able to seal us off completely. As Pedro Bissonette put it, "The land was on our side." The whole landscape was a jumble of hills, gullies, ravines, dry washes, sagebrush, and clumps of cottonwood trees. The marshals got lost in there. They also had no stomach for nighttime, hand-to-hand, guerilla-style fighting. They were technological, long-range killers. So there was a lot of sneaking through the perimeter, a lot of coming and going. Indians from Denver, New Mexico, and L.A. trickled in, a dozen or half-dozen at a time. A group of Iroquois from New York joined us for a while. Most of them were guided in by some of our local Sioux who knew every bush and every little hillock around us and who could find their way blindfolded. Usually people started walking in from the Porcupine area about eight or nine miles away. Some carried heavy packs of food. The government had their APCs out and illuminated the nights with their flares. They also kept the whole area under steady fire, shooting blindly. A continuous stream of red-glowing tracer bullets crisscrossed the whole prairie around us. It never stopped the brothers and sisters from coming. Among the groups walking in were some Northwest Coast people, Pullayups and Nisquallies, led by Sid Mills who had fought so long for native fishing rights in Washington State. These were among our toughest fighters.

One time Sid and two or three other guys went out to bring in some food. They walked and walked the whole night and never made their contact. When dawn came they discovered that they were barely a few hundred yards away from the Sacred Heart Church. The whole night they had been walking around in circles, never getting more than a stone's throw away. Dennis conducted an honoring ceremony for them. Instead of an eagle feather Sid got a compass. He earned his eagle feather anyway.

Another time a young Indian in our little Datsun chased one of the government's huge armored cars. He was banging on the armor with a stick, "counting coup." The APC did not know what to do and lumbered off, the little Datsun harassing it all the way to the roadblock.

Some young Oklahoma boys brought off a big coup by raiding a government bunker, stealing all their supplies— coffee, eggs, cigarettes, K-rations, bread, and sausages. The marshals must have been drunk or sleeping. On another occasion some of our guys made a big show of burying a number of large, empty film containers left behind by a TV crew. Immediately you could hear the alarm spreading on the feds' shortwave: "Those Indians are planting Teller mines!" All the APCs took off in a hurry and we had scored another coup. So the siege had its humorous aspect, too.

All the time we were in communication with the other side, bantering back and forth, calling each other names, doing a lot of teasing. Then suddenly we heard the voice of the chief marshal: "The fun and games are over!" The ring around us was tightened. Elements of the 82nd Airborne were brought in, waiting their turn at nearby Hot Springs—just in case. A 'copter called *Snoopy* suddenly had a sniper in it taking potshots at us. Heavy 50-caliber MGs opened fire on our perimeter. Our telephone lines to the outside world were cut, all except the one connecting Wounded Knee with the marshals' headquarters. Special kill-and-destroy teams were being flown in, with attack dogs and infrared gun scopes which enabled the government sharpshooters to see us in the dark. Trip-wire flares saturated the whole area around us. If we touched the wire a flare would go up, bathing the whole landscape in a strange, ghostlike light. Press was no longer admitted. One of the last reporters to leave asked Russel, "Do you think you'll still be around tomorrow morning?" Russ Means answered, "That's up to the government."

Our reinforcements and supplies dwindled down to a trickle. Beyond our perimeter, the scene was right out of a cheap World War I movie. The feds were building themselves regular sandbag positions with stoves and all the comforts of home. They had radios and even TVs to entertain themselves. We could hear the rock 'n' roll music drifting in from their bunkers. They wore light blue Day-Glo man-from-Mars jumpsuits or camouflage outfits. Their positions were surrounded by ever-growing mounds of empty shells and beer cans. Their armored cars were fitted out with high-powered strobe searchlights and M-79 grenade launchers.

We had little to put up against this sort of war technology. Ammo was as short as food. During a typical firefight the feds would be pouring in upon us some five to ten thousand rounds while we would answer them with maybe twenty-five or thirty shots. Whatever ammo we could scrape together was piled up on the altar of the Sacred Heart Church.

The men came out of their bunkers from time to time to fill their pockets with bullets. The trouble was that they had a hard time finding the right kind of ammo to fit their oddball weapons, some of them real antiques that should have been in a museum. In spite of all their sophisticated weaponry I had the feeling that the feds were in a strange way afraid of us. While we were relaxed, as Indians usually are, they were nervous and trigger-happy. One night when we played Indian music—grass dance songs and powwow stuff—the marshals thought these were our death songs and got all worked up, expecting a banzai charge. One day Dennis found an old stovepipe and attached a thing to it that looked like a gunsight. We set it up and started a rumor that we had acquired a rocket launcher. This, too, upset the feds. We always had the moral edge, but they had the hardware.

Again I come back to the old Cheyenne saying: "A nation is not lost as long as the hearts of its women are not on the ground." As the siege went on our women became stronger. One bunker was held by a married couple. When the husband was hit by several bullets, the wife insisted on holding the position alone. Women "manning" a bunker got into a two-way radio argument with some marshals. The girls finally took up a megaphone, shouting across no-man's-land so that everybody could hear: "If you SOBs don't shut up, we'll call in the men!" One girl got hit in the white church. A bullet ricocheted and grazed her hand. It was just a flesh wound. She went on as if nothing had happened. During a firefight there was one young woman in particular who held off seven marshals while some of the men got behind shelter. All she had was an old pistol. She used that to scare them off. That was Gray Fox's wife. She was really good with a gun. I guess some of the men did not like her because of that. Especially, I think, those who scrambled to safety while she covered them.

One of the good things that happened to me at Wounded

Knee was getting to know Annie Mae Aquash, a Micmac Indian from Nova Scotia who became my close friend. She was a remarkable woman, strong-hearted and strong-minded, who had a great influence upon my thinking and outlook on life. I first noticed her when an argument arose among some of the women. One group, as I remember, called themselves the "Pie Patrol." Why, I do not know. There were no pies and they did not do much patrolling as far as I could see. They were loud-mouth city women, very media conscious, hugging the limelight. They were bossy, too, trying to order us around. They were always posing for photographers and TV crews, getting all the credit and glory while we did the shit work, scrubbing dishes or making sleeping bags out of old jackets.

Annie Mae gave these women a piece of her mind and I took her side. So we hit it off right away and became instant buddies. Annie Mae taught me a lot. She could make something out of nothing. She made nice meals with seemingly no provisions except dried beans and yellow peas. After I gave birth she made a tiny Wounded Knee patch for little Pedro. She was older than I and already a mother, divorced from a husband whose heart was not big enough for her. Annie Mae found among us Sioux an Indian culture her own tribe had lost. She was always saying, "If I'm going to die, I'm going to die. I have to die sometime. It might as well be here where I'd die for a reason." She had a premonition that her militancy would bring her a violent death, and in this she was right. She had heard the call of the owl. When we left Wounded Knee at the end of the siege she handed me a .38 and a knife, just in case we should run into the goons instead of surrendering to the feds. If we met Wilson's gang we might have to fight for our lives, she told me.

My brother was with us at Wounded Knee. He walked out one night to get food and ammunition and got busted. He had all his weapons taken from him, but the police had no proof against him and soon he was back at the Knee starting a new cycle of comings and goings. He brought me presents, things only a brother would risk his life to give to a sister—a little coffee, cigarettes, candy bars, and stuff like that, cheap, everyday articles but precious to one besieged, pregnant lady. At that time snipers with nonbarking attack dogs were harassing us. The feds could not see our men at night, but the dogs would smell them. It was a Vietnam vet, one of our few white brothers at the Knee, who told us how to fix those mutts. The thing to do was to have some pepper in your pocket and to urinate in one place and stomp and rub your feet in it. Walking off, one could start a good, hot urine trail for the dog to follow and then, after a few hundred yards, put a big pile of pepper on one's tracks. When the dog got a noseful of that he was useless for the rest of the week. Oddities among our warriors were two brothers, Charles and Robert. They were great-grandsons of General George Armstrong Custer, whom we Sioux, together with our Cheyenne brothers, wiped out at the Little Big Horn in 1876. When Custer surprised a peaceful Cheyenne village on the Washita, killing most of the men, one of his prisoners was a young girl, Maotsi, called Monaseetah by the whites. She caught the general's eye. She was told to be "nice" to him, otherwise he would be hard on her people—and she had seen just how hard he could be. When Maotsi got pregnant Custer kicked her out. He had no further interest in her or her offspring. A son was born who survived the famous death march of the Cheyennes and later married a Sioux woman, moving in with his wife's tribe into which he was adopted.

Thus it happened that the great-grandsons of Yellow Hair, Custer, were counting coup on the Blue Coats of 1973. For them Wounded Knee was a grudge fight. Some of the reporters who did not like us called Wounded Knee a "guerilla theater." A theater is make-believe, but the siege was very real, and so were the wounds and deaths. The Knee sure was dramatic, however, both in the many things that happened there and in the people who participated.

Politicians, celebrities, and civil rights leaders came to Wounded Knee early in the siege when the feds were still letting VIP visitors and reporters through the roadblocks. Our South Dakota senators Abourezk and McGovern were among them. Abourezk was supportive, which ruined his chances to run for a second term. McGovern was not. He is a great liberal anywhere but in South Dakota, because being friendly with activist Indians would cost him his reelection. At one time he seriously proposed storming Wounded Knee, which must have pleased his white constituents. He came up to me while I was doing dishes and held out his hand. He had a sour face. He said, "Hello, I'm George McGovern." I just looked at him and said, "So what," turned around, and went on scrubbing dishes.

Under the Fort Laramie Treaty of 1868 the Sioux had been recognized as an independent nation. The government had unilaterally abrogated this treaty without asking the Indians who were a party to it. On March 12, 1973, a big day, Wounded Knee declared itself a sovereign territory of the independent Oglala Nation. Anybody of goodwill, Indian or white, could become a citizen. Whatever one might say about AIM, it was never racist. As Crow Dog expressed it: "We don't want to fight the white man, but only the white man's system."

Periodic meetings were held between our spokesmen and various government negotiators to arrive at a peaceful settlement. These usually took place inside a tipi in no-man's-land. Always an altar was set up and the pipe smoked before the discussions started. Some government people could not relate to this. One of them said, "Imagine having to sit on the

earth around a buffalo skull in order to talk to those people."
The talks always came around to which came first, the
chicken or the egg. The government negotiators said: "Disarm and surrender, then we'll consider your grievances."
Always we replied: "Let's talk about our grievances first,
then we'll disarm and come out." Crow Dog proposed a
compromise. Instead of surrendering our arms outright, we
would stack them all inside the tipi while the negotiations
went on. The tipi entrance would be barred by the sacred
pipe, then nobody would touch these weapons. The government people rejected this proposal. They had no faith in the
pipe. As a matter of fact, there was little that was sacred to
them. They had no strong beliefs of their own, except a faith
in naked power, numbers and paragraphs. And so the siege
continued.

Some of the most memorable events at the Knee were the
two air-drops. The first airlift dropped four hundred pounds
of food into the perimeter—powdered milk and Similac for
the children, dried beans, flour, rice, coffee, tea, sugar, bak-
ing soda, and cigarettes, as well as bandages, antibiotics, and
vitamins. The single plane came in very low. It almost got
caught on a telephone wire, but managed to duck under it
and come in for a hard landing on the road close to the
trading post. As soon as it touched down, everybody ran up
and unloaded it. To me it seemed as if it was done in a minute
or less. It all happened so fast that the plane took off before
the feds had a chance to react. The airlift came as a complete
surprise to them. We saw them running about, gesticulating,
shaking their fists at the sky. The pilot and copilot were both
Vietnam vets. The copilot had been one of our medics for
almost a month and he could show the pilot the way by
picking out landmarks. He was white with a tiny bit of
Mohawk in him. He had made a Sioux-style flesh offering
before going on this mission.

The second air-drop was carried out by three planes,

Piper Cherokees, which was sure a good name for planes flying in support of Indians. Each plane carried four parachutes; each chute had two heavy duffel bags of food attached to it. Altogether the planes dumped one ton of supplies. They came in at first light on April 17. The men who flew these small machines were very brave. They flew very low through night and bad weather, expecting at any moment to be intercepted by government jets. One of the chutes did not open. I watched it hit the ground. It was full of flour, so when it hit there was a big white cloud and some overexcited people screamed that we were being bombed. The whole drop lasted about five minutes and then the planes vanished. The day of this air-drop was the day Clearwater was killed.

Two of our men were killed at Wounded Knee and many were seriously wounded. On the other side no one was killed and only one marshal badly wounded. For all I know he might have been caught in the feds' own crossfire. The marshals reacted very quickly to the second airlift. A helicopter flew over in no time and from it a sniper opened fire on a few of our people still busy carrying food to the trading post. Our men shot at the copter and that started a firefight which lasted almost two hours. Frank Clearwater had arrived the day before with his pregnant wife Morning Star. She was Apache and he was Cherokee. He was resting on a bed inside the church when a bullet crashed through the wall and smashed into his head. When it became known that one of our brothers had been badly hurt we used the two-way radio to ask the marshals for a cease-fire. They promised to hold their fire and two of our men and some nurses went up the hill to get him. They were waving a white flag. The nurses wore arm bands and had a red cross painted on their helmets, but they were immediately shot at by the marshals and pinned down for two hours until it was dark and the firing ceased. Three brothers from a nearby bunker finally managed to get Clearwater on a blanket and carry him down. They came under fire all the way. Clearwater was brought up to the roadblock and, after some negotiations, the feds made a helicopter available which flew him to Rapid City where he died a few days later without ever having regained consciousness. His wife was kept overnight in jail. She wanted him buried at Wounded Knee, for which he had given his life, but Wilson and the government would not allow it "because he was not a Pine Ridge Sioux." In the end Crow Dog buried him on his own land in the Indian manner, with the pipe and Grandfather Peyote.

On April 27, Buddy Lamont, a thirty-one-year-old Oglala Sioux, an ex-marine Vietnam vet and only son, was shot through the heart and died instantly during a heavy firefight. Buddy was shot in an abandoned house next to the community center. I guess a sniper in one of the fed bunkers had pinned him down. He lost patience and ran out of the building, drawing more fire, possibly so he could shoot back, and just when he was coming out of the building he was hit. Again the medics were shot at. Again the relatives coming out with his body were arrested and wound up in Pine Ridge jail. Buddy received his honorable discharge from the Marine Corps just about the time a government bullet killed him. He is buried on the hill by the ditch, joining the ghosts of all the other Sioux killed at Wounded Knee. His headstone says: "Two thousand came to Wounded Knee in 1973. *One stayed.*"

CHAPTER 10

The Ghosts Return

Eighty-five years ago
the ghost dancers thought
that by dancing
they could change the earth.
We dance to change ourselves.
Only when we have done this
can we try to change the earth.

—*Crow Dog, 1974*

I t was the Ghost Dance religion which was at the core of
the first Wounded Knee, and Indian religion as much as
politics was also at the heart of the second Wounded Knee in
1973. By common consent, Crow Dog was the spiritual
leader inside the Knee, and together with medicine man
Wallace Black Elk he performed all the ceremonies. Crow
Dog's influence upon the spiritual and physical well-being of
the occupiers was very, very strong. Outside, and not far

from Wounded Knee, the oldest and most respected Sioux holy man, Frank Fools Crow, acted in support of us from his place at Kyle, doing as much for the Sioux people outside as Crow Dog did inside. All the medicine men of the Sioux Nation visited and supported us, but it was Crow Dog who revived the Ghost Dance, outlawed for over eighty years, right at Wounded Knee, during the siege.

Leonard did so many things. He performed the rituals and prayers, took a major part in all negotiations, operated upon gunshot wounds, healed the sick, and even took over for a while as chief engineer. The fires for the sweat lodge were kept going twenty-four hours a day, and almost every night we had a ceremony, such as a yuwipi or, on a few occasions, a peyote meeting. On solemn occasions men and women made flesh offerings by cutting pieces of skin from their arms, just as Sitting Bull had done in 1876, a few days before the Custer battle. Some of the leaders pierced their breasts as is done during a Sun Dance, thinking their suffering could help the people through spiritual power.

Every evening I went to a ceremony. These rituals were quiet, very quiet. One evening, after a ceremony, I was walking back to the other side of Wounded Knee where I stayed, and all along the creek I heard women crying, babies screaming, cannon shots, and the hooves of horses drumming on the earth. I was walking along Cankpe Opi Wakpala where our women and children had been killed in 1890. It was so strange, reliving this tragedy in a half dream, this recurring of a vision I had as a young girl after a peyote meeting. I still do not know what to make of it. Is it the vision of a tragedy still to come, of history repeating itself?

Every evening all the warriors took sweat baths to purify themselves. Leonard put his friend Wallace Black Elk in charge of most of these inipi ceremonies. One night Leonard himself was running the sweat, and when he and the others came out of the lodge the feds opened up on them, hitting the lodge and the tipi with their M-16s. Some men jumped into the shallow bunker nearby, but Crow Dog got stuck between the fireplace and the bunker and had to lie there, very exposed, for about two hours before he had a chance to make a dash for shelter. It was a miracle nobody got killed that day.

Before we had our first meeting with the government representatives trying to negotiate a settlement, everybody asked Leonard to perform a sunrise ceremony at Big Foot's grave. He set up an altar and said: "Our most sacred altar is this hemisphere, this earth we're standing on, this land we're defending. It is our holy place, our green carpet. Our night light is the moon and our director, our Great Spirit, is the sun."

Leonard was our chief doctor and all the white medics and volunteer M.D.s deferred to him. The white doctors had come to the Knee expecting to treat children's and respiratory diseases. They had not thought that there would be firefights. They had no surgical equipment. So Leonard did all the operating. When Buddy Lamont got killed there were three other men with him in the bunker. One of them was hit four times, three times in the arm and once in the foot. The second man was shot in the hand and the third, Milo Goings, got a bullet in his knee. Leonard doctored them all. It took him less time than it would have a white doctor to take a bullet out and there never were any infections. He was using Indian medicine to treat the wounds. To take a bullet out, he first used porcupine quills and an herb, redwood, to make the flesh numb. Once this kind of Indian anesthesia began working—and it acted very fast—he went in with the knife, the same knife he uses to pierce the Sun Dancers. He sewed the wounds up with deer sinew and stopped the bleeding with sacred gopher dust, a medicine Crazy Horse had preferred above all others. To prevent infections and speed up the healing process, he used taopi tawote, wound medicine, I think in white botany it is called yarrow. He employed an herb called wina wazi hutkan, burr root, to stop internal hemorrhages. He treated respiratory diseases with the sweat bath and with teas made of several varieties of sage, and reduced fever with hehaka pejuta, the elk herb which the whites call horsemint. This is also a powerful love medicine. These were some of the Indian herbs which Leonard used. Pat Kelly, a white doctor from Seattle who came to the Knee to help us, had complete faith in Leonard. He always said that wounds treated by Crow Dog healed twice as fast as those treated by the white medics with their modern medicaments.

Rocky Madrid, a chicano medic, was hit in the stomach. It was a miracle that he did not get his guts blown out. He managed to walk back to the hospital and Crow Dog took the bullet out. Luckily it had not penetrated all the way into the stomach. Rocky said that Leonard was in and out with his knife almost before he knew it and that with Indian anesthesia he did not feel a thing. Leonard taught the white medics how to use his natural medicines and to say the proper prayers before treating a patient.

It was strange that Crow Dog was called upon to doctor machines as well as men. After Bob Free resigned as chief engineer, Leonard took over his job, too. When things broke down he fixed them. He had a real gift for that kind of work. As a kid he had learned how to repair cars. At the Knee he repaired the gas pumps and kept the electricity going. During the last few weeks it was cut off and we had to make do with kerosene lamps which we had found in the store. Part of Leonard's job as chief engineer was to put up defense works. He supervised the building of bunkers, all of which had individual names, such as the Strong Heart or the Sitting Bull bunker. He engineered a defensive circle of mines. He put some boys to work pounding a hundred pounds of coal from the store into charcoal. Also from the store he got about a thousand light bulbs. These he filled with charcoal and battery acid. He put all these tiny light bulb bombs on one fuse, all the way around the perimeter, connected to a battery. They were strung on a wire and when one of the feds touched that it set off a spark which exploded the bulbs. Individually his tiny mines could not do much damage but they served well in keeping the marshals at a respectful distance. One thing Leonard did not do was to take up a gun and shoot. His being a medicine man forbade it.

The most memorable thing Leonard did was to bring back the Ghost Dance. I think he did this not only for us, the living, but also for the spirits of those lying in the mass grave. As I mentioned before, the Ghost Dance tradition has always been strong in our family. Leonard's great-grandfather, the first of the Crow Dogs, was not only one of the earliest Ghost Dancers among the Sioux, but also one of their foremost leaders.

Back in 1889 a man came and told Crow Dog: "A new world is coming. A new power will strip off like a blanket this world which the wasičun has spoiled, and underneath will be the new world, undefiled and green. Walking on it we will meet our dead relatives whom the wasičun has killed, come to life again, coming to greet us. The buffalo, who have all disappeared into a great hole in a mountain to get away from the wasičun, will come out from their caves beneath the earth to fill up the prairie again with their countless herds. The father says so." That man was Short Bull from our own Brule tribe, a famous warrior who had fought Custer.

Many men were soon traveling silently at night, on foot, on horseback, hidden in cattle trains, wandering hundreds of miles across the new railroad tracks and over the barbed-wire fences, traveling ghostlike, unseen and unheard by the wasičuns, spreading the same message from tribe to tribe.

Short Bull and his friends Kicking Bear and Good Thunder had received this message from Wovoka himself, the Paiute holy man to whom the Ghost Dance religion had been given in a dream on the day the sun had died. Wovoka had let them look inside his black Uncle Joe hat. In it they had seen the universe. They had looked into the hat and understood. The Piute dreamer made them die and walk on the new world that was coming. Then he made them come to life again. Wovoka had given them a new dance, new songs, and new prayers. He gave them a sacred eagle feather, an eagle wing, and scarlet face paint. Of the four songs he gave them, the first brought fog and white mist, the second brought snow and icy cold, the third, gentle rain, and the fourth, sunshine and warmth.

Life was so hard for our people—starving, fenced in, without horses or weapons. The message brought them hope. And so they began to dance and sing, to bring back the buffalo, to bring back the old world of the Indians which the wasičun had destroyed, the world they had loved so much and for whose return they were praying.

Crow Dog, together with his friends and relatives Two Strikes and Yellow Robe, joined Short Bull's camp of Ghost Dancers, bringing all his followers along. They moved to Pass Creek where a sacred tree stood, which was good to dance around. They were dancing, too, at Sitting Bull's camp at Standing Rock, at Big Foot's place near Cheyenne River, even at Pine Ridge right under the wasičuns' noses. The Ghost Dance was a religion of love, but the whites misunderstood it, looking upon it as the signal for a great Indian uprising which their bad consciences told them was sure to come. The whites were afraid, and the agents called in the army to put this new religion down.

At Pass Creek, Crow Dog's people danced in a circle holding hands, wrapped in upside-down American flags symbolic of the wasičuns' world of fences, telegraph poles, and factories which would also be turned upside down, as well as a sign of despair. They also dressed in special Ghost Dance shirts painted with star and moon designs and with the images of eagles and magpies. These shirts, the people believed, would make them bulletproof. Whirling in a circle for hours and hours, some dancers fell down in a trance, "died," and in death wandered among the stars, spoke with their long-dead relatives, and experienced wonderful things which they described afterward.

Grandpa Dick Fool Bull was a child when he witnessed the Ghost Dance, but he remembered it well. A few years before he died over a hundred years old, Leonard taped him. This is what Dick Fool Bull said on his tape: "To start with I'll tell you what I remember started the trouble, the big trouble. I happened to be at Rosebud, camping at Rosebud under guard—soldiers, cavalry—they rounded up all the fathers and grandfathers to make sure they don't get away and mix up with that hostile bunch.

"My father was hauling freight from Valentine with his ox team. He'd go down there in the morning and camp down there and then he'd come back to Rosebud and unload. We heard there was a Ghost Dance going on, north of us by the falls at an Indian village called Salt Camp. My mother's youngest brother took sick somehow and he wanted to see the dance, thinking that it might cure him. So they hooked up the team, the buckboard, and I rode over there with my uncle and my mother and my sisters. We got up there and when we got to level ground and could see the village we saw a lot of commotion going on, a lot of people on horseback and running around. When we got closer we could see a big circle of women and men, no children, just men and women clasping hands like they do now in a round dance.

"They all sing the ghost song, go round and round. I remember one fellow, he has a cartridge belt and a butcher knife, and a woman on each side of him. He acted like he was drunk, weaving back and forth, then he keeled over, falling on his face. Then he turned over. He lay there like dead and two men, the dance leaders, went over to him. One came with a fire, a pan full of glowing coals, and a big eagle wing. He put something on the fire which made a good-smelling smoke and with his big wing he fanned that smoke over that dancer, the one who was lying on his back. As he fanned the man he came to and sat up. The leader asked him what he had experienced.

"He said: 'Well, there was a road from here to over there, a ghost road. I could not see it but I knew it was there and I walked on it. I came to a hill and a lone man stood there. When he saw me he sat down and waved to me to sit down beside him. I went up the hill and he showed me a big Indian camp, tipis, buffalo, horses, men hunting, women tanning, like in the old days, and that man told me, "That is your people over there, that's where you're going to be. That's how you shall live. Now you go back. Teach your people. Teach them to live the old way." ' And he gave that dancer a new song to remember when he woke up.

"And there was another dancer, not from our tribe, an Arapaho I think, and he got into a trance. He was like hypnotized, like not being where he was but somewhere else. In those days they had rifles and they wore shirts that were made out of canvas. And on the back they had the sun and the half-moon painted on each one. And the fringes were painted. They hung up those shirts on posts and they took their rifles and shot at them. And the bullets don't pierce the shirts but are falling on the ground. And one man puts a ghost shirt on and says, 'Come on, shoot at me,' and they do and when the bullets hit the shirt they just fall harmlessly on the ground and the man isn't hurt. And he tells the people, 'With that sacred shirt, when you wear it, no bullet can hurt you.' That's the way it was." This is how old Dick Fool Bull remembered it.

When you go toward Parmelee, in the bed of the Little White River, you come to a place where Leonard's great-grandfather had a Ghost Dance in 1890. You can still make out the circle made by many footsteps. During that dance an old man called Black Bear swooned and fell down in a trance. He lay like dead for some time. All of a sudden he woke up. They saw this man standing, his arms raised and outspread. And in broad daylight they saw lightning strike and go into his hand, and when they cedared him, and he came to, he had a little rock in his hand, a rock from the stars.

So the soldiers were chasing the dancers, driving Crow Dog's band deep into the Badlands, where they sought refuge on top of a snow-covered butte littered with the bones of long-extinct animals. There was nothing to eat. They were cold and hungry. The children were crying and the few ponies had become so thin they could hardly stand up. Crow Dog was dancing in the snow, naked except for a loincloth. He was singing:

> They are butchering cows here,
> They are killing buffalo cows.
> Make your arrows straight.
> Make arrows.

He shot a sacred arrow high into the sky. He received a vision that he had to give himself for his people. But the dead and the buffalo did not return. The appointed time had not come yet. The soldiers found Crow Dog and his people in their hideout and Crow Dog surrendered to save the lives which were entrusted to him. They survived. Others were not so lucky. Sitting Bull and his companions were killed in a big shootout with tribal police which left the snow red from the blood of the slain of both sides. Big Foot also surrendered, but he and his people were massacred all the same.

Leonard always thought that the dancers of 1890 had misunderstood Wovoka and his message. They should not have expected to bring the dead back to life, but to bring back their ancient beliefs by practicing Indian religion. For Leonard, dancing in a circle holding hands was bringing back the sacred hoop—to feel, holding on to the hand of your brother and sister, the rebirth of Indian unity, feel it with your flesh, through your skin. He also thought that reviving the Ghost Dance would be making a link to our past, to the grandfathers and grandmothers of long ago. So he decided to ghost-dance again at the place where this dance had been killed and where now it had to be resurrected. He knew all the songs and rituals that his father Henry had taught him, who himself had learned them from his grandfather. All through the night women were making old-style Ghost Dance shirts out of curtains, burlap bags, or whatever they could find. They painted them in the traditional way and they were beautiful.

On the evening before the dance, Leonard addressed the people. We got it down on tape. This is what he said: "Tomorrow we'll ghost-dance. You're not goin' to say 'I got to rest.' There'll be no rest, no intermission, no coffee break. We're not going to drink water. So that'll take place whether it snows or rains. We're goin' to unite together, no matter what tribe we are. We won't say, 'I'm a different tribe,' or, 'He's a black man, he's a white man.' We're not goin' to have this white man's attitude.

"If one of us gets into the power, the spiritual power, we'll hold hands. If he falls down, let him. If he goes into convulsions, don't be scared. We won't call a medic. The spirit's goin' to be the doctor.

"There's a song I'll sing, a song from the spirit. Mother

Earth is the drum, and the clouds will be the visions. The visions will go into your mind. In your mind you might see your brothers, your relations that have been killed by the white man.

"We'll elevate ourselves from this world to another world from where you can see. It's here that we're goin' to find out. The Ghost Dance spirit will be in us. The peace pipe is goin' to be there. The fire is goin' to be there; tobacco is goin' to be there. We'll start physically and go on spiritually and then you'll get into the power. We're goin' to start right here, at Wounded Knee, in 1973.

"Everybody's heard about the Ghost Dance but nobody's ever seen it. The United States prohibited it. There was to be no Ghost Dance, no Sun Dance, no Indian religion.

"But the hoop has not been broken. So decide tonight— for the whole unborn generations. If you want to dance with me tomorrow, you be ready!"

For the dance, Leonard had selected a hollow between hills where the feds could neither see the dancers nor shoot at them. And he had made this place wakan—sacred. And so the Sioux were ghost-dancing again, for the first time in over eighty years. They danced for four days starting at five o'clock in the morning, dancing from darkness into the night. And that dance took place around the first day of spring, a new spring for the Sioux Nation. Like the Ghost Dancers of old, many men danced barefoot in the snow around a cedar tree. Leonard had about thirty or forty dancers. Not everybody who wanted to was able to dance. Nurses and medics had to remain at their stations. Life had to be sustained and the defenses maintained.

On the first day, one of the women fell down in the snow and was helped back to what used to be the museum. They smoked the pipe and Leonard cedared her, fanning her with his eagle wing. Slowly she came to. The woman said she could not verbalize what had happened to her, but that she was in the power and had received a vision. It took her a long time to say that much because she was in a trance with only the whites of her eyes showing. On one of the four days a snowstorm interrupted the dancing, but it could not stop it. Later, Wallace Black Elk thanked the dancers for their endurance and Russel Means made a good speech about the significance of the rebirth of the Ghost Dance.

The Oglala holy man Black Elk, who died some fifty years ago, in his book said this about Wounded Knee: "I can still see the butchered women and children lying heaped and scattered all along the crooked gulch as plain as when I saw them with eyes still young. And I can see something else died there in the bloody mud, and was buried in the blizzard. A people's dream died there. It was a beautiful dream.

"And I, to whom so great a vision was given in my youth—you see me now a pitiful old man who has done nothing, for the nation's hoop is broken and scattered. There is no center any longer, and the sacred tree is dead."

In that ravine, at Cankpe Opi, we gathered up the broken pieces of the sacred hoop and put them together again. All who were at Wounded Knee, Buddy Lamont, Clearwater, and our medicine men, we mended the nation's hoop. The sacred tree *is not dead!*

CHAPTER 11

Birth Giving

Ho! Sun, Moon, and Stars,
All you that move
In the Sky,
Listen to me!
Into your midst
New Life has come.
Make its path smooth.

—*Omaha prayer for a newborn child*

On Friday, April 5, Crow Dog left Wounded Knee for about one week. He had been chosen to go on a four-man embassy to Washington in the hope of being able to see the president in order to reach a settlement we could live with. As it turned out, trying to reach a settlement in Washington was just as futile as at Wounded Knee. At this time Crow Dog was not yet my husband and lover, but I had great confidence in him, believing in his powers as a medicine

man, and I had hoped he would be around when I had my
baby. Now he was leaving just when I was about to give
birth and I felt let down. I was very self-centered, or rather
belly-centered. Washington and Nixon could have been
swallowed up by a flood or an earthquake as far as I was
concerned. My baby seemed a helluva lot more important.

The Sioux language has a number of words for pregnancy.
One of them means "growing strong." Another means "to be
overburdened." I felt both strong and overburdened at the
same time. I wanted to have my baby at Wounded Knee, but
was not sure whether that could be, because sometimes a
person would come and say, "Negotiations are coming on
real good. We'll all be out of here in a day or two. We're all
gonna go home." I always answered, "We'll either be out of
here or we'll die. Whatever, I'm going to have my baby right
here, the Indian way." But I was a lot less confident than I
sounded.

I was determined not to go to the hospital. I did not want a
white doctor looking at me down there. I wanted no white
doctor to touch me. Always in my mind was how they had
sterilized my sister and how they had let her baby die. My
baby was going to live! I was going to have it in the old Indian
manner—well, old, but not too old. In the real ancient tradition our women stuck a waist-high cottonwood stick right in
the center of the tipi. Squatting, holding on to that stick, they
would drop the baby onto a square of soft, tanned deer hide.
They themselves cut the umbilical cord and put puffball
powder on the baby's navel. Sometimes a woman friend was
squatting behind them, pressing down on their stomach, or
working the baby down with some sort of belt. They would
rub the baby down with water and sweetgrass and then wipe
it clean with buffalo grease. I did not think that I was quite
that hardy or traditional to do it exactly in that way. And
where would I have gotten buffalo grease?

Somebody should also have given me a fully beaded and quilled cradleboard and two turtle or lizard amulets to put the navel cord in—one to hide somewhere in the cradleboard and the other to display openly so that the bad spirits would think the navel cord was in that one, and they would try to bewitch it and would be fooled. Keha, the turtle, and Telanuwe, the sand lizard, are hard to kill. They live long. Their hearts go on beating long after they are dead. So these fetishes protect and give long life. My aunt, Elsie Flood, the turtle woman, would have made such a charm for me, but that was not to be.

I should have found a winkte, that is a gay person, to give my baby a secret name. Winktes were believed to always live to a great old age. If they gave the newborn such a hidden name, not the one everybody would know him by, then the winkte's longevity would rub off on the little one. Such a winkte name was always funnily obscene, like for instance Che Maza, meaning Iron Prick, and you had to pay the name-giver well for it. Well, I had no money and how was I going to find a winkte at Wounded Knee? I could not very well go to every warrior and ask him, "Are you by any chance gay?" This is not to criticize winktes. We Sioux have always believed that a person is free to be what he or she wants to be. I know a winkte who is incredibly brave. At the Sun Dance he chooses the most painful way of self-inflicted suffering. He pierces at the same time in two places in front and two spots in the back. Then he stands fastened between four poles with little space to move. He cannot tear himself loose by running a few steps and then making a sudden jump. He has to work the skewers through his flesh slowly, excruciatingly. But somehow, I cannot believe in the winktes' power of longevity. In the old days the winkte lived so long because he wore women's clothes and was tanning and beading and cooking while the other men went on a war party and got themselves killed. I have a suspicion that nowadays the winktes live no longer than anybody else.

So I could not be quite as traditional as all that. When I say that I was determined to have my baby the Sioux way, I simply meant with an Indian prayer and the burning of sweetgrass and with the help of Indian women friends acting as midwives, having it the natural way without injections or anesthesia. I did intend to have my baby inside the ceremonial tipi, but was persuaded not to. It was too exposed and often under fire.

I did not always have lofty thoughts about traditional birth giving on my mind during the last week before I went into labor. More often I was preoccupied with much more earthly things such as getting safely to the toilet. Being in my ninth month I had to urinate frequently. The women had cleaned out a garage and with the help of some men made it into a four-way ladies' room. It was really weird. You always met a number of girls lined up, waiting their turn. Seeing my big belly they usually let me go ahead. Sometimes tracers were all around us like lightning bugs as the bullets kicked up the dust at our feet. Somehow or other this shooting did not seem real. The girls remained standing in line, chatting and giggling. There was never any panic. Somebody would come and shout, "Is everybody all right? Anybody need tranquilizers?" Imagine being in a place where you needed tranquilizers to go to the can! We did not take them anyway. My problem was that in my condition I had to go two or three times as often as the others, and I was in more of a hurry.

One evening I was inside the trading post. I had just cleaned up when that Pine Ridge man came in and sat down. He kept looking and looking at me and finally said, "Are you gonna have your baby here?"

I told him, "Yeah, if I have to. Are you going to stay to the end?"

He said, "No. I got work to do on the outside."

"Gee," I told him, "you're an Oglala. This is your land. You're supposed to stick it out. I'm from the next reservation, Rosebud, a Brule woman and pregnant. But I'm staying. You're not going to accomplish much."

He gave me a long look. "Wow! You're gonna have your baby here the Indian way. That's pretty heavy." I had to agree with him.

On another occasion my brother told me, "You shouldn't be here, pregnant as you are. I should put you across my knee and spank you for having come." I told him to mind his business, and did he have a cigarette.

There was another pregnant woman with me at the Knee, Cheryl Petite. She also planned to have her baby inside the perimeter. She was a great big woman. Some of the guys were betting which of us would pop first. She went into labor on Sunday, three days before I did. Her husband was a loudmouth and he came to tell me, "She beat you. We're gonna have our baby first."

I answered him that I did not care who was having her baby first. This was no sports event. I wasn't in a race. But he kept on bragging all over the village that Cher was going to beat me to it. She was in labor for two hours. When her pains were about ten minutes apart he started worrying: "Maybe it would be better to go to the hospital. Maybe she's too small. Maybe he's not in the right position. Maybe it's gonna be a breach baby." So they got themselves all worried and he started negotiating at the roadblock, and the marshals let them through to have their baby at the Pine Ridge Hospital. The people inside the village felt bad. Many came to me saying, "Mary, you're our last chance now to have a baby born at Wounded Knee." I did not want to disappoint them.

Shortly before Crow Dog left for Washington, he put on a peyote meeting. I was glad to be able to participate in it just when I was on the point of giving birth—exactly a week before I went into labor, as it turned out. I took medicine. When the sacred things were passed around I took hold of the staff and prayed with it, prayed that my child and I would come through it all safely. And at the time of midnight water Leonard stood up and said, "It's gonna be all right. Good things will happen to you." And I told him how much strength the meeting was giving me. While I was praying it had rained, a sort of foggy, misty-white rain. But then it stopped and when the meeting ended the sky was clear. I left confident, feeling good.

Monday, just as the morning star came out, my water broke and I went down to the sweat lodge to pray. I wanted to go into the sweat but Black Elk would not let me. Maybe there was a taboo against my participating, just as a menstruating woman is not allowed to take part in a ceremony. I was disappointed. I did not feel that the fact that my water had burst had made me ritually unclean. As I walked away from the vapor hut, for the third time, I heard that ghostly cry and lamenting of a woman and child coming out of the massacre ravine. Others had heard it too. I felt that the spirits were all around me. I was later told that some of the marshals inside their sandbagged positions had also heard it, and some could not stand it and had themselves transferred.

After that nothing happened until Tuesday morning when some stuff came out of me. At four o'clock in the afternoon I began having spasms at intervals of half an hour. They made me lie down then. At nine o'clock at night the cramps became severe. The pains lasted all night. On Wednesday morning they became harder. A firefight started, but I was too preoccupied to pay it any attention. My friends kept me strong. Pedro Bissonette, who was later killed by BIA police, was pacing the floor, pacing and pacing. Every now and then he would look in on me to see how I was doing, trying to reassure me: "An ambulance is waiting for you. Just in case anything should go wrong. It's ready to take you through the roadblock to the hospital. Just give the word."

"No," I said, "it's all right." But it wasn't. The pains were bad and they lasted so long. And they were so real, blotting out everything else. I was too tired to push, too tired to live. Then I got lonesome. I missed my mother with whom I had never gotten along, missed my sisters, missed Grandma. I wished that there had been a father waiting for me and the baby. And yet I was so lucky in having such devoted women friends standing by, helping me. Josette Wawasik acted as the chief midwife. She was a seventy-two-year-old Potawatomy lady from Kansas who had been at the Knee from the very beginning and had also taken part in the BIA building takeover half a year before. Ellen Moves Camp and Vernona Kills Right were assisting her, and naturally Annie Mae Aquash was there, too. Mrs. Wawasik had delivered thirteen babies before and Ellen Moves Camp had delivered three or four, so they knew what they were doing. Ellen's case was tragic; she was such a strong-hearted woman, and later had to see a son turn into an informer against us. Their hands were gentle. I had no injections, or knockout medicine, just water. I gave birth inside a trailer house. As I said, I had wanted to deliver inside the tipi but that would have been risking all our lives. Well, my labor lasted until 2:45 P.M. and then it went zip, easy, just like that.

A couple of hours before Pedro was born a cow gave birth to a calf. The old-style Sioux are proverbial gamblers and they had been betting which would come in first, the cow or me. And the cow had beaten me by a length.

When the baby was born I could hear the people outside. They had all come except the security manning the bunkers, and when they heard my little boy's first tiny cry all the women gave the high-pitched, trembling brave-heart yell. I looked out the window and I could see them, women and men standing there with their fists raised in the air, and I really thought then that I had accomplished something for my people. And that felt very, very good, like a warmth spreading over me.

Dennis Banks came in and hugged me, saying, "Right on, sister!" and he was crying, and that made me cry, too. And then Carter Camp and Pedro Bissonette came in with tears streaming down their faces. All those tough guys were weeping. And then my girl friends came in, taking turns holding the baby. Grandma Wawasik went to the window and held up the baby and a great cheer went up. They were beating the big drum and singing the AIM song. And that led to another song, many songs, and my heart beat with the drum. They wrapped my baby up and laid him beside me. They brought in the pipe and we prayed with it, prayed for my little boy whom I named Pedro. I am glad I did because this way Pedro Bissonette's name is living on. And right away after my son was born he lifted up his little, soft head and so I knew that I had a strong child, because they don't do that until they are two weeks old. And the macho Sioux men said, "For sure, that's a warrior." As I looked at him I knew that I was entering a new phase of my life and that things would not, could not ever be the same again. More and more people crowded in, pumped my hand, and snapped my picture, and I wasn't even done yet. Grandma Wawasik and Ellen Moves Camp had to throw them all out so that I could have my afterbirth. Out of the window I could see smoke. The feds were burning off the sagebrush to deprive our guides of cover. The whole prairie around Wounded Knee was burning. Vernona said, "They're sending up a smoke signal for you." I was very, very tired and finally slept a little.

The drumming and singing and cheering had gotten the marshals excited. As was usual with them, they thought we were getting ready for a banzai charge. They were running in all directions, waving their M-16s about. Soon half a dozen APCs came lumbering up, closing in on our positions, and started a firefight. Luckily nobody got hit. That would have taken the joy out of the day, April 11, a good day for all of us. And so, though I was hardly grown-up myself, I had become a mother.

A few days after the baby was born came the air-drop, and among other things, I got an onion. I was so happy, after two months inside Wounded Knee, to see a fresh, real-life onion again. My good mood did not last long, however. Over the two-way radio I heard a guy saying, "A man got hit in his head. He's bleeding. He's not going to make it. Hold your fire so we can get him to some facility, we got to get him to a hospital." I felt so sad then, but at the same time I felt that in some mysterious way I had given a life to replace the one that had been lost. The fatally wounded brother was Clearwater, a Cherokee.

When the firefight started on that day, I happened to be in the trading post to which I and the baby had been trans-ferred. The bullets were going right through, coming through one wall and tumbling out through the other. Every-body was telling me to take my boy and get the hell out of there to a safer place. I was told to go with Roger Iron Cloud over to the housing area and hide in a basement. So I bun-dled up the baby and got his diapers together and we started running. We got into a crossfire and had to hit the dirt three times. I was scared, really scared, the only time during the siege—not so much for myself as for the baby. I was pray-ing: "If somebody has to die, let it be me, grandfather, but save him!" I was concentrating upon survival, upon getting us out of this situation alive. I was lying on top of my child to shield him. Sometimes Iron Cloud interposed his body, putting it where he thought it would do myself and little

Pedro the most good. That's the type of Sioux macho I can appreciate. Well, we made it safely into the basement. I had experienced a moment of panic thinking that the voices I had heard, the vision I had received years ago, might mean that I and my baby would have to join the spirits up on the hill. Those bastards! Forcing me to run like a track star four days after giving birth! My knees kept shaking for quite a while. More from the running, I like to brag, than from anything else. Well, that was Pedro's baptism of fire.

Leonard sneaked back into Wounded Knee a few days after Pedro was born and gave him an Indian name. He also held a peyote meeting for us. I took medicine and all the pain I still had went away. I also gave baby a little bit of peyote tea. Some people from California sent my child a sacred pipe and a beautifully beaded pipe bag, which made me happy and him well equipped on the road of life.

I left Wounded Knee the day Buddy Lamont got shot, roughly a week before the siege ended. I was resting with the baby in my room and some guy came in and said, "Somebody got killed." I asked him if he was sure and who had been hit. He told me it was Buddy and I said, "Oh, no, that's my uncle!" I went over to where Kamook, Dennis's wife, was staying and found her crying, with Dennis holding her in his arms. I was so mad, I could not cry. I did not want to believe it. A friend took me over to our improvised hospital to see Buddy and I held his hand. It was still warm. His relations asked me to come out of Wounded Knee with them and help with the funeral. I went into Wounded Knee poor and I left it poor. All that my baby and I had was the clothes on my back and a bundle of diapers and a blanket for him. Of course, we had also the pipe, but it was not an auspicious start for setting up a mother-baby establishment.

I had been promised that I would not be arrested, but the moment I passed the roadblock I was hustled to the Pine

Ridge jail. They did not book me, just took all my things away and were about to take my baby too. They told me I would have to wait, they could not put me in the tank before the Welfare came for my baby. Being poor, unwed, and a no-good rabble-rouser from the Knee made me an unfit mother. The child would have to be taken to a foster home. I was not going to give up my baby. I would never see him again. I was ready to fight to the death for my child, kick the shit out of the Welfare lady, scratch the guard's eyes out if necessary. Luckily Cheyenne, Buddy's sister, showed up just then and persuaded them to let her take care of the baby until I came out. I do not know what I would have done without her. Instead of helping her in her grief, she was helping me. Then one of the marshals came in in his pretty blue outfit and said, "Why are you so ornery? Why don't you try to be nice to me?"

I told him that I did not talk to pigs, which turned him off sufficiently to leave me alone. Because I could not nurse, my breasts swelled up and became hard and painful. So I was not too happy in that jail which the goons jokingly called "Heartbreak Hotel." They told me I was being held for questioning and debriefing, but I would not talk to them. I was not allowed to make any phone calls, send out messages, or talk to a lawyer. After twenty-four hours they finally let me go because the baby had to be nursed. Some of the government press officers said it was bad PR to hold a nursing mother. As I left the jail I found my mother waiting for me. I had not seen her in a long while. She was crying, telling me over and over again that I should not have come to Wounded Knee, or at least I should have come out early before things got tough and when I would not have been arrested. I told her there was nothing to cry for. She said, "Those militants you are hanging out with are no good. They'll get you killed. Why on earth can't you settle down, have a nice home, lead a peaceful life." But then suddenly she stopped weeping and went on in a completely different vein: "Those goddam sons of bitches, doing that to my daughter and grandchild! They are not supposed to be doing that, jailing you just after delivery and taking your baby away. Why doesn't somebody shoot a couple of them for a change?"

I said, "Yes, I'm a mother now and made you a grand-mother." Suddenly we got along very well and could under-stand each other. Her anger did not last and somehow things were better between us after this.

I was not free to go, though. I and the baby were taken to Rapid City to wind up in the old, buggy Pennington County Jail, but only for a few hours because they saw that nothing could be gotten out of me. That is how the state and the feds kept their promises that I would not be subject to arrest. It did not surprise me. They gave up on me and just let me go. After I got out I had to hitchhike about a hundred and fifty miles to get home to Grass Mountain. I got picked up by a goon called Big Crow and he tried to take me to his house and to bed with him. I held the baby tight and jumped out of his pickup truck, rolled over easy, and ran like hell into the sagebrush, hiding myself in a culvert. He was fat and winded, so I had gained on him. Also it was dark. He could not find me. I could hear him muttering and cursing until he drove off. I did not dare come out of hiding for two hours because I was afraid he was playing a trick upon me and would double back. It was dark, spooky, and very cold in the ditch and I had a hard time keeping the baby from crying so that he would not give us away. It was like in the old days when our women with their babies had to hide themselves from the cavalry, except for the culvert of course. In the end a nice old skin gave me a ride home and that was the end of Wounded Knee for me.

For Crow Dog, the end came about a week later when an agreement had finally been reached. Inside the Knee some warriors wept when the agreement was signed, saying, "Just another treaty to be broken. We made a commitment. This is a copout." One man said, "Why don't you just kill us and make our bodies plead guilty?" There were only some hundred and twenty people left to surrender: the others had all walked out, forty of them on the last night by way of a route that was not being watched because it was so open that it was almost suicide to take it. And even on that last evening there was still a firefight. The hundred twenty remaining could have walked out too but chose to stay to the end. Among the leaders who stayed to the last was Leonard. He was the last one out, I think. He was taken off in handcuffs by helicopter to the Rapid City jail. The feds were not satisfied with the twenty-odd old rifles that were surrendered, and the head of the government negotiating team proclaimed, "They just turned in a lot of old crap. I feel the White House need not fulfill its commitment to AIM because of this violation."

Two years later, seven of us who had all been at the Knee went to see the movie *Billy Jack*. There was a superficial similarity to Wounded Knee—an Indian making a last stand inside a white clapboard church surrounded by a lot of state troopers—but afterward Crow Dog was joking, "That Billy Jack had it easy. He was besieged for only twenty-four hours and there were no heavy MGs or APCs. And he was taken out with just a pair of handcuffs on him while they trussed us up with manacles, leg irons, and waist chains like something out of a medieval torture movie. Yeah, Billy Jack had it easy."

The little white church on the hill burned down in a fire which has never been explained, though I have heard that it has since been rebuilt. The trading post is flattened out like a stomped-on tin can. The museum is gone. Of the great

Gildersleeve trading empire only a huge, rusty open safe remains in which wasps have made their nest. It is the only sign of the white man's "civilization." Everything is gone. No landmark is left. The feds bulldozed our bunkers as well as their own and only the spirits remain up on the hill, roaming in the night by their ditch. If you are lucky you might still find a .50-caliber shell or an empty trip-wire flare canister in the sagebrush. I believe that the government tried to extinguish all visible reminders that Indians once made their stand here. It will do them no good. They cannot extinguish the memory in our hearts, a memory we will pass on to generations still unborn. Today the perimeter looks very much as it did before the white man came, as it looked to Sitting Bull, Crazy Horse, and Big Foot. Maybe that is as it should be.

CHAPTER 12

Sioux and Elephants Never Forget

A beautiful tepee is like a good mother. She hugs
her children to her and protects them from heat
and cold, storm and rain.

—Sioux proverb

After Wounded Knee I became Crow Dog's wife. I think
he had had his eye on me for a long time, but I didn't
have my eye on him. I was not even eighteen years old and he
was about a dozen years older. So he seemed to me to belong
to another generation. Also I looked upon him with a certain
kind of awe. He was a medicine man and the spiritual leader
of the American Indian Movement. Also I called him uncle
after the Indian fashion, and he called me niece. So I did not
look upon him as I would have upon one of the wild young
warriors I was used to going with.

Now, in many ways the Sioux are prudes. They have a horror of nudity. They are in a way bashful. Boys and girls feel inhibited about showing affection for each other. Their fear of incest and the taboos connected with it are so severe that in traditional families a son-in-law will never speak to his mother-in-law, while a father-in-law will not behave in a familiar, easygoing way with a daughter-in-law. On the other hand the approach of a man to a woman is very simple and direct, and sex is taken for granted, as something natural or even sacred. Also medicine men are not supposed to be holier than other people, or sanctimonious like white preachers. As old Lame Deer used to say, "They respect me not because I am such a good boy, but because I have the power." When it comes to women, medicine men are supposed to behave like everybody else.

I met Leonard at the Rosebud Fair and Rodeo. He took me for a ride in his old red convertible. Suddenly he had his arm around me and was kissing me. We were going to a party. I did not want to stay long. I did not want to be with him. I wanted to leave. I had a date with a young man from Oklahoma. But Leonard grabbed me by the arm and somehow maneuvered me out of the house down to the pasture, lifting me across the fence. Nobody was there. So in the end I went home with him. But I had not made up my mind about him. I was not ready to be tied down. So the next day I told his mother that I was going away, to another state. She said that Leonard had told her that I would be his wife for sure. I told her that I was not right for him. And I did not stay with him then. That came later.

At Sun Dance time Leonard approached me. He said he needed my help and my family's pickup truck to go into the hills for tipi poles. I went and borrowed a pickup from my brother-in-law. Leonard took me way up to the highest hill. It was pretty up there. I stood and looked around, admiring the beautiful view of the whole valley of the Little White

River spread out before us. But there were neither tipi poles on that hill nor lodgepole pines. Leonard said, "Give your uncle a kiss." I kissed him. We stayed up on that hill for a considerable time. Again he asked me to be his wife, and once more I told him, "No, I won't."

After Wounded Knee, on the day the AIM leader Clyde Bellecourt was shot, we all got him to the hospital in the town of Winner where he was operated upon. Leonard was there and old Lame Deer, to pray and smoke the pipe for him. Then we drove in a caravan back to Rosebud and the Crow Dog place where Leonard held a big ceremony for Clyde's recovery. Everybody vowed to drink no more and to quit the wild life. After the ceremony he asked me to stay. I said, "No, I am going to leave." He cornered me and would not let me go. Again and again he said, "Be my wife." My ride had left in the meantime and so I ended up staying—for good.

Years ago Old Man Henry, Leonard's father, had somehow gotten hold of an enormous truck tire, as tall as a man. He had put this near the entrance gate and painted on it in big white letters: CROW DOG'S PARADISE. This paradise, Crow Dog's allotment land, is beautiful. The Little White River flows right through it. It is surrounded by pine-covered hills. In the sky overhead one can see eagles circling. Sometimes water birds, sacred to the peyote people, fly over it with their long necks outstretched. There are horses to ride. Everywhere on this land one is close to nature.

The paradise is not just a one nuclear family place, but rather a settlement for the whole clan, the whole tiyospaye. In 1973, when I moved in with Crow Dog, it consisted of two main buildings. The biggest one was the house in which Leonard's parents lived. Old Man Henry had built it himself out of whatever odds and ends he had been able to find—tree trunks, rocks, parts of an old railroad car, and tar paper. Some windows were car windows from wrecked vehicles. It was large with a big, old-fashioned iron stove, an old wood-burning kitchen range, and an ancient, foot-powered sewing machine. Herbs, sacred things, and feather bustles hung down from the beams of the ceiling which was held up by two tree trunks. Right at the entrance stood the bucket with cool fresh spring water with the dipper for everyone to use. Coffee was always brewing on the range. On the outside Henry had painted the whole structure sky-blue with red trimmings. Nothing was at a right angle. Everything was bulging or sagging somewhere. There was no other house like Henry's. It stood for forty years and all Henry's children and most of his grandchildren were raised in it. It burned down under suspicious circumstances in 1976 while Leonard was in prison. Nothing is left of it now but the memory.

The other building is the one Leonard, I, and our children lived in. It was a flimsy thing, more in the nature of a bungalow than a house—a kitchen–living room and two tiny bedrooms. There was no cellar. The walls were thin and in winter it was hard to keep warm. It looks exactly like a few hundred other houses on the reservation built by the government under the OEO program. We call them "poverty houses." It is painted bright red and looks nice if you don't come too close.

There are always a few tipis around with people living in them, and somebody with no place to go who has made the outdoor cook shack his home. A white friend's camper was totaled a few years ago, and now a couple is using the shell for a home.

I now had a place and a man to stay with, but it was not always paradise in spite of the legend on the huge truck tire. I was in no way prepared for my role as instant wife, mother, and housekeeper. Leonard had three kids from his previous marriage—two girls, Ina and Bernadette, and one son, Richard. The girls were old enough to know that I was not their real mother, old enough to judge my performance. They had it in their power to accept or to reject me. I did not know how to cook. I did not even know how to make coffee. I did not know the difference between weak coffee and strong coffee, the kind that the Sioux like which will float a silver dollar.

Sioux always drop in on each other and stay over—a day or a week, as the spirit moves them. People eat at all times, whenever they are hungry, not when the clock says that it is eating time. So the women are continuously busy cooking and taking care of the guests. Indian women work usually without indoor plumbing, cook on old, wood-burning kitchen ranges, wash their laundry in tubs with the help of old-fashioned washboards. Instead of toilets we have out-houses. Water is fetched in buckets from the river.

Leonard is a medicine man as well as a civil rights leader. This means that we have ten times more guests than the usual Sioux household. The whole place is like a free hotel for anyone who cares to come through. The red OEO house in which I and Leonard live simply began to come apart from all the wear and tear. When I moved in, the place was a mess. Nobody tried to clean up or help out. They all came to eat, eat, eat, expecting a clean bed and maybe to have their shirts and socks washed. I spent a good many years feeding people and cleaning up after them. It is mostly men who stop by at the house, and only very few women, and you cannot tell men to do anything, especially Sioux men. I even sometimes moved my bed outside the house into the open to get some sleep, because the men stay up all night, talking politics, drinking coffee, and gossiping. Sioux men are the worst gossips in the world. I would wash dishes for the last time at midnight, go to bed, and in the morning all the dishes would be dirty again.

Most other medicine men do not go all out as Leonard does. They keep their homes tight, a little more to themselves. They do not fall into the trap of making their houses into dormitories and free hotels. Leonard pities people. Whenever we go to town we pick up somebody who is walking, and then usually we have him for dinner, and then breakfast. Some come and stay for days, weeks, or even months. Many Indians have no place to go, no one to feed them, so they come to Crow Dog's Paradise. If we see somebody who is out of gas, Leonard stops and syphons some off into his tank, and then we ourselves get stuck five miles from home. If Leonard notices someone having car trouble, he stops, takes out his tools, and fixes the car—an automobile medicine man on top of everything else. Money I am supposed to use for food or household things he gives away to anybody who asks. Years ago he got almost four thousand dollars in residuals for a TV commercial he did. That money was to buy a pickup truck. So, of course, there was a big giveaway feast. The friends and relatives—sixth cousins, seventh cousins, people very distantly related, strangers claiming kinship, one hundred and fifty of them— came. They came in rattletrap cars, in buggies, on horse-back and muleback, on foot, in trucks. One came on a motorbike. Sides of beef were being barbecued. Women were engaged in an orgy of cooking. People went up to Crow Dog: "Kanji, cousin, I need a headstone for my little boy who died." "Uncle, I am crippled, I sit at home all day. I need a TV." "Nephew, my children need shoes." When the giveaway feast was over, Leonard had two dollars left to buy the pickup with.

Leonard's great-grandfather had seven wives to do the cooking and tanning and beading for giveaway feasts, and the buffalo meat was free, but those days are gone. Naturally, Leonard is much admired for his old-style Sioux generosity. At the Sun Dance of 1977 they put the war bonnet on him and made him a chief. They call him a wicasha wakan—a holy man—but confidentially, it can be hell on a woman to be married to such a holy one.

Beside being tumbled headfirst into this kind of situation, still in my teens, with a brand-new baby and totally unprepared for the role I was to play, I still had another problem. I was a half-blood, not traditionally raised, trying to hold my own inside the full-blood Crow Dog clan which does not take kindly to outsiders. At first, I was not well received. It was pretty bad. I could not speak Sioux and I could tell that all the many Crow Dogs and their relations from the famous old Orphan Band were constantly talking about me, watching me, watching whether I would measure up to their standards which go way back to the old buffalo days. I could tell from the way they were looking at me, and I could see the criticism in their eyes. The old man told me that, as far as he was concerned, Leonard was still married to his former wife, a woman, as he pointed out again and again, *who could talk Indian.* Once, when I went over to the old folks' house to borrow some eggs, Henry intercepted me and told me to leave, saying that I was not the right kind of wife for his son. Leonard heard about it and had a long argument with his father. After that there was no more talk of my leaving, but I was still treated as an intruder. I had to fight day by day to be accepted.

My own family was also against our marriage—for opposite reasons. Leonard was not the right kind of husband for me. I was going back to the blanket. Here my family had struggled so hard to be Christian, to make a proper red, white, and blue lady out of me, and I was turning myself back into a squaw. And Leonard was too old for me. I reminded them that grandpa had been twelve years older than grandma and that theirs had been a long and happy marriage. But that was really not the issue. The trouble was the cultural abyss between Leonard's family and mine. But the more our parents opposed our marriage, the closer became the bond between Leonard and myself.

I came to understand why the Crow Dogs made it hard for me to become one of them. Even among the traditional full-bloods out in the back country, the Crow Dogs are a tribe apart. They have built a wall around themselves against the outside world. For three generations they have lived as voluntary outcasts. To understand them, one must know the Crow Dog legend and the Crow Dog history.

Kangi-Shunka, the founder of the clan, had six names before he called himself Crow Dog. He was a famous and fearless warrior, a great hunter, a chief, a medicine man, a Ghost Dance leader, a head of the Indian police, and the first Sioux—maybe the first Indian—to win a case before the Supreme Court. As Leonard describes him, "Old Kangi-Shunka, he was the lonely man of the prairie. He goes by the sun and moon, the stars and the winds. He harvests from the earth and the four-legged ones. He's a buffalo man, a weed man, a pejuta wichasha. He sees an herb and he hears the herb telling him, 'Take me for your medicine.' He has the kind of spirit and words out of which you create a nation."

For most people, what their ancestors did over a hundred years ago would be just ancient history, but for the Crow Dogs it is what happened only yesterday. What Kangi-Shunka did so long ago still colors the life-style and the actions of the Crow Dogs of today and of their relations, of the whole clan—the tiyospaye, which means "those who live together." Sioux and elephants never forget.

Some of the Crow Dogs trace their origin back to a certain

Jumping Badger, a chief famous in the 1830s for having killed a dozen buffalo with a single arrow, for having counted fourteen coups in war, and for distinguishing himself in fifteen horse-stealing raids. It is certain that the first Crow Dog belonged to a small camp of about thirty tipis, calling themselves the Wazhazha or Orphan Band, which followed a chief called Mato-Iwa, Scattering Bear, or Brave Bear. Kangi-Shunka was born in 1834 and died in 1911. He was raised in the bow-and-arrow days when the prairie was covered with millions of buffalo and when many Sioux had still to meet their first white man. He died owning a Winchester .44 repeating rifle with not a single buffalo left to use it on. He lived long enough to ride in a car and make a telephone call. At one time he was a chief of the Orphan Band. He played his part in the proud history of our tribe.

As Old Man Henry tells it, Crow Dog got his name in this way: He was taking his people to Hante Paha Wakan, to Cedar Valley, to hunt. Before riding out he had a vision. He saw a white horse in the clouds giving him the horse power, and from then on his horse was Shunkaka-Luzahan, the swiftest horse in the band. And he heard the voice of Shunk-Manitu, the coyote, saying, "I am the one." Then his horse suddenly raised its two ears up and the wind got into the two eagle feathers Crow Dog was wearing, and the feathers were talking, the feathers were saying, "There is a wichasha, a man up ahead on that hill, between the two trees." Crow Dog and his companions saw the man clearly. The man raised his hands and suddenly was gone. Crow Dog sent out two scouts, one to the north and one to the south. They came back saying that they had seen no one. Had this man on the hill been a wanagi, a spirit, trying to warn Crow Dog?

Crow Dog told his men to make camp near a river. He said, "Put the tipis close to the bank, so that the enemy cannot surround us." They did this. During the night Crow Dog could hear the coyote howl four times. Shunk-Manitu was telling him, "Something bad is going to happen to you." Crow Dog understood what the coyote was saying. Crow Dog got the men of his warrior society together, the Kit Foxes. They were singing their song:

> I am a fox.
> I am not afraid to die.
> If there is a dangerous
> deed to perform,
> That is mine to do.

They painted their faces black. They prepared themselves for a fight, for death.

At dawn the enemy attacked—white settlers led by a white and many Crow scouts, with many Absaroka warriors helping them. With Crow Dog were many famous warriors. Numpa Kachpa was there, Two Strikes, who got his name when he shot down two white soldiers riding on the same horse with one bullet. Kills in Water was there, and Hollow Horn Bear's son, and Kills in Sight. Two Crows had wounded Kills in Sight and unhorsed him. Crow Dog came in on a run, killed the two Crows, and put Kills in Sight on his horse. He whipped the horse and it took off with Kills in Sight hanging on to it. The horse was fast and got Kills in Sight safely home.

Crow Dog was looking around, hoping to catch himself one of the riderless Crow horses, when he took two enemy arrows, one high on his chest right under the collarbone and the other in his side. He broke off the arrows with his hands. Hollow Horn Bear's son and two others of his men came to help him. They were wounded, and their horses all had at least one arrow stuck in them. Crow Dog told them, "I am hurt bad. I cannot live. No use bothering with me. Save yourselves."

They rode off. Crow Dog managed to get hold of a horse and got on it, but he weakened soon. He became so weak he fell off this pony. He was lying in the snow. He had hardly strength to sing his death song. Suddenly two coyotes came, hooping gently. They said, "We know you." They kept him warm during the night, one lying on one side and one on the other. They brought Crow Dog deer meat to make him strong, and they brought him a medicine. One of the coyotes said, "Put this on the arrow points." Crow Dog did what the coyote told him. The medicine made his flesh tender and caused it to open up so that he could take the arrowheads and what was left of the shafts out. They almost came out by themselves.

The medicine the coyotes gave him cured Crow Dog. The nourishment they brought made him strong. The coyotes brought him home to his camp. A crow showed the way. Crow Dog said, "I was already walking on Ta-Chanku, on the Milky Way, on the road to the Spirit Land, but the coyotes led me back." And so he took on his seventh and last name, Kangi-Shunka, Crow Dog. Of course, it should have been Crow Coyote.

Years later, he was on his way to join Sitting Bull in Canada, and near the sacred Medicine Rocks he and his men were jumped by white soldiers. Crow Dog was hit by two bullets. His companions tied him to his horse and managed to get him home. This time a medicine man by the name of Sitting Hawk saved him. He told Crow Dog, "I will put my wound medicine into you. But I will not take the bullets out. One day you will die and go back to Mother Earth and the bullets will still be in you. Your human body will dissolve but the bullets will remain as evidence of what the wasičun have done to us."

This is the legend of Crow Dog, which Old Man Henry has told me many times. The first Crow Dog was a great warrior though he never took part in a big battle, such as the Little Big Horn. He preferred to do his fighting as a member of a small war party made up of warriors from his own Orphan Band. He fought the wasičun and Pawnee and Crow warriors.

Crow Dog had been a close friend of Crazy Horse. Together with Touch the Clouds, White Thunder, Four Horns, and Crow Good Voice, he accompanied Crazy Horse when this Great Warrior surrendered himself at Fort Robinson in 1877. After Crazy Horse was treacherously murdered, it was Crow Dog's cool head and bravery which prevented a general massacre. As the enraged Sioux faced the soldiers who were only waiting for a pretext to start the killing, Crow Dog rode back and forth between them, pushing back the over-eager warriors and soldiers with the butt end of his Winchester.

Crow Dog was most famous for his having shot and killed Spotted Tail, the paramount chief of the Brule Sioux. They were cousins and when they were young, they had been friends. Later, their paths diverged. Spotted Tail said, "It's no use trying to resist the wasičun." He cooperated with the whites in most things. Crow Dog was like Sitting Bull; he stuck to the old ways. The so-called "friendlies" gathered around Spotted Tail, and the so-called "hostiles" around Crow Dog. This led to rivalry and rivalry led to trouble, big trouble that was slowly building up between the two men.

On August 5, 1881, Crow Dog was hauling wood in his buckboard with his wife beside him when he saw Spotted Tail coming out of the council house and getting on his horse. Crow Dog handed his wife the reins, took his gun, which was hanging beside him out of its scabbard, got down from his seat, and faced the chief. Spotted Tail saw him. He said, "This is the day we settle this thing which is between us like men." Spotted Tail went for his six-shooter. Crow Dog knelt down and fired, beating Spotted Tail to the draw. He hit the chief in the chest. Spotted Tail tumbled from his horse and died, the unfired six-gun in his hand. Turning Bear shot at Crow Dog's wife, but missed. Crow Dog drove back to his home with his wife. A man called Black Crow prepared a sweat lodge to purify Crow Dog. He loaded up the Winchester and shot it into the sacred rocks four times, saying, "Now Spotted Tail's spirit won't bother you." They then purified themselves with water.

A judge in Deadwood sentenced Crow Dog to be hanged. He asked leave to go home to prepare himself. The judge asked, "How do we know that you will come back?" Crow Dog said, "Because I'm telling you." The judge let him go. For a month Crow Dog prepared for his death. He made up a death song and gave all his things away. What little he had, his horses, wagon, chickens, he gave to the poor. His wife prepared a white buckskin outfit for him, plain, without beads or quillwork. He wanted to be hanged in this. When all was ready he hitched up his last horse to an old buggy and with his wife drove the one hundred and fifty miles to Deadwood for his own execution.

When he arrived at Deadwood his lawyer was waiting for him with a big smile: "Crow Dog, you are a free man. I went to the Supreme Court for you and the Court ruled that the U.S. government has no jurisdiction over the reservation and that there is no law for punishing an Indian for killing another Indian." Crow Dog said, "You're a damn heap good man. I have driven a hundred and fifty miles for nothing." Then he went home with his wife.

Black Crow told Crow Dog: "Cousin, the blood guilt will be upon you for four generations. From now on you will not smoke the pipe with other men. You will smoke a small pipe of your own, and you will smoke alone. You will not eat from a common dish; you will eat alone from your own bowl. You will drink from your own cup. You will not drink water from the dipper when it is handed around. You cannot eat from other people's dishes and they will not eat from yours. You will live apart from the tribe. Cousin, yours will be a lonely life."

Kangi-Shunka paid blood money. He gave the Spotted Tail family many horses and white-man dollars. That made peace between the families, but not between the Crow Dogs and the spirits. They suffered their ostracism with a certain arrogance. They were weighed down by Crow Dog's deed, but at the same time they were proud of it. Theirs was a proud sort of shame. The first Crow Dog was an outcast but also something of a hero. The Crow Dogs wrapped themselves in their pride as in a blanket. They turned guilt into glory. They began speaking of the royalness of their bloodline. The first Crow Dog had shown them the way. As a chief he had the right to wear a war bonnet, but he never did. Instead he found somewhere an old, discarded white man's cloth cap with a visor and to the top of it he fastened an eagle feather. And that he wore at all times—the lowest and the highest. He used to say: "This white man's cap that I am wearing means that I must live in the wasičun's world, under his government. The eagle feather means that I, Crow Dog, do not let the wasičun's world get the better of me, that I remain an Indian until the day I die." In some mysterious way that old cap became in the people's mind a thing more splendid than any war bonnet. And it was into this clan that I married.

The shock of having to deal at the same time with the myth and the reality, with trying to break through the Crow Dog buckskin curtain, and having to take care of the needs of so many people as well, was too much for me. I broke down.

I got sick. I was down to ninety pounds. My body just collapsed. I could no longer stand up. If I tried, my legs would cramp up and hurt. My joints ached. I told Leonard, "I don't feel good. I can't sleep, and if I do I dream about people who have died, my dead friends and relations. Every time I close my eyes I see those who have been killed. I am sad, always. I think I am going to die too."

Leonard said he would do a doctoring meeting for me. He put up the peyote tipi for me. Another road man, Estes Stuart, came to help him. I ate the sacred medicine. I kept eating and eating. I was so weak I could not sit up. They made me lie down on a blanket. Leonard gave me some peyote tea to drink. It was old tea and very strong. I drank two whole cups of it. At midnight Estes prayed, and he talked while the water was going around. He said that since he was a peyote man he had X-ray vision, X-ray eyes which could see into my body, and he could not detect any sickness in me except one—love sickness. I felt so bad that tears came to my eyes. I thought, "Here I am, sick unto death, and they are making fun of me." I think I was a little paranoid. Estes had not been making fun at all. He explained later that what he meant was that mine was not a sickness of the body, but of the mind. That I felt that nobody loved me, not Leonard, not his family, not the people I cooked and washed for. I was sickening for want of love.

Suddenly people were all around me, talking to me, comforting me. Old Man Henry was patting my cheek, calling me "daughter." All those present were praying for me. All through the night I ate peyote. And Grandfather Peyote was calling me daughter.

When the sun rose, I rose too. I suddenly could sit up, even walk. I stepped outside the tipi and all around me I could see strange tropical birds flying, birds of metallic, fluorescent rainbow colors leaving trails of gold and silver. I went inside the house to lie down. I went to my bed, drew aside the blanket, and my legs turned to water. In my bed lay a strange woman, her hands crossed over her breast, her face stiff and white, her eyes unseeing. She was dead!

I got very scared. All of a sudden my whole body stopped. My heart quit pumping. My blood froze. I could not breathe.

Then I saw that the strange woman lying dead in my bed was me. Myself. And a great weight was lifted from me. I could breathe again. My heart was beating. I felt good. What was dying, what had died, was my former self, but I would go on living. Leonard came in and asked how was I doing. He put his arm around me and kissed me. He told me to lie down in the bed. As I did, the dead woman disappeared. The peyote power got hold of me. I started laughing. I kept on giggling and giggling. My ribs were sticking out, I had grown so skinny. I was all bones. But I kept on laughing for an hour. I would be all right.

CHAPTER 13

Two Cut-off Hands

They won't let Indians like me live. That's alright.
I don't want to grow up to be an old woman.

—*Annie Mae Aquash*

Nobody could ever say anything bad about my friend
Annie Mae, because she never did anything bad in
her life. She never walked into my home, she always burst
in, full of energy. She was a small woman, hardly more than
five feet tall, but she dominated those around her by the
force of her personality. She was pretty, too, with her wide,
smiling mouth, her Indian eyes and cheekbones, her flowing
black hair.

She was always the first up in the morning, making sure
that everybody got fed. She saw to it that all the men had
clean clothes. She often took dirty clothes to the river and
washed them herself. She combed and braided all the men's
hair. Whenever she saw young girls just sitting around and

gossiping, doing nothing all day but lying on a couch putting on makeup, she would tell them to get off their asses and start doing something worthwhile. She was happy to clean house, have everybody sweeping up and mopping. She was a good cook. She taught me and a lot of other women some good Indian recipes. Once she danced into my kitchen, danced around the table with a whole basket full of frogs she had caught in the river and killed. She cooked us up some frog's legs French-Canadian style. She would do fine bead-work for you. All you had to do was ask her. She learned how to make Sioux moccasins from Leonard's mother. She was gifted and had a flair for designing clothes, for creating very imaginative Indian fashions. She even modeled them for white customers. She was a natural-born leader. She had held responsible positions as director of Indian youth and antialcohol programs. She played a very active role within the Indian movement, both at national AIM headquarters in Minneapolis and on the West Coast. For me she was a rock to lean on, a rock with a lot of heart. She did not deserve to die.

Annie Mae was a Micmac Indian, born and raised on a tiny reservation in Nova Scotia, not far from Halifax. Though she lived in Canada, two thousand miles from Rose-bud, her life was almost a copy of mine, or of that of thou-sands of other young Indian girls and women. Instead of on a reservation, she lived on a reserve. Instead of a Bureau of Indian Affairs regulating and interfering with her existence, it was a department. The white boss lording it over the Micmacs was an agent, not a superintendent. The men who harassed her were mounties, not state troopers. Otherwise everything was the same north of the border. She lived in the same kind of tar paper shack that I did. She too had to do without electricity, indoor plumbing, central heating, run-ning water, and paved roads. She too was often hungry, down to one meal a day, eating anything she could find. Her mother had the same name as I—Mary Ellen. All she could tell me about her father was that he was a good fiddler who one day vamoosed. Her mother then married a good, hard-working, sober-minded man, but he got sick and died. Her mother then came apart, did hardly anything but gamble and smoke, and took off to marry again, abandoning her half-grown children, leaving them to fend for themselves.

Annie Mae had two sisters and one brother. One of the sisters, Mary, was especially close to her. She told me that Mary was very much like herself. The kids helped each other, Annie Mae having to take the part of her absent mother. Annie Mae could live off the sea, clamming and fishing. She worked as a berry picker and spud picker at one dollar per hour. Spud picking was back-breaking work. When she was seventeen she decided there was nothing to hold her on the Micmac reserve. She was eager and determined to make something of herself, to find out things. For many Micmacs, Boston was the mecca, the big city with a capital B, and to Boston she went.

She had met a young Micmac, Jake Maloney, and married him. They had two daughters. For a while she lived like a white middle-class housewife in a middle-class home. She was a sharp dresser, even wore dyed beehive hairdos, but she wanted to remain an Indian. She wanted her daughters to grow up as Indians. Jake's and her beliefs conflicted. They started to quarrel. He beat her. She left and divorced him. She had to fight him for the custody of her daughters. In the end she won. Her own children, at one time, told her that they preferred living with their father because he could give them the many things they wanted, things Annie Mae would not be able to give them if they lived Indian style on Boston's skid row. They preferred their white stepmother to their real one. Annie Mae grew into a Native American militant. She got into the same kind of fights that Barb and I had fought. She gave herself to the cause and that meant giving her children to her sister Mary to care for. That was hard and heart-wrenching. It was the sacrifice Annie Mae made to the movement—her motherhood. One thing she got out of her marriage: her husband was a martial arts freak and a professional karate teacher. Annie Mae became his sparring partner and learned some good chops and kicks. She knew when and on whom to use them.

Annie Mae met her first AIM people on November 26, 1970, when Russel Means and two hundred militants buried Plymouth Rock under a ton of sand, as a "symbolic burial of the white man's conquest." Among the tribes represented were New England Wampanoags, Narraganset, and Passamaquoddy, as well as a group of Micmacs, Annie Mae among them, calling themselves the "first victims of the wrath of the WASP." Later Annie Mae was among those who with war whoops boarded *Mayflower II*, the replica of the vessel that had brought the pilgrims to the New World. She watched Russel climb up the rigging, waving a pirate's blunderbuss, shouting: "Don't let us pick this up! We don't want to take up the gun again. But if you force us to, watch out!" This first meeting with AIM had on Annie Mae the same effect my first encounter had on me. It decided her fate. It decided when and how she would die.

In the beginning of 1972, or thereabouts, Annie Mae found herself a lover, Nogeeshik Aquash. Nogeeshik was a Canadian Indian who, Annie Mae told me, came from an island in the Great Lakes area. He looked and acted like an Indian, but at the same time was unlike any other Indian I knew. He was good-looking in a sinister way. His face was very pale with a sort of Fu-Manchu mustache and a tiny, scraggly goatee. He was very slim, elegantly emaciated. He had the movements of a cat, or maybe a spider. Paleness contrasting with his black hair, he sometimes reminded me of a handsome ghost. He is a good artist and lithographer. He dressed Indian, but again in a strange, unique way. He always wore a special sort of little, flat black hat with a feather stuck in it. Together they worked in the movement. On the side they started Indian fashion shows and became involved in exhibiting and sponsoring Indian crafts and jewelry. Annie Mae took part in the takeover of the BIA building and later she and Nogeeshik went to Wounded Knee. Right after Annie Mae helped me give birth, she and Nogeeshik were married in the Indian way. As Leonard was then with Russel Means in Washington trying to arrange a cease-fire, our friend the medicine man Wallace Black Elk performed the ceremony. They were joined together with the pipe and the star blanket. They were cedared up and smoked the sacred tobacco while four men and four women made a flesh offering for them. "A marriage like this," Black Elk told them, "lasts forever."

It did not work out that way. Their relationship turned sour. For a while they lived in Ottawa and that town was not good for them. Nogeeshik did a lot of barhopping and sometimes took Annie Mae along. He was moody to begin with, but when drunk he became abusive. Annie Mae told me, "He was torturing my mind. He did not treat me right." White women were attracted to him and he flaunted them in Annie Mae's face. Once or twice, she said, he beat her, or at least tried to. She could take care of herself if it came to physical confrontations. They split up a few times but always got together again until finally she got to a point where she could not take it anymore. She told me, "We had a quarrel and he broke the pipe, the sacred pipe we were married with at the Knee. For no reason at all. Then I knew that it was all over and I left him for good."

After that she stayed on and off with us at Crow Dog's

Paradise. She got very high up in the councils of AIM, to the extent of helping set movement policies. She had no luck with men. She was a very strong-hearted woman and that made some men uncomfortable. In the months before her death she got really close to Leonard Peltier. She admired him, and could not do enough for him. I still think that he would have been the ideal man for her, but things turned out tragically for both of them.

Annie Mae came to us to take part in the 1974 and 1975 Sun Dance. She came alone. She put up a tipi in back of our house and there she lived. She liked being with us Sioux. She tried learning to speak our language. She started making Sioux arts and crafts. Tough in a fight, she was gentle and comforting to any of the people who were sick or in despair. Everybody liked her, and many depended on her. She pared her existence down to the very basics, to the simplest way of tipi living.

At that time many other people besides her were camping on our place, and someone stole a necklace and earrings she had, worth about five or six hundred dollars. She said, "I have no need of such things anymore. Whoever took them is welcome to the stuff. I am only sorry that skins are ripping off skins." She came over to the house and dumped all her clothes and possessions on the table, telling me, "Keep these. This is for you. I'd rather not have anything at all, just whatever I have on my back. That's good enough for my execution." Ever since Wounded Knee she had had premonitions of approaching death. "I've fought too hard," she said. "They won't let Indians like me live. That's all right. I don't want to grow up to be an old woman." She talked that way often, almost cheerfully, without a trace of sentimentality. All she was left with then were her jeans, ribbon shirt, and Levi's jacket. That was all.

She wanted to take Leonard and me to the Micmac country, to Nova Scotia, to Shubenakadie, to Pictou's Landing, to all the tiny Micmac reserves which, as she jokingly said, are not much larger than a football field—the king-size ones. She told me that her Micmac people were losing their culture and their language. She said that every year her people go to an island and have ceremonies there, but that these rituals are becoming Christianized. She wanted to take Leonard to her tribe to teach them, to let them see that the old Indian ways still exist.

Leonard taught her the way of Grandfather Peyote. She liked to come to the meetings and was learning the songs. During a half-moon ceremony she had a vision. She was sitting beside me when it came to her. She said that she saw the moon turn into a prison, a jail with round walls, and inside it she saw the tiny figures of Indians leaving this prison, walking toward a big fire, walking right into the flames. And inside the fire was a man beckoning to her. And so she also walked into the flames. She told me: "I have experienced pain and the ecstasy and the glory of the fire which will consume me soon. A fire that will make me free."

Annie Mae still traveled a lot. Wherever Indians fought for their rights, Annie Mae was there. She helped the Menominee warriors take over a monastery. She told me that she was packing a gun. She said, "If any of my brothers are in a position where they're being shot at, or being killed, I go there to fight with them. I'd rather die than stand by and see them destroyed." No matter how often Annie Mae left us, she always showed up again at our place.

I read somewhere in an anthropology book that we Sioux "thrive on a culture of excitement." During the years from 1973 to 1975 we had more than enough excitement for even the most macho warrior, more than we could handle. Wilson, the tribal chairman at Pine Ridge, had established a regime of terror. Being shot at or having one's house fire-

bombed were daily occurrences Pine Ridge people had to
live with. Pine Ridge and our own reservation have a common border, and the violence spilled over onto Rosebud.
Many people who either opposed Wilson, belonged to AIM
or OSCRO, or had been at Wounded Knee were brutally
murdered. Some estimate that as many as two hundred and
fifty people, women and children among them, were killed
during this time—out of a population of eight thousand!
Between forty and fifty of these murders have been listed in
official government files. The vast majority of these killings
were never investigated. Among the victims was one of our
best friends, Pedro Bissonette, leader of OSCRO, the Oglala
Sioux Civil Rights Organization. He was shot to death by
tribal police on a lonely road, "resisting arrest" as they
claimed. One of his relatives, Jeanette Bissonette, was shot
and killed driving home from the burial of another victim.
Byron De Sersa was shot to death on account of an article
critical of the Wilson regime his father had written in a local
Indian newspaper. Wallace Black Elk's brother was killed in a
mysterious explosion when entering his home and turning
on the light. Our oldest and most respected medicine man,
Frank Fools Crow, was firebombed and had his horses killed
and his sweat lodge with all his sacred things destroyed.
Leonard's family suffered too. His niece, Jancita Eagle Deer,
was killed in an unexplained "accident" after having been
savagely beaten. She had last been seen in the car of her
lover, who later turned out to be an informer and who had
brutally mistreated her many times before. Jancita was then
suing a high South Dakota official for rape. Her mother,
Delphine, Leonard's older sister, wanted to take up the suit,
but was beaten to death by a BIA policeman who claimed
"drunkenness" as his excuse. Her battered corpse, her arms
and legs fractured, was found in the snow, the tears frozen
on her cheeks. A nephew went up into the hills and never

came back. His body was found with a bullet in it. And so it went, on and on.

It came to a point where nobody felt safe anymore, not even in their own homes. Once, when a car backfired near our house, all of our children immediately took cover under beds and behind walls. They thought the goons had arrived. The situation was aggravated by the fact that the movement became an object of attention for the FBI's Cointelpro and Cablesplicer projects. AIM was infiltrated by a number of informers and agents provocateurs. I hardly think that AIM deserved that much attention. This infiltration, together with the never-ending violence, brought on a general state of paranoia. The agents stirred up mistrust among us until nobody trusted anybody anymore. Husbands suspected their wives, sisters their brothers. Old friends who had fought many civil rights battles together began to be afraid of each other. Those inside prisons suspected those who remained free. Men sentenced to longer terms suspected those who were released sooner. Even some of the leaders began doubting each other—and by then Annie Mae was a leader.

It did not surprise me when the rumors started that she was an FBI undercover agent. People were saying: "Look at that woman, she is always traveling. Wherever something happens, she's there. So she must be an informer." Annie Mae came to me and cried. She said, "The goons are after me. They might kill me as they have killed so many others. I don't know what to do. If I get killed I don't want my children to think that I died working for the enemy. Promise me, if the goons blow me away, to tell my girls that I died true to my beliefs, fighting for my people."

For a while Annie Mae stayed at the point of greatest danger. She was helping Sioux women intimidated by the goons in Oglala, on the Pine Ridge Reservation, where Dennis Banks had set up a camp of opponents to Wilson's rule. That was like going into the lions' den. On June 26, 1975, the FBI invaded the little settlement in force under the pretext of investigating, of all things, the theft of an old pair of boots. Whether the FBI people were just dumb or whether they wanted to provoke an incident, I cannot say. What is sure is that their wading into that explosive situation was the spark that blew up the whole powder keg. A firefight started. It ended with one Indian and two agents dead. It may have been pure coincidence that this happened on the ninety-ninth anniversary of the Custer battle. Among those accused of having shot the feds was Leonard Peltier, Annie Mae's close friend. The witnesses against him later withdrew their testimony, saying that they had been nowhere near and that they had testified against him only under threats and compulsions. Peltier is now doing two lifetimes in the white man's prisons.

In the aftermath of this incident, the situation at Pine Ridge got totally out of hand. The whole reservation was in a state of panic. Annie Mae did not even dare use her own name anymore. She took refuge with us, again staying in the tipi behind our house. She was at Crow Dog's place when the big bust occurred. On September 5, 1975, the whole SWAT team, about a hundred and eighty agents in bulletproof vests with M-16s, rubber boats, helicopters, heavy vehicles, and artificial smog fell upon our and Old Man Henry's homes, as well as upon Annie Mae's little tent and the cabin of Crow Dog's sister and brother-in-law, less than a mile away. It was an Omaha Beach type of assault, like the movies one saw on TV of actions in Vietnam. We found out, much later, that the FBI thought that Peltier was hiding out at our place, which was completely untrue.

When the feds saw Annie Mae, they said, "We've been looking for you." They handcuffed her, throwing her around like a rag doll. When they were dragging her into the squad car she smiled at me and gave me the Indian Power sign with her fists even though she was handcuffed. They questioned her and questioned her although she had not been anywhere near the scene of the shootout. The FBI was convinced that she knew where Peltier was hiding. They knew how close she was to him. Then, suddenly, they let her go for lack of evidence. She came to see me. She related to me what had happened to her. The agents had told her that she would not live long if she did not tell them every-thing she knew and some things she could not have known—where some people had gone to ground, for instance. If she did not talk and if she did not do everything they wanted, she wasn't going to live. They would make sure she'd be dead—or put her away for the rest of her life, which would be worse.

She said to me: "They offered me my freedom and money if I'd testify the way they wanted. I have those two choices now. I chose my kind of freedom, not their kind, even if I have to die. They let me go because they are sure I'll lead them to Peltier. They're watching me. I don't hear them or see them, but I know they're out there somewhere. I can feel it."

I told her to stay with us if she wanted to, she was wel-come to move in with me anytime. I told her to take care of herself. She said: "Maybe this is the last time we can talk together. Remember, your husband is an important man to his people. Love him and protect him from all bad things. Don't let this white man's culture destroy him. Don't let him drink. Don't let him go with people who might do him harm. Watch him. He is a good man. He is needed."

I saw her one more time in Pierre, South Dakota, when Leonard went on trial. She had come to support him and to comfort me, to give us courage. We were all staying at the

Holiday Inn. She came to my room. She did not say anything much, she was just sitting on the bed looking at me.
She said, "I just wanted to see you. You won't see me again."
We talked about a few unimportant things, said our good-
byes, shook hands, hugged each other, and she cried and
cried. That was the last time I saw her. It was as if she had
heard Hinhan, the owl, hoot for her, death calling her. She
knew and she accepted it.

In the last days of November 1975 she just disappeared.
Everybody said, "Annie Mae has gone underground." At the
same time I had to take leave of my husband, who was sent to
prison on Wounded Knee–related charges. Leonard was
held in Lewisburg, Pennsylvania, a maximum-security
prison. I went with my little son Pedro to New York to stay
with white friends so that I could be close to him, within
visiting distance. It was there, in New York, in early March
1976, that I got a phone call from a friend in Rapid City,
telling me that Annie Mae Aquash had been found dead in
the snow at the foot of a steep bluff near Wanblee on the Pine
Ridge Reservation. The FBI was there at once, swarming
over her. They shipped her to Scotts Bluff for an autopsy.
They cut her hands off to send to Washington for identification—a needless cruelty as they could have made fin-
gerprints on the spot without mutilating her. It seems that
those who killed her had also raped her. She was buried in a
pauper's grave. After the FBI had identified her, an official
report was issued that she had died of exposure. The impli-
cation was that here was just another drunken Indian passing
out and freezing to death. But no alcohol or drugs had been
found in the autopsy.

Annie Mae's friends and relatives were not satisfied. They
obtained a court order to exhume the body and had their
own pathologist perform a second autopsy. He at once found
a bullet hole in her skull, found the bullet, too, a .32-caliber

slug. He also found the cut-off hands thrown with the body into the coffin. William Janklow, the attorney general of the State of South Dakota, had said that the only way to deal with renegade AIM Indians was to put a bullet through their heads, and someone had taken the hint. Leonard could occasionally call me collect from the prison. When I told him that Annie Mae had died, and how, he wept over the phone. We cried together. He would have liked to be the one to bury her, but that could not be.

Annie Mae Aquash is dead. Leonard Peltier is doing two lifetimes. Maybe the prison hacks let him wear the moccasins she made for him. Nogeeshik was in a bad car accident and is now a wheelchair case. Leonard and I still have a lot of things she once treasured, which she gave to us. Someday I am going to find out who killed this good, gently tough, gifted friend of mine who did not deserve to die. Someday I will tell her daughters that she died for them, died like a warrior. Someday I will see Annie Mae. In a strange way I feel that she died so that I, and many others, could survive. That she died because she had made a secret vow, like a Sun Dancer who, obedient to his vow, pierces his flesh and undergoes the pain for all the people so that the people may live.

CHAPTER 14

Cante Ishta –
The Eye of the Heart

You got to look at things
with the eye in your heart,
not with the eye in your head.

—*Lame Deer*

Some of our medicine men always say that one must view the world through the eye in one's heart rather than just trust the eyes in one's head. "Look at the real reality beneath the sham realities of things and gadgets," Leonard always tells me. "Look through the eye in your heart. That's the meaning of Indian religion."

The eye of my heart was still blind when I joined Leonard to become his wife. I knew little of traditional ways. I had been to a few peyote meetings without really understanding them. I had watched one Sun Dance, and later the Ghost

Dance held at Wounded Knee, like a spectator—an emotional spectator, maybe, but not different from white friends watching these dances. They, too, felt emotion. Like myself they did not penetrate through symbolism to the real meaning. I had not yet participated in many ancient rituals of our tribe—the sweat bath, the vision quest, yuwipi, the making of relatives, the soul keeping. I did not even know that these ceremonies were still being performed. There were some rituals I did not even know existed.

I was now the wife of a medicine man who had been a finder and seer since boyhood, because the elders of the tribe had noticed his spiritual gifts when he was still very young, about eight years old. They had said, "Watch this boy. He's the one," and had taught and prepared him for his future life as a medicine man. Because going to a white school would spoil him for the role the elders had chosen for him, Old Henry had driven the truant officers away with his shotgun, telling them, "I will rather go to jail before I let this boy go to your school!" Now Leonard would teach me to be a medicine man's wife, and I was eager to learn.

I think it was not easy for him to teach his wife. She knows him during the day and during the night, too. Knowing his strengths, she cannot fail to see his weaknesses also. And he knows the good and the bad in her likewise. We were under stress from the outside all the time, and so we had our ups and downs. Also, with the kind of life I had before, I did not respect him just because he was a man, as some Sioux women do. Some of those old macho Sioux proverbs like "Woman should not walk before man" I did not think were meant for me. We loved each other, and sometimes we fought each other. Under the conditions under which we had to live, how could it have been otherwise? But always, always I felt, and was enraptured by, his tremendous power—raw power, spiritual Indian power coming from deep within him. It was raw because, never having been at school and being unable to read or write, there is no white-man intellectualism in him. At the same time, his thinking and ideas are often extremely sophisticated—unique, origi-nal, even frightening.

I was at first very unsure about the role of a medicine man's wife, about the part women played, or were allowed to play, in Indian religion. All I knew from childhood was that a menstruating woman had to keep away from all rituals, and the thought intimidated me. Leonard helped me overcome these feelings of insecurity. He told me about Ptesan Win, the White Buffalo Woman, who brought the sacred pipe to our tribes. He told me about medicine women. He said that in 1964 he went to Allen, South Dakota, to take part in a number of ceremonies. While there he met a medicine woman. She said good things to the people at this ceremony. Her name was Bessie Good Road. She used a buffalo skull in her rituals, and always a buffalo came into her meetings. She had the spiritual buffalo power. Every time the buffalo spirit moved his legs, his hoofs struck sparks of lightning. Every time the buffalo grunted, flashes of light shot from his nos-trils. Every time the buffalo swung his tail, one could see a flaming circle. "I took my drum and sang for her," he told me. "I had never seen a medicine woman before and I was awed by her power." She told him: "Someday I won't be here anymore. I want to leave these things, this power for my people to stand on. We are losing many sacred things, losing sacred knowledge, but to this place the buffalo spirit still comes."

The medicine woman did not talk much. She had to wait a long time until she could use her medicine, until she no longer had her moon time. He was not ashamed to have this holy woman teach him. Hearing this made me feel good.

In this way Crow Dog talked to me. It did not matter where. Riding in a car, at the table eating fry bread and hamburger, around the stove with other people listening, or at night lying by his side. He taught me how to listen. Sound is important. Our sound is the sound of nature and animals, not the notes of a white man's scale. Our language comes from the water, the flowers, the wild creatures, the winds. Crow Dog believes that the newborn child can understand this universal language, but later he forgets it. He teaches about harmony between humans and the earth, between man and man and between man and woman. He always says: "What's the saddle good for without a horse? Get the horse, and a saddle blanket, and the saddle together. That's what the sacred hoop means."

Tunkashila, the Grandfather Spirit, has filled this universe with powers, powers to use—for good, not for bad. We only have to suffer this power to enter into us, to fill us, not to resist it. Medicine men, Leonard told me, have a sort of secret language. Sioux, Crow, Blackfeet medicine men, before they start talking, they already know what they'll be saying to each other. I guess that goes for medicine women, too.

I had to learn about the sweat bath, because it precedes all sacred ceremonies, and is at the same time a ceremony all by itself. It is probably the oldest of all our rituals because it is connected with the glowing stones, evoking thoughts of Tunka, the rock, our oldest god. Our family's sweat lodge, our oinikaga tipi, is near the river which flows through Crow Dog's land. That is good. Pure, flowing water plays a great part during a sweat. Always at the lodge we can hear the river's voice, the murmur of its waters. Along its banks grows washte wikcemna, a sweet-smelling aromatic herb—Indian perfume.

The lodge is made of sixteen willow sticks, tough but

resilient and easy to bend. They are formed into a beehive-shaped dome. The sweat lodges vary in size. They can accommodate anywhere from eight to twenty-four people. The bent willow sticks are fastened together with strips of red trade cloth. Sometimes offerings of Bull Durham tobacco are tied to the frame, which is then covered with blankets or a tarp. In the old days buffalo skins were used for the covering, but these are hard to come by now. The floor of the little lodge is covered with sage. In the center is a circular pit to receive the heated rocks. In building a lodge, people should forget old quarrels and have only good thoughts.

Outside the lodge, wood is piled up in a certain manner to make the fire in which the rocks will be heated—peta owihankeshni—the "fire without end" which is passed on from generation to generation. After it has blazed for a while, white limestone rocks are placed in its center. These rocks do not crack apart in the heat. They come from the hills. Some of them are covered with a spidery network of green moss. This is supposed by some to represent secret spirit writing.

The scooped-out earth from the firepit inside the lodge is formed up into a little path leading from the lodge entrance and ending in a small mound. It represents Unci—Grandmother Earth. A prayer is said when this mound is made. A man is then chosen to take care of the fire, to bring the hot rocks to the lodge, often on a pitchfork, and to handle the entrance flap.

In some places men and women sweat together. We do not do this. Among us, men and women do their sweat separately. Those taking part in a sweat strip, and wrapped in their towels, crawl into the little lodge, entering clockwise. In the darkness inside they take their towels off and hunker down naked. I was astounded to see how many people could be swallowed up by this small, waist-high, igloo-shaped hut.

The rocks are then passed into the lodge, one by one. Each stone is touched with the pipe bowl as, resting in the fork of a deer antler, it is put into the center pit. The leader goes in first, sitting down near the entrance on the right side. Opposite him, at the other side of the entrance sits his helper. The leader has near him a pail full of cold, pure water and a ladle. Green cedar is sprinkled over the hot rocks, filling the air with its aromatic odor. Outside the entrance flap is a buffalo-skull altar. Tobacco ties are fastened to its horns. There is also a rack for the pipe to rest on.

Anywhere from twelve to sixty rocks can be used in this ceremony. The more rocks, the hotter it will be. Once the rocks have been passed into the lodge, the flap is closed. Inside it is dark except for the red glow of the rocks in the pit. Now the purification begins. As sage or cedar is sprinkled on the rocks, the men or women participating catch the sacred smoke with their hands, inhaling it, rubbing it all over their face and body. Then cold water is poured on the rocks. The rising cloud of white steam, "grandfather's breath," fills the lodge. A sweat has four "doors," meaning that the flap is opened four times during the purification to let some cool outside air in, bringing relief to the participants.

Everybody has the privilege to pray or speak of sacred things during the ceremony. It is important that all take part in the ritual with their hearts, souls, and minds. When women have their sweats, a medicine man runs them—which is all right because it is so dark inside that he cannot see you.

The first time I was inside the oinikaga tipi, the sweat lodge, when water was poured over the rocks and the hot steam got to me, I thought that I could not endure it. The heat was beyond anything I had imagined. I thought I would not be able to breathe because it was like inhaling liquid fire. With my cupped hands I created a slightly cooler space over my eyes and mouth. After a while I noticed that the heat which had hurt me at first became soothing, penetrating to the center of my body, going into my bones, giving me a wonderful feeling. If the heat is more than a person can stand, he or she can call out "Mitakuye oyasin!"—All my relatives!—and the flap will be opened to let the inside cool off a bit. I was proud not to have cried out. After the sweat I really felt newly born. My pores were opened and so was my mind. My body tingled. I felt as if I had never experienced pain. I was deliciously light-headed, elated, drunk with the spirit. Soon I began looking forward to a good sweat.

Once we were in California testifying for an Indian brother on trial in Los Angeles. Some of the local Indians invited us to a sweat somewhere in the desert eighty miles from L.A. As I was hunkering down inside the lodge, they started passing in the rocks. When about twenty were in the pit, the usual number for a woman's sweat, I expected them to close the flap and start the ceremony. Instead more and more rocks, a big heap, were coming in. I stared at the huge pile of glowing, hissing rocks rising higher and higher. I tried to back away from the rocks, but there was no room. My knees started to blister. Already the heat was terrific and they had not even poured the water yet. I cringed at the thought of what cold water on this big mound of fiery rocks would do. Then it came, the water. I thought I would die. Never, never thereafter would I eat lobsters, knowing what these poor creatures have to go through. I felt I could not cry out to have the flap opened. After all, I represented the Sioux women on this occasion. As the hissing steam enveloped us there rose a chorus of cries: "Ow, ow, ow, Great Spirit, we thank you for making us suffer so. We are suffering for our poor brothers in jail. Make us suffer more!"

"Jesus Christmas," I thought, "these people don't sweat to purify themselves. They sweat to suffer." There were some anguished cries: "All my relatives!" The door was opened, but it was so hot outside in the desert that it brought me no relief. The flap was closed again and more water poured. The prayers started. I was praying too, silently: "Please make the prayers short," but they were long. When it was all over we could not get out quickly enough. Some women were in such a hurry they did not even wrap their towels around themselves and came out stark naked. The relief of being out of that particular sweat lodge was indescribable. Leonard told me that they had used more stones in the men's sweat than in ours. I could not see how that was possible.

Once Leonard ran a sweat in New Jersey for New York Indians—just a good, normally hot Sioux sweat. As Leonard poured the water those New York Indians began to scream. They tore apart the back of the sweat lodge, clawed their way out, and ran away in all directions. If that had happened in Sioux country it would have been a serious desecration of a religious ceremony. Leonard just gave the kind of laugh he reserves for tragicomic situations. "I forgive these people," he said. "They just don't understand Indian ways. They have to be taught."

I have to admit that Leonard's sweats are very hot. He has been in so many of them that he does not seem to feel the searing heat. During a peyote ceremony, I saw him picking up glowing embers with his bare fingers to put them back into place. Because he is no longer bothered by intense heat, he thinks everybody is like him in that respect. People are always dropping in to meet a medicine man, or to learn from him, or simply out of curiosity. One such visitor was a young black man called Jamesie. He made himself into a slave for me, chopping wood, fetching water, helping in the kitchen. That was nice. Then he wanted to take part in a sweat. Unfortunately for him, it was one of those in which men want to suffer for a brother in the slammer. That meant not only that it would be excruciatingly hot, but that there would be no crying "All my relatives!" and no opening of the flap during the ceremony. When the heat got to poor Jamesie he started screaming: "I'm dying, I'm dying!" Crow Dog told him that it was the most wonderful thing in the world to die during this ceremony, the most beautiful end a man could wish for. It was but little comfort to Jamesie.

I often tell Leonard, "Purify them, but don't cook them!" And Leonard always answers, looking innocent, "But it wasn't hot at all. I can't understand these people. There must be something wrong with them."

Leonard is also a yuwipi man. Yuwipi is one of our oldest, and also strangest, ceremonies. I had never been to a yuwipi until I met Leonard. It is an unexplainable experience. How can you explain the supernatural for which there is no rationalization? When the first yuwipi ceremony that I took part in was being prepared, I became apprehensive, and once it was in progress, I was even scared. I was still reacting like a white woman.

A yuwipi is put in motion when a man or woman sends a sacred pipe and tobacco to a medicine man. That is the right way to ask for a ceremony. Some person wants to find something—something that can be touched, or something that exists only in the mind. Maybe a missing child or the cause of an illness. The yuwipi man is a finder. He is the go-between, a bridge between the people and the spirits. Through him people ask questions of the supernaturals, and through him the spirits answer back. The person who sent the pipe is the sponsor. Yuwipi men do not get paid for their services, but the sponsor has to feed all comers who want to participate and take advantage of the ritual.

A dog feast is part of the yuwipi ritual, and dog meat is the holy food that is served at the end of the ceremony. This did not bother me. I had eaten dog many times as a child—not in a sacred way, but simply because we were so poor that we ate any kind of meat we could get our hands on—dog, gopher, prairie dog, jackrabbits—just about anything that walked on four legs. The dog feast is an almost human sacrifice. In the old days, young men from the warrior societies would go through the camp selecting dogs for a dog feast. Sometimes they would pick the dog of a great chief or famous hunter. It would have been very bad manners for the owner to object or let his face betray his feelings. It was an honor bestowed upon the owner as well as the dog. Whether they always appreciated the honor is another matter. It is because we are so fond of our dogs that the feast takes on the character of a sacrifice. They scent the dog, paint a red stripe on its back, and strangle it so that its neck is broken and it dies instantly.

I remember a funny incident. We were all staying at a white friend's home in New York. Somebody had a strange dream, and that called for a yuwipi ceremony. We had everything necessary for it except the dog. Henry was standing at a window overlooking Broadway. He pointed out to our host a man walking a young, plump dog. "Just the right kind," said Henry. "Go get him!" "No way," said our friend. "Go, tell the man," urged Henry, "what a great honor it is. Also tell the dog that it is a very great honor and that he won't feel a thing." "New York dogs have no sense of honor," replied our friend and we all had to laugh. So we used beef.

The way I remember my first yuwipi, young girls started it by making tobacco ties, tiny squares of colored cloth, each containing a pinch of Bull Durham tobacco, that were being tied into one single string more than thirty feet long. They made four hundred and five of these little tobacco bundles, one for each of the different plants, "our green brothers," in our Sioux world.

While the girls made tobacco ties, others prepared the biggest room in the house for the ceremony. All furniture was removed, the floors swept and covered with sage. All pictures were taken from the walls. Mirrors were turned around because nothing that reflects light is allowed to remain during the ceremony. For this reason participants must remove jewelry, wristwatches, even eyeglasses before entering. All windows were covered with blankets because the ritual takes place in total darkness. Blankets and bedrolls were placed all along the four walls for everybody to sit on.

The string of tobacco ties was laid out in a square within the room. Nobody was allowed in this sacred square except the yuwipi man. All others remained outside. At the head of the square, where the sponsor and singer with his drum had taken their seats, were put a large can filled with earth and two smaller cans on each side. Planted into the big can was the sacred staff. It was half red and half black, the colors separated by a thin yellow stripe. To the top half of the staff was fastened an eagle feather and to the lower half, the tail of a black-tailed deer. The red of the staff stands for the day; the black, for the night. The eagle feather represents wisdom because the eagle is the wisest of all birds. An eagle's center feather will make the spirits come into the ceremony.

The deer is very sacred. Each morning, before any other creature, the deer comes to the creek to drink and bless the water. The deer is medicine. It is a healer. It can see in the dark. If any doctoring is to be done, the deer's spirit will enter. Leonard uses a certain kind of medicine from behind the animal's ears to cure certain diseases. It is very powerful. So that is what the deer tail stands for.

In the smaller, earth-filled tin cans were planted sticks with colored strips of cloth, like flags, attached to them. These represent the sacred four directions, red for the west, white for the north, yellow for the east, and black for the south. In front of the staff was put the buffalo skull, serving as an altar. There was also a small earth altar, representing

Grandmother Earth. On it was placed a circle of tobacco ties. Inside this circle, with his finger, Leonard traced a lightning design, because on this occasion he also wanted to use lightning medicine. It is believed that if a spirit comes in and then backs away from a person, that person cannot be cured.

Against the horns of the buffalo skull rested the sacred pipe. Also used were two special, round finding stones and three gourd rattles. Out of the tiny rocks inside the gourds come the spirit voices. These rocks, not much bigger than grains of sand, come from ant heaps. They are crystals, agates, and tiny fossils. They sparkle in the sunlight. Ants are believed to have power because they work together in tribes and don't have hearts but live by the universe.

Everybody then received a twig of sage to put behind their ears or into their hair. This is supposed to make the spirits come to you and to enable you to hear their voices. Then the yuwipi man was brought into the center of the square. His helpers first put his arms behind his back and tied all his fingers together. Then they wrapped him up in a star blanket, covering him completely. A rawhide thong, the kind once used to make bowstrings, was then wound tightly around the blanket and secured with knots. Then the yuwipi man was placed face down on the sage-covered floor. On this occasion it was Leonard who had been tied up. He lay there like a mummy. I could not imagine how he could breathe. Then the kerosene lamps with the big reflectors were extinguished, leaving us sitting in absolute, total darkness. For a short while we sat in utter silence. Then, with a tremendous roar, the drum started to pound, filling the room with its reverberations as the singers began their yuwipi songs. It sent shivers down my spine.

Almost at once the spirits entered. First I heard tiny voices whispering, speaking fast in a ghostly language. Then the gourds began to fly through the air, rattling, bumping into walls, touching our bodies. Little sparks of light danced through the room, wandered over the ceiling, circled my head. I felt the wing beats of a big bird flitting here and there through the darkness with a whoosh, the feathers lightly brushing my face. At one time the whole house shook as if torn by an earthquake. One woman told me later that in one of the flashes of light she had seen the sacred pipe dancing. I was scared until I remembered that the spirits were friends. The meeting lasted almost until the morning. Finally they sang a farewell song for the spirits who were going home to the place from which they had come.

The lamp was lit and revealed Leonard sitting in the middle of the sacred square—unwrapped and untied. He was weeping from emotion and exhaustion. He then told us what the spirits had told him. Then we ate the dog, and afterward wojapi, a kind of berry pudding, drank mint tea and coffee, and of course smoked the pipe, which went around clockwise from one person to the next.

The white missionaries have always tried to suppress this ceremony, saying it was Indian hocus-pocus and that the yuwipi men simply were mountebanks after the manner of circus magicians. They tried to "expose" our medicine men, but the attempt backfired. During the 1940s the superintendent at Pine Ridge had Horn Chips, our foremost yuwipi man, perform the ceremony in full daylight in the presence of a number of skeptical white observers. He had Horn Chips tied and wrapped by his own BIA police. To the disappointment of the watching missionaries, the mystery sparks appeared out of nowhere and the gourds flew around the superintendent's head. The result was that many Christian Indians went back to the old Lakota religion.

One of the strangest yuwipi ceremonies took place in New York when Leonard was visiting there. Dick Cavett some-

how got wind of a yuwipi man being in town and asked for a
ceremony in the proper ritual way. Cavett was born and
raised in Nebraska, close to the Pine Ridge Reservation, and
he believes in the power of yuwipi. As usual Leonard had all
his sacred things with him, but he had no drummer or singer
and, of course, no dog meat. The dog could be dispensed
with, but having neither drummer nor singer was a problem. Leonard solved it by getting hold of a tape recorder and
taping his own drumming and singing before the ceremony.
He instructed one of the New York Indians to turn the
recorder on the moment the lights went out. He had timed
the whole ceremony on his watch. He also taught some
Mohawk Indians how to tie him up. He told Cavett and the
Indians who had come to participate that he doubted very
much that the spirits would come in under such unusual
circumstances, but they did appear and it turned into a very
good meeting. As Leonard used to say: "I am a guitar and the
spirits are the strings who make the music."

In May 1974, Old Henry and Leonard put on a Ghost
Dance. After the one at Wounded Knee this is only the
second time during this century that the dance has been
performed. We held it on a lonely mesa which has served the
Crow Dogs as their sacred place and vision-quest hill for
generations. It was supposed to be a ritual for Sioux only,
but somehow, through the "moccasin telegraph" which always spreads news among Indians in a mysterious way,
everybody seemed to know about it, and many native people
from as far away as Alaska, Canada, Mexico, and Arizona
suddenly appeared in order to participate. Strange things
happened. Observation planes flew over the sacred dance
ground. One of our young security men pointed his gun at
them to drive them away. The pilots finally took the hint.
Two FBI agents were discovered hiding behind some nearby
trees. They wore very stylish, mod clothes and told us they

were insurance agents. Though we were angry at their desecration of our ceremony, we had to laugh. It was so ridiculous. There is no house for miles up there, and no road. The
only living things to sell life insurance to on that pine-
studded hill are coyotes and porcupines. We made a citizens'
arrest and took the two snoopers to tribal court, where they
were put on bail for peddling on Indian land without a
license. They bailed themselves out with hundred-dollar
bills which they peeled off from a fat roll of green frogskins
that they carried in their pockets. It was funny, but the
presence of the planes and the agents gave me premonitions
of bad things to come.

The weather was fine throughout, with the sun shining all
the time. We had a great many dancers, among them a
sixteen-year-old white girl, the daughter of friends from
New York. We also had two Mexican Indians taking part,
one a Nahua from Oaxaca, the other a Huichol from Chi-
huahua. They had come in their white campesino outfits.
The Huichol brother said that his name in Indian was Warm
Southwind. So, of course, we renamed him "Mild Disturbance." About a dozen dancers got into the power and
received visions. One young Navajo with a red blanket
wrapped around him suddenly began to dance with the
movements of a bird. It seemed almost as if an eagle had
taken possession of his body. The best thing that happened
was the appearance of a flight of eagles toward the end of the
dance. Nobody had ever seen so many of these sacred birds
together at one time. They circled with outspread wings
over the dance ground and then flew off in an undulating
line, like a long plumed serpent gliding through the clouds.
It made us happy.

The Crow Dogs have always believed that they are under a
kind of curse on account of the first Crow Dog killing Spotted Tail over a hundred years ago. They see the face of the

dead chief in their drinking bowls. Leonard always says that Spotted Tail's blood is still dripping on him, loading him down. He says that the guilt lasts for four generations, that only his sons will be free from it. Thinking of all the bad things that happened in the months following the Ghost Dance, one could almost believe that Spotted Tail's anger is still unappeased. (At a give-away feast in 1989, Crow Dog put a war bonnet on the present chief Spotted Tail, and both families decided to be friends forever from that day on.)

CHAPTER 15

The Eagle Caged

Grandfather, I pray to you.
Grandfather, don't let me be
taken away.
My people need me,
as I need them.
Grandfather, I ask you,
don't let them put me
in a penitentiary.

—*Crow Dog*

After the Ghost Dance of 1974, Leonard was in a good mood for a while. He watched sacred water birds flying over Crow Dog land and was happy seeing eagles circling in the sky. He liked to go for rides on Big Red, his favorite horse, and went tearing off at a gallop, enjoying the wind in his face, the sense of freedom one experiences flying on horseback over the prairie. But already he felt prison walls closing in on him. After Wounded Knee he was free on borrowed time. He could not understand why the government was after him. He did not consider himself a radical. He was not interested in politics. He never carried a gun. He thought himself strictly a religious leader, a medicine man. But that was exactly why he was dangerous. The young city Indians talking about revolution and waving guns find no echo among the full-bloods in the back country. But they will listen to a medicine man, telling them in their own language: "Don't sell your land, don't sell Grandmother Earth to the strip-mining outfits and the uranium companies. Don't sell your water." That kind of advice is a threat to the system and gets you into the penitentiary.

The main charge against Leonard stemmed from the occupation of Wounded Knee. Four government agents in the guise of postal inspectors tried to sneak in during a truce period. They were stopped by some of our young security guards. Afraid of being found out and roughed up, they immediately identified themselves as agents carrying badges, handguns, and handcuffs. Our young men disarmed them and took them to Leonard, who was in the museum building. They asked him, "What shall we do with them?"

Leonard said, "Well, it's breakfast time. Let's give them coffee and something to eat." He then lectured them for half an hour on the reasons for Wounded Knee and Indian civil rights in general. Then he had them politely escorted out of the perimeter.

For this he was charged with "interfering with federal officers during performance of their duties" (spying on us) and with "armed robbery" (the taking away of the agents' guns and handcuffs). The prosecutor said that the occupation of Wounded Knee was illegal, a conspiracy and a crime. That Crow Dog was a leader and therefore responsible for everything that happened during the occupation, even if he himself did not do it, or even witness it. On this ground Leonard was sentenced to thirteen years.

The government was not altogether happy because Leonard had gotten a suspended sentence, putting him on probation. He was still free. So they had to do something about that. In March 1975, Leonard and I came home late and found a bunch of white strangers in our house. One, a man called Pfersick, said he had come to see the Indian guru. He was high on drugs, actually using them in front of us. Leonard told him that drugs were not allowed in Crow Dog's home. Pfersick said: "Who the fuck are you to tell me what I can or cannot take or smoke?" A little later he made very crude sexual advances toward me, using foul language, patting me on the bottom. Leonard stepped between us, pushing him away. At that he went ape and attacked Leonard with a chain-saw blade he took from the wall. Leonard dodged it and got in a few good licks on his own. Some skins came to the rescue. They subdued the madman. Pfersick and his hangers-on were told never to come back and were thrown off our land. They brought a charge against Leonard for assault and battery. After a trial of only a few hours an all-white South Dakota jury found Leonard guilty and he got another five years. We used to say at that time that even Jesus Christ would have been found guilty in the State of South Dakota for every imaginable crime if he were an AIM Indian.

On September 2, 1975, still another incident happened. Two men named Beck and McClosky crashed their car through a wooden barrier, driving right into our yard. It was 1:30 A.M. and both were drunk. Of the two Beck was the heavy. He was a violent, murderous half- or quarter-blood. He had a long criminal record. Much later, when it no longer had an effect upon our lives, Beck murdered an inoffensive, middle-aged man called No Moccasin before witnesses and was sent to jail for it. The other man, McClosky, was comparatively harmless, simply Beck's drinking partner. They came into Crow Dog's place, making a big racket, boasting of just having savagely beaten a sixteen-year-old nephew of Leonard. Leonard was sleeping soundly and it took some time to rouse him. When he finally had put on his pants and stepped into the yard, he found some of the relatives who are always staying with us fighting off the intruders. McClosky got his jaw cracked in the process. Again someone, and you can guess who, induced Beck and McClosky to bring charges of assault and battery against Crow Dog and his relatives. We knew nothing about it.

Now it is a sad fact that on any given weekend innumerable drunken brawls take place all over the reservation. Men in a drunken stupor senselessly maim each other. Arms are broken, eyes gouged out, but this sort of thing is never investigated. On the adjacent Pine Ridge Reservation they had a civil war situation. Over a hundred people had been murdered and not a tenth of these cases was ever looked into, and then only if the police thought they had a chance of pinning the killing on some AIM member. That this endless violence was totally ignored by the government made what happened next unreal and unexplainable—at least at that time. At the break of dawn on September 5, 1975, four days after Beck and McClosky provoked the fight in our yard, I was awakened when somebody kicked our door in and shouted: "This is the United States marshal, this is the FBI, come out or we'll shoot!"

Next thing I felt the muzzle of an M-16 pressed against my head. They came one hundred and eighty-five men strong, marshals, agents, SWAT teams, making an Omaha Beach–type assault on the home of a single medicine man. It was like a newsreel from Vietnam, like seeing a bad movie in a dream. Out through the broken-down door I could see an observation plane circling over us. Choppers were landing in the yard. Across the Little White River, flowing through our property, guys in camouflage outfits came paddling rubber rafts. Some men with flak vests were aiming submachine guns at us. It was as if we were a Vietcong village overrun by a hundred and eighty-five Rambos. It would have been funny had it not destroyed our lives. Through the window I could see the SWAT team coming down the hill in extended battle line. They were actually laying down some sort of smokescreen. I heard them singing: "We've come to take you away."

Two Rambo types broke the window and climbed in. They pointed at little Pedro who was still half asleep and asked, "Is this the kid who was born at Wounded Knee?" They threw him across the room so that he hit his head against the wall. He was crying. I wanted to rush to him but one of the feds said, "One more step and I blow you away, right into the Happy Hunting Grounds!" He, too, put his gun against my temple. So now I had two M-16s on each side of my head. If these two had pulled their triggers they would not only have killed me, but also each other. A third FBI man threw a gun at my feet, saying, "Go on. Pick it up. I'm told you're such great warriors. Go on. Do it. Let's have a nice shootout!"

I saw that one of their headmen had walked in. I told him, "Yeah, you better watch your boys before they kill somebody." His face got red and he walked out. In the door he turned around and said, "I'm from Minneapolis," as if that explained the whole insane scene. He nodded to his men and they put their guns down. But they ransacked the whole place, trampled upon and broke our sacred things, and hauled men, women, and children half-naked out of their beds. They forced them to sit outside on the ground on that

raw morning with hardly anything on. Out of pure mean-
ness they shot and killed Big Red, Leonard's favorite horse,
and then blasted away at a little black colt. I asked them to
show me their search warrants. They didn't have any, just a
few blank arrest orders against "John Doe" and "Jane Doe."
  They dragged Leonard away in handcuffs together with a
few of his friends and relatives, among them my friend
Annie Mae Aquash. On the ninety-mile trip to Pierre, the
state capital, the agents had their fun and games with
Leonard. When he had to leave the car to answer a call of
nature, they put a gun at his feet, too, telling him, "You'll rot
in prison for the rest of your life. We'll make you a sporting
proposition. You've got a fifty-fifty chance. Take the gun and
run!"
  Leonard ignored them. The handcuffs they had put on
him were of a special kind which tightens and tightens with
every slightest movement. They cut off the circulation in his
arms and made his wrists bleed. In Pierre they handcuffed
him to a chair and kept at him for twenty-four hours, not
letting him sleep, asking over and over again: "Where is
Peltier? Where is Peltier?" This question made absolutely no
sense to Leonard. The whole nightmarish event made no
sense. Why the hundreds of agents? The helicopters? The
rubber rafts? The only charge against him was McClosky's
broken jaw, broken not by Leonard but by one of his
nephews. All that was needed would have been a single
tribal policeman telling Leonard, "Cousin, there's that com-
plaint about a brawl. Why don't you come to the tribal
council and clear the matter up?" That would have been the
customary approach had anybody bothered at all. Why this
Omaha Beach kind of assault? The question bothered us for
years. It was not until 1979 that we found out the reason for
this madness. Leonard went to jail for over a year simply
because the FBI had goofed and then had to justify its action
in some way.

On June 23, 1975, there had been a shootout at the tiny hamlet of Oglala on the Pine Ridge Reservation, over a hundred miles from our place. The FBI had invaded the place because it was rumored to be an AIM stronghold. A firefight erupted. One Indian and two FBI agents were killed. Hundreds of people had been killed on that reservation during these troubled days and nobody had given a damn, but two dead FBI agents were a different matter. Somebody had to be tried and convicted for their death— somebody, anybody. The FBI combed Pine Ridge for likely suspects but did not come up with anything. So-called witnesses were suborned, threatened, and browbeaten. One slightly feebleminded woman, Myrtle Poor Bear, was shown a photograph of someone's mutilated body and told, "You'll be like this unless you testify the way we tell you." The government admitted later that their witnesses had not been "believable" and that the agents had put unlawful pressure on them. In the end they picked upon Leonard Peltier, an Indian from Fort Totten, as a likely perpetrator, not because there was a good case against him, but because he was a radical AIM leader and a thorn in the government's flesh.

Crow Dog and his people were not involved. We had not even known about the events in Oglala. Crow Dog was at home when it happened, running his ceremonies. The FBI knew that very well. But someone had given the FBI a tip that Peltier was hiding out on Crow Dog's place, and they believed it—which doesn't say much for their intelligence as Peltier was half a continent away, in Oregon actually. The FBI had staged the whole Beck-McClosky incident from beginning to end, possibly threatening Beck with long jail terms for his various crimes unless he cooperated. Later they tried to justify their assault on Crow Dog's place by pressing phony charges. We found all this out much later by reading some of the briefs coming out of the Peltier case.

After the last of the agents with their rubber rafts and 'copters had disappeared, we were left stunned. Leonard's old parents, myself, the kids—we were all in a state of shock. For a year afterward the children ran to hide themselves whenever a car backfired or a plane was flying overhead, screaming, "The FBIs are coming."

The government made Leonard into a criminal for having defended his home and family against some drunken punks. To them my husband was more dangerous than Peltier because moral power is always more dangerous to an oppressor than political force. I felt unspeakably lonely. How could I go on without him? How could I handle the responsibilities which had now fallen on my shoulders? I was still so inexperienced and so very young, still in my early twenties. Leonard had taken care of all things for all the people in the Grass Mountain district, not only the healings and ceremonies but also the little everyday problems which are so important. How could I have filled the void? Leonard's parents were old and in bad health and now, when they needed their only son to run the home and help them, he had been taken away.

I went through my daily chores in a daze. Any moment I expected Leonard to walk in the door. Sometimes I imagined hearing his voice calling me, and then I remembered where he was. The children asked, "Where is daddy, why is he in jail?" and I had no answer for them.

The trials were a farce. The government had not had much luck trying Indians in Wounded Knee–related cases up to that time. Whenever there had been a proper trial outside South Dakota, under a change of venue, whenever we had voir dire—that is, the right to question prospective jurors to find out whether they were prejudiced against Indians—whenever we had proper time to develop our case before an unbiased jury, the trials ended in acquittal. The government learned from this. They forced Leonard's trial to be held in South Dakota—the state, as Annie Mae always said, where Jesus Christ himself would have been found guilty of inside trading and child molesting had he been an AIM Indian.

Leonard's trials were rushed through in a day, without voir dire and without giving the defense a chance to make their point. Leonard had no illusions. During the trial he whispered to me, "They'll find me guilty at two o'clock."

I said, "Why two o'clock?"

He gave me a sad, knowing smile. "They want their free steak and beer lunch at the court's expense. Figure it out for yourself. They go to lunch at twelve. It takes them half an hour to get there and back. They'll take an hour to eat their steaks. After they come back they'll sit around for half an hour to make it look good, as if they were deliberating. Then they'll come in with their 'guilty' verdict." And that's what happened—at two o'clock sharp.

Before we could enter the courthouse to be with Leonard at his sentencing, we were thoroughly and electronically searched. They passed a beeper between Ina's legs. She was eight years old at that time. They were afraid of us. They even stuck the beeper into Pedro's diapers, looking for a gun. All they got was a beeper covered with baby shit.

At his three trials Leonard was sentenced to a total of twenty-three years. I watched the marshals dragging him off in handcuffs and leg irons. We just kept looking at each other until the iron bars snapped shut behind him and he disappeared from view. Leonard's old Mother, Mary Gertrude, cried, "I'll go on praying for him with the pipe. I'm Indian. I'll keep praying with the pipe, making tobacco ties. And I'll tell the spirit: 'I want my son back here, where he belongs, where he was raised. I want him back in his house, in our old home where he was born. I'm old, but I won't die until he comes back here.' "

One marshal said, "Listen to that old, crazy squaw. Lady, I'm telling you, you'll be dead a long time before your son comes back."

It is hard for an outsider to understand what being in jail must have been like for Leonard, a traditional Sioux medicine man. Leonard is part of nature, a man who rides horses, who searches the hills and valleys for healing herbs, who herds cattle, who watches birds for signs, who talks to the clouds and the winds. I thought, "How will he be able to stand being cooped up in a tiny cell like a caged eagle in a zoo whose wings have been clipped?" But things were much worse than I could ever imagine, even in my nightmares. I knew little of what was going on in America's maximum-security prisons. I soon found out.

After Leonard had been taken away he was whisked from one jail to another in a totally senseless pattern. I tried to follow him everywhere and keep in contact with him, but often neither I nor his lawyers had the slightest idea where he was being kept. The government seemed to be playing a game of hide-and-seek with us: Pennington County Jail in Rapid City; Pierre, South Dakota; legendary Deadwood in the Black Hills; Minnehaha County jail in Sioux Falls; Oxford and Cedar Rapids in Iowa; Terre Haute in Indiana; Leavenworth in Kansas; Chicago; Sioux City in Iowa; Lewisburg in Pennsylvania; Richmond in Virginia; and for a short time a holding tank in New York City. They dragged Leonard all over the country while I kept tracking him down.

From the first day Leonard spent in jail his friends rallied to free him. We turned especially to our white friends. They went all out, spent their rent money and funds that should have sent their kids to college to hire lawyers and fly them to different trials and jails, but they were as ignorant about the ways of American justice as far as Indians were concerned as we backwoods Sioux. But we all learned fast. It did not take us long to find out that money was all-important. If you have two hundred thousand dollars to spend on defense, you win your case; if you have no money, you lose. The so-called adversary system is simply a lottery. If you had money and connections to hire a brilliant lawyer and were faced with a mediocre prosecutor, you won. If you had no money and had to rely upon a court-appointed lawyer, you lost. If you could get a trial shifted to an Eastern city, you generally were acquitted. If you were tried in South or North Dakota, you went to jail. Guilt or innocence did not enter into it. We never got a jury of our peers. In all the trials I witnessed I never saw an Indian juror. They say that the law is getting ever more enlightened and liberal and color-blind. That is bullshit. In 1884 the first Crow Dog won his case before the Supreme Court which, under the 1868 treaty, ruled that the government had no jurisdiction on the Sioux reservations. Almost a hundred years later the courts ruled against us on the same question. The thing to keep in mind is that laws are framed by those who happen to be in power and for the purpose of keeping them in power. That goes for the U.S.A. as well as for Russia or any other country in the world.

After everybody involved had gone broke we learned how to raise money. In the end we had the support of the National Council of Churches, the World Council of Churches, the Quakers, Amnesty International, the Center for Constitutional Rights, and the Fellowship of Reconciliation. Of course we were lucky because just then Indians were "in." A few years later the media and money would be concentrated on the environment, women's lib, the Lesbian Nation, macrobiotics, or crystal-healing. Organizations supporting minorities have a tendency to put their main efforts into backing leaders with what is called "name recognition." Thus main support was first concentrated on the cases of

Russel Means and Dennis Banks. Leonard had to wait until support shifted to the secondary leaders. He had been sentenced to a total of twenty-three years. It took some two hundred thousand dollars to get him out of jail in slightly under two years. While I was happy to see him free, I had a bad conscience thinking of the many nameless kids who had stuck their necks out in all the AIM confrontations languishing in the slammer, unable to raise money for bail or defense.

Among my favorite lawyers were Ken Tilsen of Minneapolis, Dan Taylor of Louisville, Bill Kunstler of New York, and Sandy Rosen of San Francisco who later won the Kent State case. Richard Erdoes and his wife Jean became our defense coordinators, providing a communications center and a place to eat and sleep. The phone bills alone ran to about two thousand dollars a month. Among our lawyers, Bill Kunstler was the most famous while Sandy Rosen was a "lawyer's lawyer," the best in his profession. Bill was great in preventing damage simply by winning a case at the first trial. In a courtroom he was brilliant and irresistible. I always thought of him as almost more of a first-class movie star than a lawyer. Sandy was a great repairman once an initial trial ended in conviction. He was a master at writing appeals, sniffing out pertinent points of law, following the tiniest lead—absolutely tops when it came to preparing a case. As for me, in spite of my original shyness I eventually became a good speaker, addressing rallies in auditoriums, churches, and parks.

All this did not help Leonard get better treatment in jail. He was at times totally isolated from the outside world, not able to communicate, not knowing what was done on his behalf. When he was allowed to make his first telephone call from inside jail he said, "What will they do to me? Will they kill me like they killed Crazy Horse?"

I asked him, "How are they treating you?"

He said, "I have been handcuffed, fingerprinted, and humiliated by body searches. They won't tell me where they are taking me next. They have taken everything from me. They have taken Crow Dog's land. They have taken my elements, they have taken my human body away from my people. But they have not taken my mind. My mind is still free." I tried not to let him hear me weep.

The first thing they do in jail with a man like Crow Dog is try to break his will, to make him from a person into a number. One way to do this is the "holdover." Leonard ignored all provocations. He was a model prisoner, never giving them an excuse for punishing him. But whenever he arrived at a new prison he was immediately put in isolation. At Lewisburg he was placed in a tiny cell, so small that he could neither fully stretch out nor stand upright. He asked, "Why are you punishing me? Why are you putting me in the hole?"

They told him, "We are not punishing you, we just have to process you for some weeks before releasing you into the general prison population."

It was the same in Leavenworth, which Leonard calls the "big, bad granddaddy of penitentiaries." They first took him through a maze of corridors and underground passages to a room which was just a cube of gray-green cement. Leonard had no idea in what part of the prison he was. The room had no windows, just artificial neon light which stayed on the whole two weeks he was there. Soon he no longer knew whether it was day or night, Monday or Friday, or whether the food he ate was breakfast or dinner. He had no clock or watch, and lost all sense of time. He saw only the hacks who brought him the food. To fight his disorientation, he sang old sacred Lakota and peyote songs. He said later that in this utter vacuum he taught himself an entirely new way of singing, and that is true. Since he came out of prison he sings peyote songs like nobody else, making it sound as if two or three men were singing. Also in some of these songs you can hear the voices of various birds, the cry of the roadrunner, the call of the water bird.

It takes a particular type of human being to want to be a hack. Half of their waking hours they are prisoners themselves, inmates by their own free will. Uneducated and underpaid, the only thing they have going for them is feeling superior to the helpless prisoners. Here, at last, are men they can look down upon because they have them in their power. If they encounter a prisoner who makes them feel inferior or impotent they become enraged, because he threatens whatever feelings of self-esteem they have left. They try to bring such a man down to their own level by humiliating him. Leonard called it "mind torture." So every day it was: "Spread your cheeks, chief, let's see what you got up your asshole."

Almost from the first day he got anonymous hate letters, many of them saying that while he was incarcerated I was sleeping around with every Tom, Dick, and Harry. One letter read: "Crow Dog, you dumb Indian, your wife gets fucked by your best friends. We have cameras that can see in the dark. We photographed them while they were doing it. We bugged the motel room and have all their moans and groans on tape. Whenever you get bored doing time we can send you the pictures and tapes." The guards bringing him these letters told him, "You know, mail is censored. So we can read your letters. Some wife you got. Maybe we'll look her up some time." Leonard only laughed in their faces. While he got these kind of letters promptly, some of my letters to him were never delivered.

The hacks kept hassling Leonard all the time, saying, "If you are such a big-shot medicine man, why don't you turn yourself into a bird and fly away?" They'd tell him, "Don't you realize that you are in our custody, that we can do with you whatever we want, that we can put you in the hole whenever we feel like it, that we have absolute power over you?"

Leonard would always answer, "You have no power at all. It is I who have the power. I have a legend. What legend do you have? What can you tell your children when you get home? What can you pass on to them?"

They just would not leave him alone. Leonard wears his hair in the traditional style of two long braids. They always tried to cut his hair. Our lawyers had a running battle with various wardens proving that cutting his hair would be illegal. Finally, in May 1976, the warden at Lewisburg set a day and hour when Leonard's hair would be cut, but his release on appeal was ordered just one day before the barbershop appointment.

Christian prisoners are entitled to their priests and Bibles, Jews to their rabbis and Talmud. Leonard told the warden that the pipe was his bible, that he had a right to have it. It took months of petitions by our lawyers and the Indian Rights Association until we finally got a ruling which recognized the Native American Religion and gave Indian prisoners the right to have their sacred things and to pray with them. The warden at Terre Haute called Leonard into his office: "Crow Dog, I have an order to give you your pipe. Here it is." Leonard asked, "Where are my pipe bag and tobacco?" The warden told him that the tobacco "was suspicious. It smells like some hippie drug. Sorry, chief. No can do."

Leonard tried to explain that, of course, this was a different kind of tobacco, chan-cha-sha, sacred red willow bark tobacco. The warden insisted that it was an illegal drug. Leonard told him that without the tobacco the pipe was no good to him, and gave the pipe back for the warden to keep until he was released.

The hacks also harassed Crow Dog for speaking to his

relatives on the phone in Lakota. They kept shouting at him, "Speak English so we can understand you. This is a white man's country. You're probably telling lies about us on the phone."

"You just have a bad conscience," Leonard told them.

They got back at him in other ways. One of the priests was gay and kept trying to fondle Leonard. He told the priest, "Father, maybe in your religion it's all right to do this but in our religion medicine men don't engage in this kind of activity." At Leavenworth, almost every day, the punks and buttwinkles cleaning the tiers stood before Leonard's "house" taunting him: "Come on, chief, put your dick through the bars so we can suck it. You might as well. You won't have a woman for maybe ten years."

When Leonard ignored them they threw garbage into his cell. He told me that he was not bothered by these things, but they left their mark on him all the same. Then there were the shrinks. One psychiatrist asked Crow Dog whether he had any physical complaints. Crow Dog said he had an irritation. What kind of irritation? the shrink wanted to know. Crow Dog told him that the American government was irritating him. "Have you got a cure for breaking promises? Have you got a cure for lying?" The shrink said that Crow Dog had misunderstood him. What about physical sicknesses? Crow Dog pretended that it was the shrink who wanted to be cured. He offered to cedar him and get him some peyote tea. The man mumbled something and gave up. At Lewisburg a psychiatrist insisted that Leonard take Valium and Thorazine "to make him relaxed and happy while doing time." Leonard told him that if they started that sort of psychological warfare they would lose, that with the help of Grandfather Peyote, he was a better psychiatrist than they were. "Don't mess with my mind," he told the Valium man, "or I'll mess with yours."

"You Indians are all alike," said the shrink, "hopeless!"
One day after the Bicentennial, on July 5, 1976, the shrinks at Terre Haute tried again. One of them called Leonard into his office. As Leonard later described it to me, the man greeted him with a big smile, asking, "Crow Dog, how do you feel about the Bicentennial?" Crow Dog told him that for an Indian to celebrate that day was like a Jew celebrating Hitler, or a Japanese celebrating Hiroshima.

"Very interesting," said the psychiatrist. "I'm Jewish myself. What about the great men America is celebrating?"

"Well," Leonard told him, "Washington was a guy with short silk pants, a wig, and wooden teeth, who kept slaves. Then Columbus. He thought he had landed in India—only ten thousand miles off course. Then Custer—without us, you might have had him for a president. You ought to be grateful. You people elected a Nixon, an Agnew. I'm humble. I'm satisfied with Sitting Bull and Crazy Horse."

"Well, what do you think of me?"

"I think you're using me as a guinea pig."

"Well, you're some guinea pig, Crow Dog, I'll tell you. I give up. You don't need me."

After that interview this shrink was always very nice to Leonard, wrote favorable reports about him, and helped us all he could.

Only twice during the one and a half years Leonard was in jail did he break down. The first time it happened in Lewisburg. He was standing in the yard near a group of inmates when it suddenly split up, revealing a prisoner whose throat had been slit from ear to ear with a shiv lying dead on the floor, almost decapitated. While Leonard was still shook up over this a man in a white coat, whom he took for a doctor, approached him, saying, "Crow Dog, your physical examination revealed brain damage. We have to lobotomize you. That's what they did to that guy in the movie *One Flew Over the Cuckoo's Nest.* That guy was like you. Wouldn't cooperate. Chief, your troubles are over. You'll be a happy, acculturated veggie. This week they'll take you to New York to perform the operation." This man knew that Crow Dog would be taken to New York on his way to another prison. It was his way of playing a joke on Leonard. When Leonard was in fact taken to New York a few days later, he believed that the man had spoken the truth. I was in New York at that time to be as close to Lewisburg as possible. I could have taken a cab and been with him in fifteen minutes, but they would not allow me to see him. They let him phone. He was weeping. "They're going to lobotomize me," he said. "They're going to take my mind away, take from me my medicine knowledge, make me into nothing." Then he really broke down.

I talked to him the whole night through, trying to cheer him up. Richard and Jean Erdoes told him over the phone, "They can't do this to you, they'd need special permission, including yours." Leonard repeated over and over again, "You don't know what it's like to be in the penitentiary. They can do anything they like. They have that power. You just don't know." We were on the phone from eight o'clock in the evening until six in the morning. We were totally exhausted, physically and mentally. We had roused one lawyer from his bed in the middle of the night, and sometime the next day he found out that the whole lobotomy threat had been a hoax. The cruel joke backfired. When we made the story public there was a general outcry. Support for Leonard really began rolling as the National Council of Churches adopted his case, calling him a "persecuted and unjustly incarcerated religious leader."

The second-worst day for Leonard was November 19, 1976, when the old Crow Dog home was completely burned to the ground under mysterious, or rather highly suspicious, circumstances. All during the 1970s numbers of homes of

Indian civil rights leaders were destroyed by fires or fire bombings. Of the wonderful old picturesque Crow Dog place absolutely nothing was left except black ashes covering the bare ground. All the invaluable relics, sacred things, ancient treaties, and buckskin costumes perished in the flames. Leonard's parents barely escaped with their lives. Many ceremonies, peyote meetings, yuwipi rituals, and giveaways had been held in that old house. Now it was gone—a piece of Indian history and heritage was no more.

Leonard took it very hard. He dictated a letter for us: "Is it right for me to be kept from my people, from my earth? The house of my mother and father has been burned down. This is where seven generations of Crow Dogs have lived. I am in the penitentiary and could not help my family save the house. I can only watch the iron bars. But even here, today, I can feel my grandfather's heartbeat and hear the echo of the drum."

They made life hard for him in so many ways. Things that make life easier for the ordinary con—TV, reading, playing cards—meant nothing to him. He was thrown entirely upon his own inner resources. Then there were the sheer distances they put between him and his family and friends. First they put him into Lewisburg, Pennsylvania, half a continent away from his Dakota home. So I moved to New York together with little Pedro to stay with friends. If I started out by car early in the morning on visiting days, I could see Leonard and still be back in New York by nightfall. The prison system decided to make it more difficult for me to visit my husband and transferred Leonard to Terre Haute, Indiana, exactly halfway between New York and Rosebud. Now, no matter where I stayed, I had to travel nine hundred miles to see him. Each time it cost several hundred dollars.

Though I felt lonely and lost without Leonard, weighed down by responsibilities I felt too weak and inexperienced to confront, I had a comparatively easy time. The nights were bad, but at least for an average of eighteen hours a day, I was kept too busy to brood. I traveled, I was in places I had never seen before, I composed leaflets, talked to lawyers, newspapermen, organization heads, made tapes, held speeches, and took care of my baby. It was now that I met and learned to like white people who were on our side. I made many friends: besides the Erdoes family, the Belafontes, the actor Rip Torn and his wife Geraldine Page, Dick Gregory, Brando, Ossie Davis and Ruby Dee, the musicians David Amram and Charlie Morrow, the writer-editor Ed Sammis, the Puerto Rican author Piri Thomas, Ambassador Andy Young, Bishop Lou Walker, Ping and Carol Ferry who always supported Indian political prisoners, the Osage artist Jeffe Kimball, attorneys Bill Kunstler and Sandy Rosen, the filmmakers Mike Cuesta and David Baxter, who made a documentary about Leonard's imprisonment. I learned a lot from these new friends, was exposed to new ideas and lifestyles. I enriched my vocabulary as my horizon expanded. I was stuffed with good food, strange and delicious, was given nice clothes, and was taken to shows and parties. There seemed to be a conspiracy to keep me so occupied that I had little time to feel sorry for myself. Most important, I had many shoulders to cry on. And always, wherever I was, I was visited by skins from many tribes who showed up in the most unlikely places.

Leonard survived through his spiritual power. Even in his cement cell with the steel bars, the bucket, and the naked light bulb which was kept burning all the time, he went on a vision quest. When he got to Terre Haute, as the bus stopped at the prison gate he heard an eagle-bone whistle. With it came a voice saying: "You hear me, you feel me, you see me, you know me. Hold on to your ancient ways and learn to bear the unbearable." Leonard told me that he communicated with birds outside his window or in the yard. They seemed to him to be spirit messengers and they cheered him up. Once a crow perched on his windowsill and that made him feel good. He thought it was a Crow Dog spirit come to visit him. Another time it was a yellowhammer which to him represented the Peyote Church. During a parole hearing he saw two eagles through the window circling in the clouds and he took this for a good sign. He always felt the presence of the spirits, even when he was in the hole. "Tunkashila is watching over me," he told me one time. "I have a hot line to the Great Spirit. I got a built-in amplifier for talking to Tunkashila."

He enjoyed the respect and affection of his fellow prisoners. When he got into Leavenworth the whole tier of prisoners ran to the bars of their houses, banging against them, chanting rhythmically, *"Crow Dog, Crow Dog, Crow Dog!"* The whole tier was a wall of outstretched hands welcoming him. In Terre Haute a black fellow inmate made up a song about Leonard. He sang it to me over the phone, accompanying himself on his guitar. It was a typical black blues song. It was beautiful. Leonard got many letters. Indians often send him poems.

He made friends with black, white, and chicano inmates. He felt especially close to the lifers. He simply could not understand how a human being could be put in a cage for a lifetime. He told me during one of my visits to the jail, "I know how these lifers feel with nobody to support them. Some haven't had a visit for years. They been here for ten, fifteen years. They don't have any idea of what's happening on the outside. Through their windows some of them can see the watchtowers with their sharpshooters, and maybe cars passing by on the distant highway, or a plane flying high in the sky. And that's the limit of their world. They don't even know whether their relatives still remember them, whether they're even alive. Lifers are the living dead."

In the spring of 1976 Leonard got a break: he was released for three months pending appeal. Rip Torn and Richard Erdoes drove us to Lewisburg to get him out. He was supposed to be released in the morning, but the hacks had their usual fun and games, taking all day with one nitpicking thing after another to delay his release. It was as if they could not bear to let him go. They even played their miserable little power games with us, the visitors, shouting down from their watchtower over a loudspeaker, "Put your car over there. No, ten yards to the right. No, put it over there on the left. No, back up forty feet. No, come forward. Now turn the car around . . ." and so on and on for a full hour. Rip has a fierce temper and I was afraid he was going to explode, but he managed to control himself though trembling with rage. When they finally released Leonard late in the afternoon they stipulated that he could not walk out. He had to be driven by the owner of the car. Nobody else could be in the car. Nobody was allowed to wait for him at the gate. Everybody, except Leonard and the driver, had to walk one mile and wait outside the prison perimeter.

So we waited, not letting all this pettiness bother us. Outside the prison grounds the hacks' power ended. We found a nice spot by the road. There was a brook, grass, flowers, trees. I spread out Leonard's sacred things—the pipe bag with Indian tobacco, the buffalo skull, the eagle wing. We had brought a fine young Lakota singer, Steve Emery, and when the car finally drove up and Leonard stepped out, Steve pounded the drum and sang an honoring song. Then he sang the AIM song as I draped my husband's red-and-blue prayer shawl around his shoulder and put the red beret with the eagle feather on his head. Then we sat down in a circle and smoked the pipe. When we were ready to go, Erdoes asked, "Crow Dog, what do you want for dinner?"

Leonard surprised us by saying, "For months I have dreamed about good Chinese food."

Erdoes found a phone booth and made a call to his wife, Jean. When we got to New York a feast awaited us, a table loaded with double-fried pork, Szechuan shredded beef, shrimps in lobster sauce, beef curry, Chinese dumplings, pork with snow peas, egg foo yong, Hunan spiced chicken. On the way to New York our car had hit a pheasant. Rip had picked it up saying, "This is good meat." So, in addition to all this Oriental food, Rip cooked a gourmet pheasant dish for us. It was great. But after dinner Leonard could not relax. He was sleepless for nights. He paced the streets. When we made love he felt the hacks were watching us. When he did manage to sleep he had nightmares. He said, "Mentally I'm still in prison."

Our friend the artist-writer Ed Sammis has a little house by a mill pond in Westport, Connecticut, a few hundred feet from Long Island Sound. He said, "Leonard, we've got to debrief you. You've got to get out into the country, smell some sea air." So we all went to Ed's house. He had a stuffed crow on one side of his mantelpiece and a stuffed toy dog on the other. In between was a handwritten sign: WELCOME CROW DOG. He must have gone to a lot of trouble to find that stuffed crow. Ed makes the best Bloody Marys in the world, and he is a good cook. He makes "steak outrageous," "beans outrageous," and "chicken outrageous," meaning that he douses everything with large quantities of brandy. He had prepared a big dinner, but Leonard fell asleep after a few mouthfuls. He staggered over to a couch and fell upon it face down. He slept for thirty-six hours. Then we traveled home to Rosebud. It was a bittersweet homecoming. The old Crow Dog house was gone, but the small, red, jerry-built "poverty house" was still there, terribly run down from all the wear and tear. Leonard tried to start his former life as a medicine man all over again, but after three months we got a notice that Leonard's appeal had been denied and that he had to go back to prison. With his acute sense of history Leonard surrendered himself at the courthouse in Deadwood, South Dakota, because it was at this same courthouse that his great-grandfather had surrendered himself in 1884.

So my husband was again dragged off in handcuffs for another year. We appealed to Judge Robert Merhige for a reduction of sentence to time served under Rule 35. Merhige was the judge who had sentenced Leonard in the phony assault-and-battery cases. He looked like a tiny, mean, gray-haired owl with a sharp beak. In the courtroom he had been a veritable tyrant and we had hated him. In his own court, at Richmond, Virginia, he was known as a fair and liberal judge. The government had picked him out of the blue and sent him to South Dakota to clear up all Indian cases in record time. I believe they picked him because Merhige knew absolutely nothing about conditions on the reservations. Probably he had never met an Indian before. During the trials the prosecution had made it impossible to develop the background to the case.

But now Merhige was receiving armloads of letters and petitions pleading for Leonard. Some of these letters came from clergymen, Indian tribal presidents, anthropologists, doctors, and teachers who knew Leonard and were familiar with conditions at Rosebud and Pine Ridge. Richard Erdoes even went to Merhige's bishop, explaining Leonard's ordeal and asking for a letter of support. Richard found the bishop, a genial Irishman, in undershirt and underpants soaking his bunions in a tub of hot water. An elderly housekeeper kept bringing teakettles of more hot water when the water in the tub cooled off. The good bishop listened and exclaimed,

"Holy Moses, what are they doing to this poor man?" He instantly fired off a letter to the judge. Richard, who is an artist, had sent Merhige an illustrated letter, describing to him the background of the story which the prosecution had hidden from the court. The illustrations showed all the crazy things that had happened to Richard as nonlegal head of the defense team—groupies climbing naked into his motel bed, rednecks taking potshots at him, having to live on fry bread and dog soup. "Dear judge," he wrote, "if you have no pity on Crow Dog, at least have pity on me." He made the illustrations as good as he could, as if they had been a job for *Life* or *Saturday Evening Post*. When he told the lawyers about it, they were aghast. They told Richard that he had blown the case, that he had dared interfere with a sitting judge, that he could be held in contempt, go to jail. But nothing happened.

With all that information pouring in upon Merhige, the judge began feeling twinges of conscience. He called us to his court in Richmond. A long trestle table in front of his bench was piled two feet high with petitions on behalf of Crow Dog. The judge pointed to this mass of papers, saying with a grin, "This is just the tip of the iceberg. We don't have enough space in this courtroom to bring them all out. We have letters here from Nigeria, Java, Greece, Japan, Sweden, Peru, and Austria. I just wonder how folks so far away can know more about this case than we do." Then he said in a low, matter-of-fact voice: "I resentence Crow Dog to time served. I order his instant release."

One of our lawyers, still oppressed by his bad experiences in South Dakota and convinced that Crow Dog would never get justice, protested loudly: "Your honor, this is the height of cruelty to keep this innocent man in jail!" He went on and on in this vein while we desperately tugged at his jacket. The judge repeated, grinning, "Didn't you hear me? I ordered

Crow Dog's release." Finally the good news sank in. It was a big moment for us. The judge invited us into his chambers, saying, "Gentlemen, this calls for a little libation." He had changed into a very nice, smiling little owl. When we entered his chamber we saw that he had framed some of Richard's illustrations. He told him, "You are very loyal but don't try to be a lawyer." He shook hands all around, commending us for our perseverance. He said, "Do something in return for me. Get my bishop off my back."

We phoned Leonard in prison, giving him the good news. "You'll be free in a few days," we told him. But it did not turn out that way. It still took weeks of red tape, of lawyers traveling back and forth. Once the prison system has somebody in its power it holds on to him like a miser to his money. It actually took almost three months until Leonard walked out as a free man—well, not quite free, because he remained on parole.

The whole tribe turned out to welcome Leonard home. All the medicine men, the tribal chairman and council members, even some missionary priests came to honor Crow Dog. But the most heartwarming were the many poor fullbloods. Slowly, solemnly Leonard directed the circle of dancers while the drums roared and the singers intoned the chief-honoring song. As Leonard passed them by, all the women made the spine-tingling, pulsating brave-heart cry. Even Leonard's old mother joined in and her cry was like that of a young woman. During this feast they honored me, too. Two medicine men, Wallace Black Elk and Bill Eagle Feathers, led me into the center of the circle, fastened an eagle plume in my hair, and gave me a new name: Ohitika Win, "Brave Woman." It made me proud and happy.

In the film that was made about Crow Dog's prison ordeal, Bill Kunstler summed up Leonard's case in a short speech: "All Indian persecution goes back to those who rule this country and what they are doing, or have done, to our native people. You push them off the land because of human greed and then you fight every attempt, however hopeless, to re-suscitate themselves and come back in some form. Like Crazy Horse and Sitting Bull, Crow Dog became a symbol.

"I guess you hate the people most who make the most justifiable demands. Because they go to the heart of our psyche. We know they are right, and therefore we have to destroy them if we can. I think a lot of people are really afraid of justifiable Indian claims to land and resources. They're most afraid of the fact that the claims are morally right, because when you are confronted with a moral imper-ative against an immoral imperative on your part, you've got to hate the people who assert that moral imperative. And I think there is an irrational, guilt-caused hatred now that is beyond my ability to analyze. We hate them because their claims are totally justified—and we know it."

It was a very good speech, but I was tired of all speeches, even good ones. All I wanted was to be back in Rosebud in our little shack, having a little privacy, making coffee for Leonard, fondling the kids, tucking them in. Go to bed, turn out the lights, make love, and rest, rest, rest.

CHAPTER 16

Ho Uway Tinkte– My Voice You Shall Hear

It was Ptesan-win, the White
Buffalo Woman, who brought
the pipe to the people and taught
them how to live.

—Lame Deer

The tremendous welcome the tribe had given Leonard upon his release from jail gave us a morale boost. A few days later came the letdown as we tried to pick up the pieces of our former lives. The square of black, charred earth and ashes on the spot where the old house once stood still gave off a burned, acrid smell. Leonard's parents and the older children huddled in the little red OEO shack in which I had set up house when I first moved in with Leonard. It was much too small to shelter all of us. It had been vandalized and overused to the point of collapse. Once it had contained a bath and flush toilet and a kitchen sink with tap water, but nothing worked anymore. It looked as if a tornado had swept through it. So Leonard fixed up the old cookshack into a tiny house for his parents. Made up of whatever had come handy, it was not much of a home, rather a flimsy hut like so many others on the res. In the year and a half that we had been away from the place the children had grown, shot up like mushrooms. Ina and Bernadette now looked more like young women, no longer the little girls I remembered from before. They were fresh and wild. The old folks had aged. They had become too feeble to handle the kids the way Leonard and I would have done. We all had become almost strangers to each other. We would have to get reacquainted with them on a grown-up to grown-up basis.

Leonard's sons, Richard and Quanah, looked at their father with big eyes. Who was this stranger with the sunken cheeks? Could this be their daddy? Suffering had given Leonard a spiritual look. He was rather handsome that way. I felt almost sorry when, due to his craving for glazed doughnuts, he regained the fifty pounds he had lost in prison. We, too, had to get reacquainted. We felt awkward and shy with each other. We had seen each other only about a dozen times while he was in the penitentiary, sometimes through a wire mesh with a guard standing by, more often sitting in a sort of telephone booth, seeing one another only as a blurred image through layers of greenish glass and plastic, the phones distorting our voices.

The long months of Leonard's incarceration had changed us both. Mostly the change was good, but we had to get used to the fact that we had become different persons. At times it seemed to me as if I had never left Grass Mountain; at other times, I felt as if I had been absent for an eternity. I had spent almost one year in New York with little Pedro. There I had enjoyed my private room with a private bath, with all the amenities of a big modern city. People had made a big fuss over me, treating me like a celebrity. Now it was back to outdoor privies, to getting water from the river and doing the laundry in a tub with the help of an old-fashioned washboard.

Most of the New York women who had supported us had been feminists. On some points I had disagreed with them. To me, women's lib was mainly a white, upper-middle-class affair of little use to a reservation Indian woman. With all their good intentions some had patronized me, even used me as an exotic conversation piece at their fancy parties. I disagreed with them on their notions of abortion and contraception. Like many other Native American women, particularly those who had been in AIM, I had an urge to procreate, as if driven by a feeling that I, personally, had to make up for the genocide suffered by our people in the past. But my white women friends had also taught me a lot which had influenced me in many ways. I was no longer the shy Sioux maiden walking with downcast eyes in the footsteps of some man. I was no longer an uncritical admirer of our warriors, heroes when facing death at Wounded Knee, but often six-foot-tall babies at home. Facing death or jail they had been supermen, but facing life many of them were weak. Many of them could not take responsibility for their actions. A lot of women got hurt and were left raising children without a father. Once it had been the traditional role of an Indian man to take care of and protect his family as well as old widows and young orphans. Now they said to our women, "Let's you and me make a little warrior," after which they got lost, making little warriors somewhere else. That was the reason Crow Dog was always stuck with caring for so many outsiders, young and old.

Before New York I had taken certain things for granted, almost as a normal part of daily life. But after I had been away for almost a year it no longer seemed quite so normal to me that so many Sioux men habitually beat their wives. My sister Barb came to cry on my shoulder. She was living with a boy at Porcupine. "When that boy is sober," she told me, "he's good, a right guy, but when he's drunk he becomes a monster. He beat me up. He was off drinking last weekend. He came home and vomited all over me. I told him I was going for some clean clothes for myself. He said, 'No, you're not going anywhere.' I said I could not stay like this with puke all over me, and started to leave. He ripped off a two-by-four from the fence and used it on me. He started beating me with this chunk of wood and messed up a couple of my ribs. So I left him for good."

I grinned and told Barb, "For a little thing like that, most Sioux women wouldn't leave their men."

My sister said, "Indian women are stronger than the men because they have to put up with all that shit, but I've had it."

I answered her: "Barb, we've been away for too long. We don't see things the way we used to."

Leonard was going through a similar phase of readjustment. He was feeling a lot of bitterness for what prison had done to him, and had to work it out of his system. His trials had made him famous among many Indians and whites alike. We both had to deal with innumerable letters, demands for help, money, spiritual comfort, and the performance of all kinds of ceremonies. Indian prisoners wanted him to visit them with his pipe and set up sweat lodges in their prison yards. Even white and black inmates asked for his assistance. He felt so strongly for everybody doing time that he turned them down only rarely. Wherever Indians tangled with the law, Leonard would travel there to help and I would travel with him. On top of it all he was still on five years' parole. As he put it: "They can put me back in jail just for spitting on the sidewalk." It was a great strain on both of us.

I noticed soon that Leonard was becoming more tolerant as far as women were concerned. He exhibited fewer of his old Sioux macho habits toward me and showed great understanding for my struggle to once again fit myself into reservation life, especially *his* life. I knew that it would take time before he could shake off his prison hangups. You cannot tell a person who has been fucked over for so many years just to shrug it off with a smile. We quarreled less than before. Leonard can be self-righteous, playing the holy man toward me. So I told him at the beginning of that new life of ours, "Hey, as soon as you get over your righteousness I'll get over mine. If you get mad at me, just calm down and I'll calm down too. I won't take my troubles out on you and you won't take yours out on me." He laughed and said that was all right.

I asked him, "What do you expect of me?"

He said, "You are a medicine man's wife. You are the water, you are the corn. You are the growing generation that you carry in your womb. I have a role and so have you. At the next Sun Dance you will stand there with the pipe representing Ptesan Win, the White Buffalo Woman."

Leonard tried to make me feel good by telling me about the role women play in Lakota legends and religion. Unlike in the Christian Bible where Eve is made from Adam's rib, in one of our ancient tales woman came first. As Leonard told it in his medicine talk, this First Woman was given power by the Spirit. She was floating down to the world in a womb bag and, as Leonard put it, she was four-dimensional—all the Creation rolled into one human being. She came into the world with a knowledge and with a back-carrier and in it she had all our people's herbs and healing roots.

First Woman had a dream and in her vision the Grandfather Spirit advised her: "On your left side, where your hand is, there is a stone." And when she awoke she found a piece of worked flint in her hand, the first tool ever. And then she had another vision in which a voice told her: "To the right there are some bushes. Go there! You shall bring up the generation!" She did not know what it meant but she did as she was told. First Woman went into her moon time and as she was walking a drop of her moon blood fell to the earth. Rabbit saw it. He started to play with this tiny blood clot, kicking it around with his foot, and through the power of Tkuskanskan, the quickening, moving spirit, the blood clot firmed up and turned into We-Ota-Wichasha—Blood Clot Boy—the First Man.

First Woman was given the power to create the things necessary for survival, the knowledge to plant corn, the knowledge to make fire with a flint and keep it going with the help of seven sacred sticks. She was given seven rocks to heat up in the fire to a red glow. She was given a buffalo paunch to use as her first soup kettle by filling it with water and dropping the red-hot rocks into it together with meat and some herbs. First Woman was the center of the earth and her symbol was the morning star. "Maybe she came from a star," Leonard finished his story.

Many times he also told us the story of the White Buffalo Woman who brought to our people the most sacred of all things, the ptehincala-huhu-chanunpa, the sacred pipe around which our faith revolves. This woman taught our people how to use the pipe and how to live in a sacred manner. After she had fulfilled her mission she bade farewell to the tribe, and as she wandered off the people saw her turning herself into a white buffalo calf. Then they knew that she had been sent to us by our relatives, the Buffalo Nation.

The Buffalo Calf Pipe still exists. It has been kept for many generations by the Elk Head family who passed it on to the Looking Horses who take care of it now. They live at

Eagle Butte on the Cheyenne River Sioux Reservation. The pipe's stem is made of a buffalo legbone. It is so old that it can no longer be used for smoking. It is kept in a medicine bundle together with another ancient pipe whose bowl is made of red pipestone. The bundle is unwrapped very rarely on very solemn occasions. Leonard was privileged to pray with it on several occasions.

The way he told it to me, he was strangely scared at its unwrapping. All through the ceremony there were dark clouds drifting overhead amid thunder and lightning. This made Leonard look up and say, "Grandfather, we hear you!" All present made tobacco and cloth offerings to the pipe. Old Henry Crow Dog made a fire and burned sweetgrass and cedar for incense, fanning the bundle with these herbs' fragrance. Leonard made an altar. He said that he was trembling doing this. They slowly unwrapped the bundle, layer by layer, until they beheld the holy pipe. As Leonard touched it he felt something like an electric shock, and when he took hold of it to pray he felt a great flow of power in his arms and veins filling his whole being. He wept. There were twelve men at that particular unwrapping and they all had a similar experience.

Leonard also told me that among many tribes the peyote people have a legend that the holy herb was found by an old woman and her granddaughter. They had become lost while gathering wild berries and nuts hundreds of years ago and could not find the way back to their village. Then they heard a voice saying: "Come over here!" Following it, they came upon a green round plant with a star design on it. This was Grandfather Peyote. He told them: "Eat me!" As they partook of this sacred food their minds cleared so that they found their way home. They brought the knowledge of how to use peyote to their tribe and to all the native people of this continent.

While Leonard stressed the importance of women in Indian religion, he was careful never to blur the role of men and women in traditional Indian life. When a number of AIM women formed an organization called Women of All the Red Nations, the first native feminist movement ever, he welcomed it. But when these women put on their own Sun Dance, excluding men from participating, he was angry. He said that our religion was all-inclusive. Neither men nor women should be prevented from taking part or going off by themselves. The only exception was that menstruating women should not take part in ceremonies because a woman's period is considered so powerful that it wipes out any other power and renders rituals ineffective. When, recently, a small group of women wanted to put on a lesbian Sun Dance, Leonard just freaked out. That was too much for him. Leonard has always protected the role of women in our rituals, but he has also been opposed to women doing things which can traditionally be performed only by a man. A lot of changes in thinking had occurred during his absence and he had to deal with that.

As always when facing a new turn in his life, Leonard went on a vision quest called "Crying for a Dream" in Lakota. The Crow Dogs' vision pit is situated on a high hill from which one can see for many miles in all directions. Surrounded by pines and sagebrush, it is a lonely but beautiful place where eagles nest and coyotes howl at the moon. The vision pit has been up there for many generations. It is an L-shaped hole leading into total darkness. Somehow it always reminded me of a grave. In a way the vision seeker is dead while crying for a dream, the more so because the Crow Dogs, once somebody is praying in the pit, cover the hole with a tarp strewn with sage, seemingly burying the vision seeker alive.

A vision quest lasts for four days and nights. Inside the pit you lose all sensations of having a body. Going into the earth womb, you are light-headed from the sweat bath to start with. You feel nothing but the damp earth at your back and the bed of sage under your sitting bones, and after a day or two, you feel not even that. You feel nothing, see nothing, hear nothing, taste nothing, because during a hanbleceya you do not eat or drink. It is scary to cry for a dream, to be entirely thrown upon yourself, not knowing whether you are awake or asleep, or even alive. As a woman I go on a vision quest for a day and a night or, at most, two days. I don't think I could stand it for longer, imagining the earth walls closing in on me.

Leonard told me about his first vision seeking. He was just a boy then, in his early teens. A spirit had told him to hanbleceya. Old Man Henry and an uncle helped him. They put up a sweat lodge for him and purified him in it. His oldest sister had made a flesh offering, having someone cut little pieces of skin from her arms and putting them into a gourd rattle which he took with him into the pit. It comforted him that she had made this sacrifice. They put him in there for two days and nights, not an easy thing for a young kid to undergo. He received a great vision. He told me that he heard someone walking around above him, that he heard a voice. It was telling him: "We are taking you to a place where you will be taught."

Suddenly he was not in the pit anymore. He was standing in front of a sweat lodge and all around him were tipis and horses, as in the old days. He saw flowers, deer, herds of buffalo. He had been transported into a beautiful ghost world. A man in a buckskin outfit was talking to him. He told Leonard that whatever he was experiencing his elders would interpret for him. He was not to add anything to his vision but should also not leave anything out. The strange man then gave Leonard a small medicine bundle. When

Leonard finally came out of his vision, he found an oddly shaped pebble in his clenched fist. He carries it in his medicine bag. When he went on his first hanbleceya after getting his freedom he also received a vision, but a smaller one.

Some people crying for a dream for four days and nights do not receive a vision. It does or does not happen. Also not all vision seekers use a pit. Uncle Bill Eagle Feathers used to pray for a dream by just hunkering down on top of a hill. The spot he had chosen must have been used for this purpose for a long, long time because the whole hilltop was covered with ancient sacred things—animal skulls, rattles, medicine bags, disintegrating tobacco bundles, cloth offerings. It was a place of mystery and whenever I was up there I felt unseen presences. There was always a sharp wind blowing on that place and I wondered how Uncle Bill could have stood it, fasting and praying on that exposed, stormswept spot.

One thing that impressed me, living at Grass Mountain, was that for the people among whom I lived, every part of daily life had a religious meaning. Eating, drinking, the sight or cry of an animal, the weather, a beaded or quilled design, the finding of certain plants or certain rocks, had spiritual significance. I watched, listened, and learned. The process was odd. On the one hand I was still the same footloose half-breed girl who once had ripped off stores in many big cities; on the other, I was becoming a traditional Sioux woman steeped in the ancient beliefs of her people. I was developing a split personality. But so were all the modern Sioux around me, I think.

It touched me deeply to see medicine men and elders include even small children in their ceremonies, to watch the love and patience with which they were taught to participate. I remember little Pedro sitting in on his first yuwipi ceremony. He was still so small and the spirits whirled him around and he was yelling to me out of the darkness that they had shown him a glowing, many-colored bird.

I also remember one of the first peyote meetings Leonard ran for me. There were only five of us, and I still did not fully understand the ways of peyote. I just ate it up like candy. I took about fifteen spoons and after a few hours got silly, started to giggle, and could not stop. I really peyoted up. I forgot everything around me. I closed my eyes and found myself in a tropical land full of fantastic, wonderful creatures. Something was happening to my mind. I plucked a strange, shimmering fruit from a golden tree and knew that this was the forbidden fruit of knowledge. But this was an Indian Eden. There was no snake and no angry angel with a sword chasing me away. And I saw for the first time peyote in the light of knowledge. Next to me sat a pregnant woman. She told me that the sacred medicine had gone into the baby inside her, making it dance to the rhythm of the water drum. I did not believe her. Later, when I was pregnant again, I felt my own baby dancing in my womb in harmony with the drumbeat. Leonard lets little children come into these meetings, lets them sit in his lap and listen to the songs. At the age of four little Pedro could already sing many Native American Church songs and use the gourd rattle.

At last came the time for me to sun-dance. One pledges at the end of one Sun Dance to take part in the following one. Standing right by the sacred tree I made my vow: "Next summer I shall sun-dance. I will do it so that Indian prisoners dear to me should go free." A year had gone by and I had to fulfill my promise.

Uncle Bill Eagle Feathers, who died a few years ago, was the intercessor, the living bridge between the people and the Spirit. As he called it, the Sun Dance was the granddaddy of all Indian ceremonies. He was right. Wi-Wanyang-Wacipi, the Sun Dance, is the most awe-inspiring of our rituals, occurring every year at the height of summer. In 1883 the government and the missionaries outlawed the dance for being "barbaric, superstitious, and preventing the Indians from becoming civilized." The hostility of the Christian churches to the Sun Dance was not very logical. After all, they worship Christ because he suffered for the people, and a similar religious concept lies behind the Sun Dance, where the participants pierce their flesh with skewers to help someone dear to them. The main difference, as Lame Deer used to say, is that Christians are content to let Jesus do all the suffering for them whereas Indians give of their own flesh, year after year, to help others. The missionaries never saw this side of the picture, or maybe they saw it only too well and fought the Sun Dance because it competed with their own Sun Dance pole—the Cross. At any rate, for half a century Indians could go to jail for sun-dancing or for participating in any kind of tribal ceremony.

For this reason, white historians think that there was no sun-dancing among the Sioux between 1883 and the 1930s, but they are wrong. The dance simply went underground. During all that time, every year some Sioux, somewhere, performed the ceremony. Henry and other old men still bear the deep scars on their chests from Sun Dances performed illegally in out-of-the-way places during the 1920s. All through our valley along the Little White River you can find traces of old, well-hidden dance circles. For half a century a handful of medicine men and elders kept the dance alive, passing on the songs that go with it and the knowledge of how to perform this ceremony, down to the smallest detail. Nothing was lost.

Leonard's chest is a battleground of scars from more than a dozen piercings. Since 1971 he has put on the ritual every summer on our own land. This happened in the following way: Many traditional people had become disgusted with the commercialization of the Sun Dance at Pine Ridge, with entrance fees and payments for picture taking, hot dog stands and ferris wheels, which made this sacred ceremony into a tourist attraction. So in 1971 a few medicine men, among them Leonard and Uncle Bill, Wallace Black Elk, and John Lame Deer, decided to perform the Sun Dance in the good old way instead of in a circus atmosphere. For their site they chose Wounded Knee where so many of our ancestors had been massacred by the army in 1890. They put up the arbor and the sweat lodge and after the preparation they began to dance. Then everything went wrong. A car drove up full of tribal police. Their chief told Uncle Bill and Leonard that they were forbidden to dance at Wounded Knee because "it was inflammatory and might draw people away" from their commercial Pine Ridge Sun Dance.

Leonard told the police boss, "Don't you know about freedom of religion? You're an Indian. How can you interfere with a sacred ceremony while it is going on?" The dancers, meanwhile, ignoring the police, continued dancing and blowing on their eagle-bone whistles. The police boss did not like the job he was sent to do. He was embarrassed and drove off.

On the second day the dancers were making flesh offerings when the sound of police sirens again drowned out their songs. This time the tribal police came in force with three squad cars. Their chief said, "I hate to do this but I'm ordered to arrest you." Bill Eagle Feathers wept. "I am the bad luck guy. Great Spirit, what did I do wrong?"

Leonard had a hard time keeping the dancers in line because it was a near-killing situation. Among the dancers was a group of young people calling themselves "Indians of All Tribes." They came from San Francisco where they had taken part in the occupation of Alcatraz Island. They wanted to fight the police. It took a great effort by Leonard and Uncle Bill to prevent bloodshed. Everybody was hauled off to court and fined. After a few hours the dancers were released but police occupied the dance ground to make sure that the ceremony could not be continued.

The dancers asked Leonard, "What are we going to do now?" One could not leave a Sun Dance half done. Not finishing it to the point of piercing was unthinkable. Leonard said, "We have made a vow to the Great Spirit and we must keep it." Somebody suggested continuing the dance at Rosebud, on Crow Dog's private land, where nobody could interfere with it, and all agreed that this was a good idea. But there was the problem of the tree. The sacred Sun Dance pole standing at the center of the Sun Dance circle is always a two-forked cottonwood tree. Men are sent out to scout for the most perfect tree they can find. They count coup upon it as in battle. A young maiden who has never been with a man makes the first symbolic cut with the axe. The tree must not touch the ground when falling but must be caught by the men who will carry it to the dance ground.

Leonard was disturbed. The Crow Dog place was over eighty miles distant. How could men carry the heavy tree that far? The tree is sacred. At the height of the dance sick persons lie beneath the tree to be cured. Looking at it, some dancers had already received visions. How could it be transported?

Just about that time a large truck with long-haired young white people arrived. They had come all the way from the East Coast to learn about Indian ways. One of them told Leonard, "We overheard what you said. We'll put your tree on our truck and drive it all the way to your place."

Leonard objected. The tree had to be carried on foot in a sacred manner. To put it on a truck would be very bad. But then Bill Eagle Feathers, twice as old as Leonard and a sun-dancer many times over, stepped in. He thanked all those, Indian and white, who were present. He pointed to the young, long-haired people. "Great Spirit, look at them. They are poor like us. Look at their clothes. Look at their shoes. They call me a lousy Indian. They call them lousy hippies. We travel the same road. Grandfather, Tunkashila will understand. The Sacred Tree will understand. What we are doing is good."

He smoked up the young hippies with cedar and sweet-grass. And then the Sun Dance pole was loaded on top of the truck with all the offerings still attached to it, the four direction flags streaming from it in the wind. The truck was followed by a whole caravan of decrepit Indian cars. For a few miles it was escorted by a tribal police car and in it the unhappy police chief was standing up, praying to the sacred tree with his pipe.

After arriving at Crow Dog's place the dancers planted the tree in a hole filled with buffalo fat. Henry made two figures of buffalo hide, one figure of a man and the other of a buffalo bull. They stood for the renewal of all life, human and animal, because that, too, is an aspect of the Sun Dance. In the old days these figures always had huge male organs symbolizing what the dance was about—more people and more buffalo to feed them.

Everybody pitched in to smooth down the dance circle, put up the shade cover of pine boughs, and make everything holy. It took them the whole day to get everything ready to continue the dance. The next morning, at sunrise, Bill Eagle Feathers raised his pipe and blew on his eagle-bone whistle, praying for an eagle to come in as a sign that the dance was blessed. Within minutes, an eagle flew in low over the hills from the east, circled slowly over the dance ground, then disappeared in the west. They then finished the dance among the grass and pines, without loudspeakers or electric floodlights, in the old, traditional way. At this dance Leonard for the first time revived the old custom of dragging buffalo skulls embedded in the flesh of his back. He told me, "I took five steps with those skulls and it felt as if my heart was being torn out through my back." From that day on, every summer there has always been a Sun Dance at Crow Dog's place, and always the person acting as intercessor prays for an eagle to come in to bless the dancers and always the eagle appears. I was only a teenager when that took place.

I have sun-danced myself. I did not pierce until the second year after I began living with Leonard. At first I did not understand the whole ritual, but I felt it deeply. I understood it with my heart even though not yet with my mind. I saw the tree, the people sitting under the shade, the dancers with their wreaths of sage, their red kilts, medicine bundles dangling on their chests. I heard the many eagle-bone whistles making the sound of a thousand birds. It made me feel good because I sensed the strong feeling between the different people and tribes. I looked at the men with their long, flowing black hair and at the women in their white, beaded buckskin dresses. It was so beautiful that it brought tears to my eyes. I wanted to be part of this, I wanted to feel it, spiritually and in my flesh. It was real compared to what I had known, not a hand-me-down belief but a personal reawakening which stirred a remembrance deep inside me. So I made a vow to sun-dance for four years, and the first time I found it hard to fulfill my commitment.

I began my dance by making a flesh offering. Leonard told me, "I'll cut the skin from your arm. That's a sacrifice. Your prayers go out for those suffering in jail, for friends who are sick. I will put the pieces from your arm into a square of red cloth, make a little bundle of it, and tie it to the sacred pipe. That way you'll remember this always." I made my flesh offering thinking of all the brothers and sisters who had died, who, I felt, had somehow died for me.

When the Sun Dance came out into the open again in the 1930s and '40s, and until recently when Leonard started the dance on our land, the piercing was comparatively tame. Just a small piece of flesh on the chest, over the heart, was pierced with a short skewer or eagle claw. To this was fastened a rawhide thong hanging from the top of the sacred pole, and the dancer then tore himself loose with comparatively little trouble. But under the influence of Leonard and the medicine men Pete Catches, Fools Crow, and Eagle Feathers, the self-inflicted pain has become more and more severe until now it is just like in the old Catlin and Bodmer paintings depicting the ritual of a hundred and fifty years ago. This has spread from Crow Dog's place to other dance sites and other Sioux reservations.

At a recent Sun Dance a friend of ours, Jerry Roy, an Ojibway Indian, underwent a different kind of self-torture on every one of the four days of the ritual. On the first day he pierced in two places on his chest and broke loose. On the second day he made flesh offerings from both of his arms. On the third, he dragged twelve buffalo skulls behind him. And on the last day he again pierced in two places on his chest and had himself hoisted to the top of the tree. He hung there from his breast muscles for a long time until finally some men grabbed his ankles and pulled him free.

At the same dance, Leonard "danced" with the tree. Instead of just tearing himself loose, he only pulled back until the flesh on his chest stretched out about six inches and then made the heavy cottonwood tree sway to his motion, which must have hurt him badly. He told me later, "I danced with the tree. It talked to me. Along and up those rawhide thongs I made a collect call to the Great Spirit. My body wasn't believing it. My mind wasn't believing it. But spiritually I believed." At another Sun Dance, Leonard had himself pierced in four places, two in front and two in back. Thongs were fastened in his flesh and tied to four horses, which were then driven off into the four directions.

I watched a young man dancing. He was a winkte—he was gay. He was as graceful as a young girl. He was standing between four upright poles. Rawhide ropes fastened in his flesh in front and in back had been tied to the poles. The young man had little room to move. His way of piercing had always been considered the most painful because he could not tear himself free by a sudden run or jump backward, but had to work himself free agonizingly slowly, bit by bit. He was swaying back and forth languidly, almost like a ballet dancer, his eyes closed, his face expressionless with just a trace of a smile, swaying back and forth, back and forth, the blood streaming from his wounds.

I even saw young boys, ten and eleven years old, having themselves pierced and, after the dance, proudly showing off their scars. Some anthros say that the dance expresses the macho side of Sioux culture, and I think that subconsciously some young men are competing with each other as if to prove that they can endure more than anyone else. But one has only to look at their faces, their eyes, to see that they are dancing in a trance, that they are unaware of anything but the sun, the sound of the eagle-bone whistles; that each is wrapped up in his own vision, that they are truly "out of this world."

I watched sixteen-year-old Bobby Leader Charge. He did not dance to brag about it later. He was dancing for the release of his brother from jail. He was dragging six heavy buffalo skulls. He ran and ran around the circle but the skulls would not come loose. At last he was too exhausted to run anymore. His older brothers and cousins grabbed Bobby under the arms, dragging him along as fast as they could. Still he could not break free. Finally three little kids sat down on three of the skulls like on sleds and their weight finally pulled the thongs out of Bobby's back. That was in 1977. We had eighty dancers that day. Now we always have close to two hundred.

I pierced too, together with many other women. One of Leonard's sisters pierced from two spots above her collar-bone. Leonard and Rod Skenandore pierced me with two pins through my arms. I did not feel any pain because I was in the power. I was looking into the clouds, into the sun. Brightness filled my mind. The sun seemed to speak: "I am the Eye of Life. I am the Soul of the Eye. I am the Life Giver!" In the almost unbearable brightness, in the clouds, I saw people. I could see those who had died. I could see Pedro Bissonette standing by the arbor and, above me, the face of Buddy Lamont, killed at Wounded Knee, looking at me with ghostly eyes. I saw the face of my friend Annie Mae Aquash, smiling at me. I could hear the spirits speaking to me through the eagle-bone whistles. I heard no sound but the shrill cry of the eagle bones. I felt nothing and, at the same time, everything. It was at that moment that I, a white-educated half-blood, became wholly Indian. I experienced a great rush of happiness. I heard a cry coming from my lips:

> Ho Uway Tinkte.
> A Voice I will send.
> Throughout the Universe,
> Maka Sitomniye,
> My Voice you shall hear:
> I will live!

Epilogue

The rest of the story is quickly told. I am thirty-seven years at this moment. Leonard is fifty. I'm not all that skinny anymore and he got heavier. He used to be a champion hoop-dancer, jumping through seven swiftly moving hoops. He can't do that anymore. I have borne Leonard three children: two boys, Anwah and June Bug (Leonard Jr.), and one girl, Jennifer. Leonard's daughters Ina and Bernadette also have babies of their own, making Leonard a grandfather.

Old Henry died six years ago in his late eighties. He and his wife spent their last years in a regular tribe-built house with running water, a bathtub, and a flush toilet. So, belatedly, he made the jump from the nineteenth into the twentieth century. Up to the very last Henry could still run a Native American Church meeting, ride a horse, and chop wood. He often used to say, "I am the last genuine aborigine left." Now he is gone. They found him lying in front of his door. It looked as if he had fallen asleep but it was the sleep from which one does not awake. A year later Grandma Mary Gertrude followed him to another world.

My own mother quit nursing, went back to school, got her degree, and is now teaching school at Rosebud. Now that I am a mother myself, I have more understanding of what she went through trying to raise a wild kid like me. Finally we are friends. Barb has married Jim, a good man, one of the sun-dancers. He is a carpenter and right now is fixing up my mother's house.

Pedro just had his nineteenth birthday. He has become a yuwipi man. He runs meetings and puts on sweat lodges. He is a good singer. He has pierced many times as a sun-dancer. The youngest child of our close friend Jerry Roy was stabbed to death by a member of a motorcycle gang. The poor kid was still so young, real sweet and friendly. Everybody called him Teddy Bear. Pedro has made a vow to hang from the tree at the coming Sun Dance for Teddy Bear's ghost.

As for those who were at Wounded Knee with us, the AIM leaders and the once young kids, they have calmed down considerably. Dennis Banks was for a number of years a university professor at Davis, California. At present he is running a limousine service in Rapid City, South Dakota. He has not lost his sense of humor. Russel Means is at the moment married to a Navajo lady and lives at Chinle, Arizona. He is one of the founders of a new, multiracial party. He was running for president or vice-president a while ago, but Ronald Reagan was too much competition. There are also rumors that he wants to establish an all-Indian bank. John Trudell, whose family was destroyed in a mysterious fire, has made a new life for himself as musician and song writer. I hear that he is very good. Those are the survivors. Many of the former brothers and sisters are dead. Some were killed but most died from natural causes. I think that the wear and tear of the long struggle just burned them up, ruined their health and took years off their lives. The best always die young.

As for wear and tear: Having four children, being a medicine man's wife, cooking and cleaning up for innumerable guests, most of them uninvited, listening to countless woes and problems, became just too much for me. I was going under. So a few years ago I panicked, packed up the kids, and simply ran away. My flight stopped at Phoenix, Arizona. Of course, Leonard found me. We made up.

We are now back in Rosebud, where we still have the yearly Sun Dances at the old Crow Dog place. Archie Lame Deer has taken the place of Uncle Bill Eagle Feathers as intercessor. He puts on the dance together with Leonard, runs the sweats, and does most of the piercing.

Everybody still comes to Leonard with their problems. We have been heavily involved for years helping the traditional Navajos and Hopis fight their long battle of Big Mountain. During the 1988 drought, white farmers in Ohio asked Crow Dog to perform a rain ceremony for them. He did, and the rain came down. He also performs sweat lodges and pipe ceremonies for Indian prisoners in America's penitentiaries. Wherever Native Americans struggle for their rights, Leonard is there. Life goes on.